YEH YEH'S HOUSE

ALSO BY EVELINA CHAO

Gates of Grace

Chao Tzu-ch'en (Yeh Yeh), 1888–1978.
Pictured here at approximately fifty years of age.

YEH YEH'S HOUSE

EVELINA CHAO

*To Mardi
Wishing you luck
with your violin!
Best wishes,
Evelina Chao*

ST. MARTIN'S PRESS ⚑ NEW YORK

Map by James Sinclair

Library of Congress Cataloging-in-Publication Data

Chao, Evelina.
    Yeh Yeh's house / Evelina Chao.—1st ed.
        p. cm.
    ISBN 0-312-33077-4
    EAN 978-0312-33077-4
    1. Chao, Evelina. 2. Novelists, American—20th Century—Biography. 3. Americans—China—History—20th century. 4. China—Social life and customs—1976– 5. Mothers and daughters—United States. 6. Chinese American women—Biography. 7. China—Description and travel. 8. Grandfathers—China. I. Title.

PS3553.H276Z477 2004
813'.54—dc22
[B]
                                                                    2004048381

First Edition: December 2004

10 9 8 7 6 5 4 3 2 1

To my mother,
Vera Lin Chao

CONTENTS

ACKNOWLEDGMENTS

This book would not have seen the light of day without the generosity and support of the following people, whom I thank most heartfully: R. D. Zimmerman, who steered me to Marly Rusoff, miraculous agent who extended her passionate advocacy of writers and books to me; my editor, Diane Reverand, who moved me to make ideas and words clear and right; David Cashion, who helped shape the book; Deborah Porter, for her liberating insights on the romanization of Chinese words and names; Zdena Heller, for reading, encouraging, finding niggles; Mimi Zweig, for cheering me on as always; my parents, for everything; and most of all Fred, for his enduring love, support, and joyful presence.

While I acknowledge the different systems of romanizing Chinese words and names, I have chosen to spell them as they were communicated to me by my relatives, adhering to the spirit of personal memoir and making Chinese words accessible to all readers, rather than formal political or literary practice.

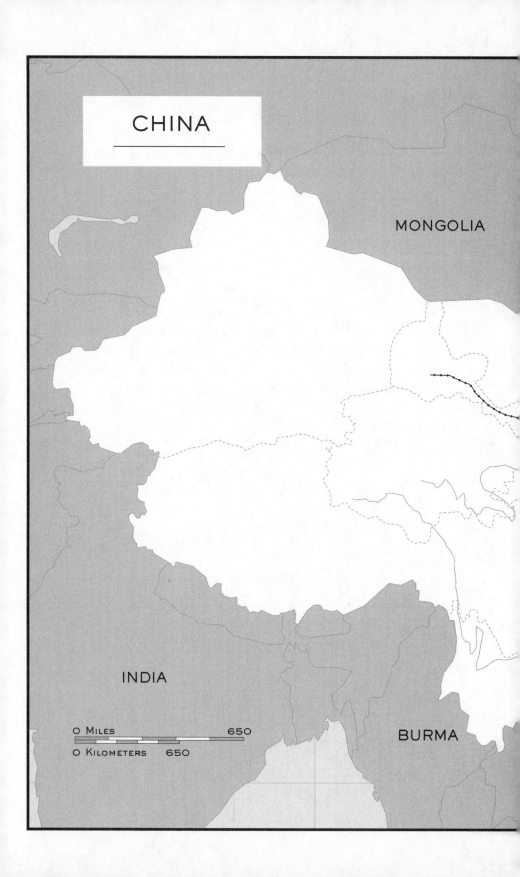

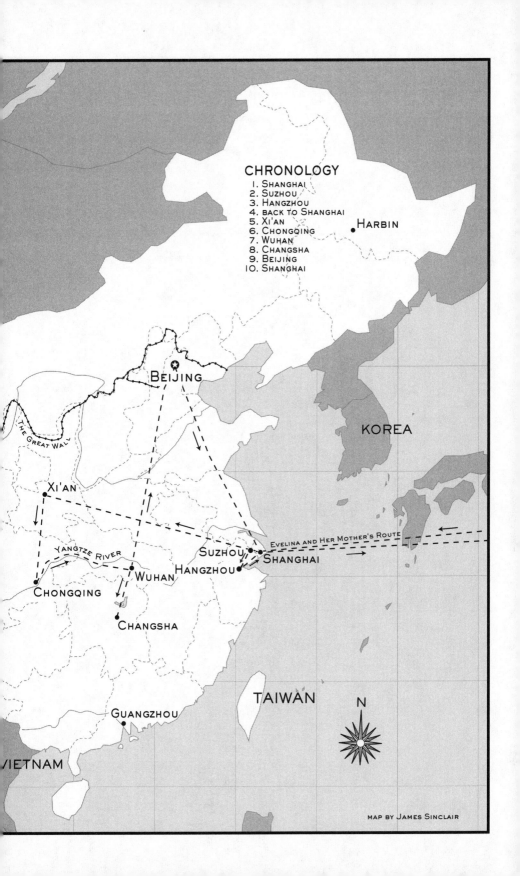

CHRONOLOGY

1. SHANGHAI
2. SUZHOU
3. HANGZHOU
4. BACK TO SHANGHAI
5. XI'AN
6. CHONGQING
7. WUHAN
8. CHANGSHA
9. BEIJING
10. SHANGHAI

HARBIN

BEIJING

THE GREAT WALL

XI'AN

KOREA

YANGTZE RIVER

SUZHOU

HANGZHOU

SHANGHAI

EVELINA AND HER MOTHER'S ROUTE

WUHAN

CHONGQING

CHANGSHA

GUANGZHOU

TAIWAN

N

VIETNAM

MAP BY JAMES SINCLAIR

PART ONE

AROUSING THE DEAF

YEH YEH, 1974

THOUGH MY FAMILY HAS BEEN IN AMERICA FOR OVER HALF A CENTURY, WE still have Peking duck for Christmas. For this holiday, in 1974, two five-pounders are roasting in the oven, sputtering and popping like firecrackers, filling the house with smoke. It is my job to make the pancakes that go with them, and I stir boiling water into flour and roll out rounds, spreading sesame-seed oil between the layers. My father and brother discuss the Redskins' chances of making it to the Super Bowl while they count out chopsticks and set the table. In the next room, my sister's young daughters make plans to go sledding the next morning as it is snowing, unusual for this time of year in Virginia. When I finish the pancakes, my mother approaches me. "Yeh Yeh told me to give this to you," she says. She has already dispensed other small gifts: a pincushion made of tangerine-colored silk, a pair of miniature Chinese scissors that fold ingeniously into the shape of a peanut. It is not lost on me that she has saved the letter for last. I take it and put it in my pocket, hardly glancing at it. My mother forgets herself for a moment, stares at me, frowning, making that small noise of exasperation in her throat.

It is more than three years since I was last home for Christmas, in 1971. We come together this time not only because of the holidays, but to celebrate my mother and younger brother's return from China. My brother was on a six-month study trip; my mother went over at the end to escort him home. Now I hardly recognize my brother. He is wearing a blue Chinese jacket and trousers, black Chinese slippers, a bad Chinese haircut that makes him look like Woodstock—the bird in the Peanuts comic strip. Somewhere along the way, caught in the flush of proletariat spirit, he must have given away his sweatshirt and jeans. He has lost weight, but seems to have gained heft with his new air of earnestness. To me he seems foreign, overly deferential; he even smells different. I am envious, though, of the way he speaks Mandarin. When he asks my mother for another pair of chopsticks his inflection is perfect, like a Chinese born on the mainland. I can tell my mother is pleased from the way she smiles and closes her hand around his when she hands him the chopsticks.

It's no secret that my brother is my mother's favorite. He has gone the farthest of us first-generation children who boomerang from adopted country to homeland, traveling to China, getting a Chinese haircut. Not that I hadn't picked up parental hints that I embark on the same pilgrimage—the sighs, the long days of silence that were the subtext of our family—but it was my brother, the only son, who had fulfilled his filial duty. He had gone to Beijing to pay homage to my grandfather and aunts and uncles, drunk from the springs of his origin, atoned for my family's desertion to America. I admire my brother for this, but I'm also relieved. He was so thorough, zealous, that I hoped he'd done the job for me, too, meaning that I wouldn't have to go on my own journey of guilt. It wasn't that I was lazy or scared. I just had other compulsions.

The ducks are done and lay on the draining racks, gleaming with burnished succulence. I slice scallions, fill small bowls with hoisin sauce. Everyone sits down and watches my father carve the ducks, after which we put pieces of skin, fat, and meat on the pancakes with slivers of scallion and dollops of sauce. I notice that my brother has gone from the table to get himself a Coke from the fridge. I roll up my pancake and bite into it, squirting duck fat all over my mouth. I chew and roll my tongue around, savoring the salt of the duck, the sweetness of the sauce, and sharp tang of scallion. It is always a miracle, this first bite.

"Duck heaven," my brother moans, raising his Coke can in salute. He has removed his Chinese jacket, revealing the Stanford T-shirt underneath. I am glad to see how quickly he is reverting to his old self.

My mother chews her pancake slowly. When she finishes, she places her hands on either side of her plate. Her thumbs are clenched between her index and second fingers, giving them the look of clasps on a valise. It is a gesture I recognize all too well, one that indicates powerful feelings that my mother, normally a stoic, has trouble stowing. She fixes her gaze on me.

"You should go see Yeh Yeh," she says.

Something in her voice makes me afraid. "He's all right, isn't he?"

My mother and brother exchange glances.

"It's not over yet," my brother says.

"What do you mean?" I say.

"The Cultural Revolution."

My brother is staring at my mother's hands, whose knuckles are white. "The Red Guards have been arresting artists, intellectuals, anyone who had contact with Western culture," he says.

"Is Yeh Yeh in trouble? Is that what you're saying?"

My brother looks at my mother again. She stares straight ahead, avoiding his glance.

"Nobody knows for sure," he says.

Though I ask more questions about my grandfather, inquiring after his health and that of his wife, Nai Nai, and whether he had come under investigation by the Red Guards, no one has any answers. After dinner we go into the living room to gather around the tree. It is trimmed with ornaments my mother has collected over the years. Among the baked-dough Santa Claus and tin-stamped reindeer are prancing pink horses, white giraffes, and yellow-and-black lions from Szechuan and Changsha. They are made of cloth, stuffed with sawdust, sewn with stitches so minute that as a child I believed the Chinese elves who made them were smaller and more clever than any at the North Pole.

My father takes out his violin. During dinner, he is silent except for the noises he makes chewing his duck. Though he has an explosive temper, he is a taciturn man with the capacity to project silence that is frightening and omnipotent. When we begin singing "Hark! The Herald Angels Sing!" accompanied by my mother on the piano, he puts the violin to his chin and suddenly his dark mood falls like a cloak dropped at his feet. A strange smile comes over his face. He closes his eyes and moves his body to the music, swaying like a concert violinist on stage. Even though he saws and moves his fingers awkwardly up and down the fingerboard, I am moved by how expressive he is, how the feelings and words he withholds flow out of him through the instrument.

After the music we clean up the kitchen, say good night and retire to our rooms. When I think everyone is asleep, I take out the envelope my mother has given me and open it. Yeh Yeh's handwriting is shaky and spidery. He is eighty-seven, and it's been a long time since I've heard from him. The letter is brief, only half a page:

> . . . I'm growing deaf. I can no longer hear the crickets chirping in my room, much less the music on the radio. Da Mama has to shout when she asks me what I want for breakfast.

And then there is the last line, which I read over and over:

> Sung Lien, come see me soon, before it is too late.

My Chinese name jumps out at me, because in all his previous letters, my grandfather addresses me by my American name. It was he who picked my Chinese name, which means "Lotus Blossom." This has caused me untold embarrassment over the years, because it sounds so un-American and because I do not think of myself as a flower of any kind. In fact, I tell no one that I have a Chinese name. Even on my driver's license it appears only as initials. Its only value is that it makes me grateful that I also have a name in English, unusual as it is. Now, my Chinese name stares up from my grandfather's letter like a hieroglyph I have only just deciphered. It reveals itself, emitting something florid, palpable, that imbues my grandfather's summons with poignancy and urgency. I feel like flying to China that very night. But the house is dark, the night is covered with snow, and on Christmas Eve nothing must stir.

Still, I move through the house, searching for the latest photographs my mother brought back from China. I find them on the kitchen table, where we had glanced through them earlier. There's one of the Beijing household, which includes Yeh Yeh, my uncle and two aunts, as well as two little grandnieces visiting from Changsha. They are wearing sweaters and vests, padded coats, scarves, and earmuffs, huddling around a charcoal brazier in the middle of their living room. They look shaggy and bulky, like yaks bunched against arctic winds, yet they are smiling, and seem healthy.

"They have such rosy cheeks!" I exclaimed when I saw the photo for the first time.

"*Rosy! Nothing!*" my father snorted, looking over my shoulder. "That's carbon monoxide poisoning, from the charcoal!"

I looked closer. In the background the walls, windows, and furniture in the house are covered with a fine white dust. Suddenly I realized it was frost.

"How cold does it get in Beijing?" I asked.

"Freezing, freezing," my mother said, wrapping her arms around herself.

The kitchen is chilly. I scoop up the photographs, bring them back to my room, and crawl under the covers of the bed I have slept in since childhood. Looking around the room, I realize I always felt relatively safe here, growing up in the fifties before the great infusion of Asian immigrants to the Washington, D.C., area. As far as I know, we were the only Chinese family living in North Arlington. At the time, I knew we were different from everybody else. Still, I thought we were American. We had a Ford sedan, a television. On Saturdays we would go pick up my mother from work, then, as a special treat, head to McDonald's for hamburgers and fries. On Sundays we watched *The Wonderful World of Disney* and my father's favorite show, *Wyatt Earp*. My favorite movie was *The Wizard of Oz*.

The photographs I've carried to my bed depict a far different world. Flipping through them, I pause at one of Yeh Yeh sitting in his study, napping. It is obvious the little grandnieces, thrilled to borrow my mother's fancy Japanese camera, have taken this one. They have managed to drape a sock on Yeh Yeh's bald head and snap the picture without him waking. Even with the sock on his head, Yeh Yeh is the picture of dignity. Dressed in his long, traditional Chinese gown and black felt shoes, he still looks imposing. Even the clumsy Chinese hearing aid sticking out of his ear like a cork and the walking cane lying across his lap don't detract from this.

When I was a child, my mother made sure I knew that my grandfather, a professor of English as well as a poet and theologian, was a very famous man in China. I discovered early on how exacting Yeh Yeh was when it came to the English language. He returned every letter I sent to him covered with red pencil marks correcting all my mistakes. It got so I began checking my letters to him over and over before putting them in the mail. I grew to think of him as a figure of incontrovertible authority, my own Wizard of Oz, a very great and scary man who lived far away in a mysterious place—a man who made me shake every time I opened the thin blue aerograms, fearing his thunderous edict: DO NOT SPLIT YOUR INFINITIVES!

But Yeh Yeh had his gentler side, too. He joked in his letters about growing old, how, being retired, he didn't know what to do with all the time he had. Sometimes, he wrote, all he thought about was the hair growing in his ears. I wrote to him about my reptile project, about our new dog, wondering all the time what he looked like. In those years there wasn't a single picture of him in our house, which I thought was strange. And though my mother talked about Yeh Yeh, my father never did, even though Yeh Yeh was *his* father. All the letters that came to our house from China were addressed to me or my mother, never my dad.

Back then, the kids in my school pulled their eyes into slits, mocking my slanty eyes, or sneered that people like me caused World War II. I was shocked at their mean and false accusations, wondering what I had done to deserve them. Sometimes I felt like an animal in the wild, a deer, which, never having been exposed to hunters, doesn't know to run or hide. I don't know what moved me to write to Yeh Yeh about these things. Perhaps putting them down on those flimsy blue aerograms to China made them seem less onerous or real. He wrote back within a month, sooner than he usually did:

> Dear Granddaughter Evelina,
> You must always be yourself, no matter what other people say or do to you. Stick to the truth. Even though life can be very hard, try not to be afraid. Study hard. Remember that modesty becomes a person best. Don't draw attention to yourself. Obey your parents. This is the best way.

I read Yeh Yeh's letter over and over. Somehow I felt that, even with him being so far away, I would be all right. After getting this letter, I began looking through our house for a picture of him. I searched the attic, the basement, through all the boxes my mother had brought in our moves from place to place. In one of the boxes I found my parents' wedding portrait, taken in China. They were both in their twenties but looked like teenagers. My mother had a blank look, as if her life had yet to come to the surface of her face. My father's smile was more of a smirk. He had thick, shiny black hair, and there was something to his high cheekbones, his narrow eyes, that gave him a wild, restless look, like a Mongolian horse rider. But I never found a picture of Yeh Yeh. The only photograph we had of any of our relatives in China was the one of Aunt Lucy, my father's older sister, which sat on my parents' dresser. Though this was not the photograph I wanted, I would still go look at it, thinking that by staring at Aunt Lucy long enough, I would somehow get a glimpse of Yeh Yeh.

This photo of Aunt Lucy had been taken at her graduation from the University of Chicago in 1950, when she received her doctorate in English literature. She looks pale, slim, her hair drawn back tightly in a bun. Dressed in a long black graduation gown, she looks severe, not unfriendly or unkind, but extremely critical, like someone you could never please, no matter how hard you tried. Her eyes seem to see everything.

"Aunt Lucy is the highbrow in the family," my mother always said, in a tone I found confusing. Later, when I understood such things, I detected the irony in her voice, expressing a quiet hurt of her own. She told me of Lucy's great achievement, publishing the Chinese translation of T.S. Eliot's poem, *The Waste Land*. Although I didn't read *The Waste Land* until I was in high school, I knew somehow that my aunt had done something miraculous and difficult and that her accomplishment bestowed great honor on our family. My young friends, who hadn't read *The Waste Land* either, much less poetry of any kind, challenged me when they caught me bragging about my aunt.

"What's so great about *The Waste Land*?" they said. "Was it on TV?"

Now I flip through the stack of my mother's photographs to the most recent one of Aunt Lucy. She is sitting in her tiny room in the house in Beijing, a book in her lap. She looks annoyed; it's clear my shutterbug grandnieces have disturbed her. Aunt Lucy looks her age now. At sixty, her hair, drawn back in the same bun, is gray. Again I wonder why it is *her* photograph that sits on my parents' bureau and not my grandfather's.

I search the covers on my bed, locate Yeh Yeh's most recent letter and read it again. *Sung Lien, come see me soon, before it is too late.* What does he mean, too late? My mother insists that, even at his age he is in good health, and though the phrase, "Cultural Revolution," has an ominous ring to it, I think Yeh Yeh ought to be safe. Why would they harm an eighty-seven-year-old man, especially one as eminent and respected as he? Even so, I make up my mind to go to China in the spring, when the music season ends and I am free to travel. It is the time when Yeh Yeh's plum tree, which he planted himself and where he sits in the shade, composing poems, will be in bloom. As pleasant as this vision is, I lie awake, beset by thoughts as improbable as the news reports filtering in on the airwaves from China about their ongoing revolution. The rumors are faint but unsettling, like earth tremors. Surely, I tell myself, wizards were beyond politics. Wizards did not suffer or die. Or did they?

2

AROUSING THE DEAF

In the spring, when I tell my string quartet I mean to go to China, their eyes pin me to the wall.

"What about London?" they shrill, reminding me of our plans to study with the Amadeus Quartet. "Where's your commitment?"

I am outvoted three to one.

I call my mother to tell her I won't be going to China with her this time.

She is silent for what seems an entire dynasty. "Well, *you* tell Yeh Yeh," she says and hangs up.

After two weeks, having begun and torn up many attempts, I mail Yeh Yeh a letter telling him of my quartet's decision to go to London. I explain how difficult it is for a young group to make its mark professionally and how playing for the renowned Amadeus Quartet may help. I end the letter promising to visit him the following spring. Afterward, I try to convince myself that my grandfather would approve of the sacrifices I was making in pursuit of high artistic ideals. Still, I feel guilty for letting him down. When I return from London at the end of the summer, I search the mail, hoping to find a blue aerogram from him, but there is nothing.

I suppose it was my father's doing that I took up the violin. He played in the evenings when he came home from work as a geologist with the Department of the Interior. For more than thirty years, he rode the bus to his lab and back. Sometimes when he got home, he would slam the door or yell at us for no reason.

Some days, getting off the bus, he headed straight for the garden, where he tended spectacular beds of red and cream-colored roses. I remember their regal, elegant names: Chrysler Imperial, Peace. In response to my father's constant pruning, watering, and feeding, the flowers grew to the size of dinner plates and were the marvel of the neighborhood. People driving by stopped to stare, and once a man got out of his car and offered to buy our house. When my father politely refused, the man walked away muttering, "I'll say one thing, you people sure know how to grow flowers." After that, my father seemed to fuss over his roses with renewed intensity, spending hours painstakingly daubing the wounds of the newly pruned canes with tar. I came out toting my jar for catching the Japanese beetles that swarmed his precious flowers, their metallic green jackets looking like malevolent jewels among the red and yellow petals. Snaring the beetles, I secretly observed my father, thinking that his hovering ministrations seemed somehow exaggerated, misplaced, as though his nursing secretly tended deeper wounds elsewhere.

Later, in the sixties, during the Vietnam War, my father watched the television news, transfixed by reports of American and Vietcong military movements. Whenever the newsman mentioned the Chinese government, he shifted uneasily in his chair and cleared his throat, acting as though the anchor held him directly responsible for all that was happening. Following the news, he took out his violin, and after playing a few notes he turned into somebody else or went someplace where nobody could see him. Everything bad that had happened to him didn't appear to matter anymore. It seemed less important that he scratched and played out of tune, than that his anger and pain seemed to wane along with the echoes of his noise. It occurred to me that while playing the violin presented certain thorny problems, it had magical, even possibly redemptive powers.

When I was eight years old, I asked for a violin of my own. That year, on Christmas morning, I poked under the tree and spied what looked like a ham. At least it was shaped like one, wide at one end, narrow at the other, wrapped in shiny green paper. I was confused, then annoyed; didn't my parents know I hated ham? When I unwrapped the thing slowly, making much ado of peeling off the tape at both ends, making sure my parents noted my disapproval, I discovered a little wooden case in which there was a half-sized

violin. Embarrassed by the fuss I had made, I was careful not to show my ela-
tion. I even resisted playing it, leaving it untouched on the coffee table for the
rest of the day. It took every ounce of my willpower to ignore it. That night,
though, when everyone else had gone to sleep, I took it to bed with me. It
was the happiest moment of my life.

Later, I was shocked to learn that my parents found a teacher from
whom I was to take lessons. This had never occurred to me, as sleeping with
my violin seemed fulfilling enough, and besides, my father seemed able to
make his noises without benefit of a teacher. But soon I went every Saturday
afternoon to study with Mrs. Greenwood, a lady who wore flowery dresses
and smelled of lily-of-the-valley, and who proved to be the most gentle and
patient teacher. She taught me how to move my bow across the strings and
my fingers along the fingerboard, giving me exercises to practice. I practiced faithfully every day, drawing my bow as she instructed, making my violin go *Gack! Gack!* like a cat coughing up a hairball.

Miraculously I made progress, so that when I was twelve, I gave a full-
length recital including works by Handel, Mozart, and Wieniawski, and sent
a tape to Yeh Yeh. A few weeks later, he sent me a poem:

> The young person was expert in playing the violin.
> The audience understood her and her music.
> A white head like me concentrated and centered my attention on the record.
> The music went high and low.
> And everywhere, it was pushing against jade and knocking at the gold.
> It was like a phoenix, soaring up the sky.
> All yellow thrushes sing among the trees.
> The colored clouds hang over the woods.
> In this way, life seemed to be like the sun sweeping away dark shadows.
> It was also like the moon shining over the tops of the hills.
> The strings of the violin describe the beauty of spring very well.
> All goblins try to hide themselves.
> The light tones hit against all that was evil.
> The high tones even arouse the deaf.
> The hitting of the notes produce thunder.

I hardly knew what to make of this, as jade and gold were not part of my
world, nor goblins. And I was vaguely insulted by the line describing where

my playing aroused the deaf. What kind of land was it where phoenixes lived? What kind of evil did Yeh Yeh refer to? I had no idea of the forces that were sweeping through China from 1950 through 1960, of Mao Zedongs's revolutionary reforms, the devastating failure of his agricultural policies. I had not heard of the Hundred Flowers Movement, when he encouraged intellectuals to criticize his policies, then brutally punished them for doing so.

Sometime during this period, Yeh Yeh stopped writing. I asked my mother why we didn't hear from him.

"You wouldn't understand," she said. I saw that her thumbs were clenched between her fingers, so I knew better than to ask again.

Although I missed Yeh Yeh's letters, I tried to follow his advice by reading as much as I could, scribbling essays and stories and poems. I imagined myself becoming a scholar like him.

Meanwhile, my father came home from his lab day after day with thunder in his face. At the dinner table, he spoke of an experiment he was developing which he believed would lead to an important new discovery, but that no one in his office understood what he was trying to do or gave him credit. *Stupid people,* he said, glaring at us as though we would know what he was talking about, but what did we know of rocks? We sat within the radius of his anger and frustration, silently pondering the rice in our bowls, as if there we would find the antidote to our helplessness.

In the evenings I went into my room, closed the door, and played my violin. As I played Bach, Beethoven, and Mozart, the vibrations of the strings traveled up my arms into my chest and down my legs, stirring every cell of my body. I felt embraced by the music, held in a place of safety, where nothing bad could happen. Even though the music was stirring and sometimes sad, it always seemed beautiful to me and soothing. At that age, I felt other feelings I was unable to identify, but even in the confusion I knew the tears that filled my eyes were of happiness and gratitude. Sometimes, when I played, the feelings would come over me so powerfully I had to stop, I was shaking so hard.

In the summer of 1963, when I was thirteen, I went to Brevard Music Camp in North Carolina. There, I spent most of the time faking Tschaikovsky's Fourth Symphony. Instead of practicing, I traipsed around in the woods with two older girls from my cabin who divulged they were at camp not because they loved music, but because their parents were divorcing and wanted them out of the way. They both had big chests and spent hours tweezing their eyebrows, shaving their legs. At night, I would wake up, thinking I heard sounds of wild animals outside our cabin, but would discover it was Barb and Renee sobbing beneath their blankets.

At camp I began to realize how different I was from the white girls. One day, after orchestra rehearsal, I went with Barb and Renee into town and, caving in to their urging, bought an eyelining pencil for thirty-nine cents. They tried to help me draw a line on my upper eyelids so I would look like I could see, as Renee put it. Except we discovered that I didn't have a fold on my upper lid. No matter how far up we drew, clear up to my eyebrows, my eyes still looked like little slits. We discovered through arduous experimentation that the more eyeliner we put on, the slittier my eyes got, like the coin slots in the camp's Coke machine. There were other differences, too. In the communal showers I was amazed at how developed the bodies of the white girls were, how their jiggly curves contrasted to my skinny brown body. It struck me that I had never seen my mother without her clothes on. Somehow, I had forgotten that I had won a scholarship and was expected to play a solo with the orchestra, Vivaldi's A Minor Concerto, a baby piece. I argued with the camp director, trying to get out of the concert as I considered it a major inconvenience, but he showed me the program that already had my name printed on it. Finally I wrote to my parents telling them about the concert. A week and a half later, I received a package from my mother. In it were a new dress she had made, low-heeled white pumps, a pair of stockings, and a garter belt, which I had never seen before, much less worn. From going to the trouble of sending all these things, she tried to make up for the fact that neither she nor my father could make the long trip to hear me play. It was okay by me, as they had heard me play many times before, and besides, this was just the Vivaldi, a baby piece.

The day of the concert, which was to take place in an outdoor amphitheater, was hot and rainy. The humidity made the varnish on my violin turn tacky like a candied apple. My violin had already become unglued because of the humidity. When I played it buzzed loudly, making the Vivaldi sound like a swarm of bees. Still, the concert went okay, although I had not practiced, thinking the piece was beneath me. By that point I had begun learning the Bruch G Minor Concerto, a grown-up work.

Toward the end of camp, my mother wrote to tell me that she was coming on a bus to bring me home. It was a long trip from Washington, D. C., to Brevard, and she intended to stay overnight in a motel before we went back together. I thought it was strange that my father was not driving with her to come get me, since they had both driven me down. She did not say why, and I didn't ask. It made me think again about what it was like at home. Both Barb and Renee had told me it had been real quiet in their homes, too, before their parents split up.

I called around town and reserved a room for my mother in a boarding-house, proud because she told me to spend less than ten dollars and I had gotten it for seven. When she arrived, she didn't seem particularly happy to see me but acted anxious and preoccupied. I felt uneasy seeing her, too. Maybe it was because I wasn't ready for camp to end. In any case, neither of us had much to say. I took her to the bunkhouse where the other parents had come to pick up their daughters. One couple had come from Georgia and had brought a huge basket of peaches. The peaches were as big as soft-balls, and when you bit into them, the juice ran all over your face and down your arms. The parents joked and hugged their daughter, crying as though they hadn't seen her in years, even though we had been at camp only four weeks. Throughout, my mother hung back by the door, looking as if she was trying to be invisible. Whenever she said something, she sounded angry or afraid. I wondered why she couldn't be relaxed and happy like the parents with the peaches.

The boardinghouse didn't serve food, so my mother bought barbequed chicken in a box for us to share. I led her to my spot in the woods, a small clearing within a stand of birch where students were supposed to practice. I had spent most of my time reading, writing letters, swinging on a swing set nearby. My mother and I ate our barbeque, not speaking. I kept thinking how different she was from the parents of my bunkmates, who chatted eas-ily with their girls. Finally, I told her that we had performed Tschaikovsky's Fourth Symphony, leaving out the fact that every week I was demoted in the violin section, because I never practiced. After that, neither of us said any-thing. We swung in the swings side by side. I swung as high as I could, jab-bing my toes in the air, as though by doing so I could kick holes through the uncomfortable feeling between my mother and me. Every once in a while I would steal a glance at her. I always knew that my mother was beautiful, with soft pale skin and shiny black hair that she wore in waves. Her eyes were gentle, not too slanty. When I was in the second grade, she came to my class to show some of the things she had brought over from China. Wearing her beautiful silk *cheongsam,* she held up her ivory brooch, cinnabar ring, and tortoiseshell hairpin, causing all the other kids to *ooh* and *ahh* in wonder. I saw how my mother was different in a way that everyone admired. I was so proud. That was why I was confused when I came home one day to find her crying by herself in the kitchen. I had never heard anything sound more awful or frightening. She had come home from her job selling drapes at a department store to pay for her classes at the community college, where she was studying to be a medical technician. She never knew I listened as she sat at the kitchen table, repeating, in a fierce, pained voice, *I'm just as good as they are. I'm just as good.*

On the morning after the last day of camp, my mother and I got on a Greyhound bus that traveled all night and into the next morning to Washington, where my father waited for us. He seemed glad to see me, but in the car going home I could feel the tension between him and my mother. It wasn't until years later that my mother told me why my father hadn't been along to get me. They had bought a new house that summer, and he had strained his back finishing the basement, so he couldn't drive or sit for long periods. I wish my mother had told me this at the time, but I'm not sure it would have explained the uncomfortable silence between her and me, or what was wrong between her and my father.

After high school, I went to Oberlin, where I signed on for a double major in violin performance and liberal arts. Even here I saw there was hardly anyone else like me. There were only three other Orientals, and they were Japanese, upperclassmen, as well. I was depressed by the small, dull college town set in the middle of endless cornfields, where everything looked yellow and flat. During winter term, I read Solzhenitsyn's *The Gulag Archipelago*. Getting out of bed in the gelid gloom of the morning, trudging through snow toward classrooms with lights shining feebly in the darkness, I imagined myself sentenced to a life term in Siberia. My liberal arts courses were boring, the lectures by the professors sounding like the drone of factory sewing machines. As a freshman in the conservatory, I was relegated to the back of the violin section, the penal colony of the orchestra. I felt isolated, bleak, hopeless.

One day during a solid month of dark clouds and snow, four other music majors cajoled me into reading the Schubert C Major Cello Quintet. It was during the slow movement, marked *Adagio,* when I realized they had stopped playing and were staring at me.

"What's the matter?" Bonnie, the cellist, asked.

Tears were running down my face. I put my bow down. It occurred to me that the notes were speaking for me, that my feelings of despair, previously unexpressed, were suddenly released in a way that no words could convey. I looked at the others, and saw that what they saw in my face made them start to cry, too.

"What's the matter with us?" Bonnie said.

We finished the *Adagio,* then the *Scherzo* and *Finale.* The final two movements were ebullient, bold, sending chills down my spine, each wave reinforcing what I knew to be clear at last: that I was going to play music, no matter what, for the rest of my life—that music was my sanctuary as well as my way out. After we finished playing, I packed my violin and ran out into the brooding afternoon, clear with the knowledge that I was leaving. In the spring I auditioned for The Juilliard School, and by August had moved to New York City.

There, in the hallways and elevators of Juilliard, I found myself at eyelash distance with the prima donnas of the future, statuesque women dressed in leopard prints, turbans, pounds of mascara and eyeliner applied like Magic Marker. When they spoke, even something simple like, "Third floor, please," their voices seemed to rise from the diaphragm of the earth, cultivated in the totality of the Western operatic tradition. Every consonant and vowel resonated with their awareness of their rare gift and their belief that the world swooned to hear them. I was in awe of this heightened level of consciousness, this ego in full bloom, thinking there was no room here for modesty, for a person intent on remaining invisible.

Those of us studying with the same violin teacher, a reknowned pedagogue, met in the school cafeteria, and, surrounded by dancers living on Diet Coke and cigarettes, discussed our artistic progress and compared notes. Within the school's competitive and paranoid atmosphere, we were careful not to indulge in actual camaraderie, only permitting ourselves the small comfort of huddling to share our frustrations with our teacher.

"She said I was ready for a recording contract with RCA," said Rudi, a violinist from Rumania.

Gunhilde, a graduate student from Iceland, raised her eyebrow. "Really? She told me that last week."

I decided not to mention that our teacher had told me the same thing that very morning.

"She was over an hour late to my lesson," complained Vivien, a red-haired English girl.

Gunhilde snorted. "You're lucky. Last week, three of us showed up at the same time. She'd gotten that far behind. She asked me to come back at eleven. Eleven o'clock *at night.*"

"Well, she's still the best," Vivien said. "Look at what she's done for Itzhak Perlman, Pinchas Zukerman . . ."

We fell silent, knowing it didn't matter if we practiced until our fingers fell off, whether our teacher showed up on time or held off lunch until midnight. Even *she* wasn't going to make any of us into a Perlman or a Zukerman.

This depressing realization drove me to take out Yeh Yeh's poem, which I carried in my violin case, to read the line, *arousing the deaf,* over and over. Though I was still uncertain of its entire meaning, I began to relate its significance to my Juilliard experience. Even while I felt oppressed by the sense of hopelessness there, I had finally begun to practice in earnest, groping like an alchemist toiling in a lab for the formula that would integrate my mind, body, and soul with music. Though the goal continued to elude me, I began gradually to take pleasure, even revel, in the process—to search for a voice, *my* voice. I knew I didn't possess a diva's instrument, or the violinistic genius of Perlman or Zukerman, but I began to sense that what I had was still worthy of discovery and expression. Yeh Yeh's poem gave me hope that this frightening and confusing time in my life contained a lesson of far greater value than any musical aim. Still, there were many days when I put down my violin, my hands and neck aching from practice, and wondered at the point of it all.

That first year at Juilliard I encountered several girls from Korea and Japan, mostly violinists who filled the ranks of the school's orchestras. In the school cafeteria they separated into their own groups and chatted in their native tongues. I learned they had their own social organizations outside of school where they met and dated Japanese and Korean men. Even so, other students perceived us as one type. I overheard a young man, an oboist from Brooklyn who affected the "Beethoven" look—wild hair, a three-day stubble of beard, a moth-eaten black coat—expound to a female violinist, who was Japanese, "You Orientals might have technique up the wazoo, but you have no spontaneity, no soul. It's not in your conformist culture. None of you can play Mozart."

Word was that we were passive, docile, and not likely to follow through on professional goals, because we would probably marry and raise families. I don't know what was more chilling: the foregone conclusion that we were working so hard to master our musical skills only to abandon them or that we were perceived as a monolithic cultural type rather than individuals.

There was one person who stood out to refute this view. Her name was Lily, a pianist from Taiwan, the only other Chinese woman at Juilliard besides myself. She had arrived in New York only two years earlier and had already established herself as one of the best recital partners around. Not only that, but rumors were that every tour she embarked on turned into a turbulent affair that left her musical partner, whether a violinist, cellist, or singer, a broken man. I kept looking for her in the way a member of a rare species seeks its own kind in the wild, but sightings of her at Juilliard were few, because she was in such demand and nearly always on tour.

One evening, late, I was rushing to the elevator on my way to my violin lesson, which had been rescheduled from that morning. The doors were closing, and I was resigned to waiting for the next elevator when an arm reached out from within and held them open. I entered to find myself alone with Lily. I knew it was she, because word was that she wore only purple. She stood there in a purple velvet bell-bottomed pantsuit and a huge floppy purple hat that looked to have come straight from Carnaby Street in London. She carried a leather bag filled with piano music, from which a page of Schubert lieder stuck out. Awed by her presence, I hugged the opposite wall of the elevator, mute. Dressed in my usual proper knit dress, I felt like a chicken next to a bird of paradise. As the elevator rose I felt panic, knowing the moment of being in Lily's presence would soon come to an end.

Suddenly she said, "You Chinese?" The sound of her voice made me jump. It was husky, deep, a baritone. I nodded.

"Not from Taiwan. Not Hong Kong," she said, assessing me. Her hair was waist-length, heavy, straight as water. It swung like a curtain in front of her face. She flung it behind her with an impatient flip of her hand.

"I was born in Chicago," I said. My usual rueful refrain, as though revealing the place of my birth actually told anyone where I was from. She stared at me from beneath the rim of her hat, her dark eyes shining bright, like those of a clever small animal. Her face was round, her nose broad, not the face of a woman who went around breaking hearts. As though she sensed I was thinking this, she smiled, revealing a set of teeth so strong and white they looked like they could crunch clamshells.

"It actually helps, being different," she said in her raspy man's voice. The elevator doors opened, she went out. I watched her spring away on high platform shoes, wishing more than anything that I could be like her.

I graduated from Juilliard in 1972, the year Richard Nixon reinstated formal relations with China, which enabled my mother and brother to travel to the mainland. It was the year I got my first job as a quartet player, and when I broke my first promise to go visit Yeh Yeh. The following spring I had to write him again:

Dear Yeh Yeh,

I am very sorry to tell you that I will not be coming to visit you this summer because I have been invited to play in a music festival on the West Coast. It begins in June, right after my teaching ends, which means I will have to leave straight away. Following that, I have a recital in Washington, for which I must prepare. . . .

This time, at the end of the summer, when I looked for a blue aerogram from him, I was not surprised there was none.

A few years passed, during which I left the quartet and began freelancing. One Christmas, my mother showed me pictures of the trip she had taken to China with my sister and her family. One was of my three nieces, then aged seven, nine, and eleven, sitting in a train compartment on the journey from Shanghai to Beijing. They had gone in July, the hottest month, and in the picture they look melted, their faces covered with heat rash.

"How hot does it get in China?" I asked.

"Roasting! Roasting!" my mother said, fanning herself.

She told me my grandfather had asked when I would be coming to see him. "You're the only one he hasn't seen now," she said.

I felt the pressure of her words, feeling as though I stood in ocean surf, fighting the inexorable pull of sand and water between my toes as the tide goes out.

"I've sent him letters," I said, as if that would make up for everything. "He doesn't answer."

"He doesn't write anymore, since Nai Nai died."

Nai Nai was Yeh Yeh's wife of more than seventy years. Their marriage, like most marriages of the time, had been arranged by a matchmaker. The first time they met was on their wedding day.

"Is Yeh Yeh all right?" I asked.

"He's nearly ninety!" my mother snapped, her patience clearly at an end. I saw in her eyes how my excuses held no water, that I was an artist all right, self-centered, self-absorbed, lacking in filial devotion, the black sheep in the family.

"I promise I'll try to go next spring," I said.

It was something I had said so often that it sounded hollow even to my own ears.

Sure enough, that spring I won an audition for a new job in the Indianapolis Symphony. I called my mother with the news.

"I have to move, find a place to live," I said. "Work starts in September."

She offered her congratulations, but did not ask me about China or if I had written to Yeh Yeh. I felt worse rather than relieved. It was clear she had given up on me.

In September, as I hurriedly scanned the mail, already late for an afternoon rehearsal, I was surprised to see the blue aerogram. The handwriting on it was wobbly, uneven, but it was Yeh Yeh's. I opened it to read the single line:

Sung Lien, come see me soon, for I am failing.

Immediately I called my mother at her medical technician's lab.

"Yeh Yeh is depressed, now that Nai Nai is gone," she said, sounding sad. "He can't hear anymore. His eyes are bad."

I hung up, called the orchestra management, which informed me they would not release me from work, as I was in the first probationary year. I searched through the schedule, discovered a week of vacation during Christmas. I called a travel agent to buy a ticket to Shanghai, cursing the fact there were no direct flights to the capital, Beijing, where Yeh Yeh lived.

Yeh Yeh did not have a telephone, so I wrote to tell him that I was coming in December. I thought of the photograph of him and my uncle and aunts sitting around the charcoal brazier with bright red cheeks, freezing. I'd bring them thick gloves, I thought, a down quilt.

I put Yeh Yeh's most recent letter in my violin case, next to his poem. They went wherever I went, to rehearsals, concerts, on tour. I began buying things for my trip to China: long underwear, packets of hot chocolate mix, and cassette tapes. September flew by.

Then, in October, I was raking leaves in my yard. It was still warm, though the air had a crisp edge to it. I had left the windows open to air out the house. I stopped raking when I heard the phone ringing. It was my mother.

"Yeh Yeh is dead."

I began to sob.

My mother was silent on the other end, seemingly preoccupied with her own thoughts. "It was too hard, without Nai Nai," she said, finally. After another long pause, she said, "He took sleeping pills."

It took me several months to realize the full impact of losing my grandfather, and even then I hardly dared think of what I had missed. Soon after my mother's call, I received a letter from Aunt Lucy. I wrote back, and she returned it covered with red pencil marks correcting mistakes in my punctuation. With a shock I felt Yeh Yeh's presence, as though, not missing a beat, he had passed his red pencil to Lucy. *Sung Lien,* she admonished, writing in the margin of my returned letter in her small, impeccable hand, *pay attention to details! Develop a good mind!* Then, at the end, she wrote, *When are you coming to see us?*

During one of our infrequent phone calls, my mother informed me that Aunt Lucy suffered from hypertension, an aftereffect of the Cultural Revolution. The Red Guards had shaved her head, shut her in a room in solitary confinement for seven months. There, she had gone mad, tearing off her clothes, shrieking incoherently until the frightened guards released her in the care of her brother, Tim, Da Bobo. It was the first I had heard this story.

"When did you find out about this?" I asked my mother.

"In 1973, when your brother and I first go back. Uncle Tim shut all the doors and windows and told us what happened. He whisper the whole time, because he still scared of spies."

"What about Yeh Yeh?" I asked. "Did they arrest him, too?"

My mother was silent, as if she, too, feared being overheard. "Ask Lucy," she said, finally. "She know everything. Go see her, before it's too late."

That spring, my boyfriend, whom I had met in the Indianapolis Symphony, and I auditioned for the St. Paul Chamber Orchestra. To our great surprise and delight we were both offered jobs. By this time, I had taken up the viola. We had to move, find a place to live. At the same time, I received another letter from Aunt Lucy. *You must come to China,* she wrote. *Only here will you learn what it means to be Chinese.* Her words shook me. What did she mean? Wasn't I already Chinese? Didn't my every experience confirm my identity as an "other" in this country? Wasn't my hard-won technique of being invisible sufficient to ensure this identity? How would going to China change anything? Perhaps, I thought, my aunt knew something about me that I had yet to discover on my own. I resolved to buy a plane ticket to China after Fred and I moved to St. Paul, but never made the call. Why? Because I couldn't speak Mandarin? Because I was afraid to face what I had missed in not going to see my grandfather? That, in going to China, I would discover that all I had done to find my voice and place in the world had been based on false premises, and I would have to start all over?

To this day I don't know how it turned out that Aunt Lucy came to visit me. Word was that she came to accept an award from her alma mater, the University of Chicago, but I couldn't help think that she undertook a dual mission to see me. She was seventy-two at the time. Probably she had gotten tired of waiting. In any case, she came, and when we met, I saw immediately that she did know all about me, and that my life up to that point had been pure subterfuge.

3

SAINT PAUL, 1982

"WHAT SHOULD I DO WITH HER?" I ASKED MY MOTHER, TWO WEEKS BEFORE
Aunt Lucy was to arrive.

My mother was silent for several seconds, which was unusual, since she is
anxious about the cost of long-distance calls and prefers to keep the conversation brisk and brief.

"Probably no problem for you," she said at last. "Aunt Lucy like books
and music. She highbrow. You two very much alike."

There was that word again. *Highbrow.* I had no better idea of what my
mother meant by it now than I had as a child. And I could tell she was not
about to explain, because she was speaking in her clam voice, the one that is
tight with the effort of being nonjudgmental, but which lets escape a tiny but
distinct note of accusation. It reminded me once again that my pursuit of my
career prevented me from going to see Yeh Yeh before he died.

"Anything else?" I said.

"Well." My mother hesitated. "Maybe try not do too much. Aunt Lucy
hypertension hurt her eyes, other things, too."

In the background of my mother's phone line I heard machines whirring.
By now she had been working as a medical technician for more than twenty
years. Her modest title belied her real talent, which is being able to diagnose
patients' diseases in a single glance. Even the doctor she works for acknowl-
edges this. I know firsthand of her powers of observation. Whenever I catch

her looking at me, I can feel her X-ray eyes scanning my weakness of character.

"Anything else?" I said.

"No."

We both listened to the silence of the phone line, then hung up.

A week before my aunt's arrival in the Twin Cities, in October, I received a letter from her explaining that the University of Chicago was presenting her with a special award in recognition of her translations of the works of Walt Whitman, adding that she had already begun research on her next subject, Mark Twain. In awe that my aunt would attempt to translate the colloquial language of Mark Twain into Chinese, which seemed like the project of a lifetime, if not an impossible undertaking, I dug in an old box of books for my copy of *Huckleberry Finn* and went to the library for Justin Kaplan's book on Samuel Clemens. I barely managed to finish it the day before her arrival.

After Aunt Lucy's plane landed at the Minneapolis-St. Paul International Airport, she emerged from the jetway, standing on tiptoes and peering around anxiously through thick black glasses. The way she stretched her neck and periscoped around, straining to see, reminded me of a prairie dog on the lookout for predators. She carried two satchels that looked too heavy for her. Fred and I approached nervously. I had sent her pictures of us, so she recognized us immediately.

"Sung Lien!" she cried, in a thin, high-pitched voice. I raised my arms, thinking to hug her, but her satchels got in the way. I took hold of one, meaning to relieve her of it, but she held on, and we awkwardly sawed it back and forth. It was then I remembered that Chinese do not hug one another, and that if it weren't for the influence of my Caucasian friends, mostly Fred, I would not have developed the habit myself. Even now it remains an unnatural act in my family. Whenever I hug my parents, they act surprised, lifting their arms awkwardly, like adults who are attempting something that is much easier learned in childhood. So instead of hugging, my aunt, Fred, and I ended up patting one another on the shoulders and back, excitedly shouting inanities. In our frenzy, Fred and I patted each other.

On the drive back to our house, Fred answered Aunt Lucy's questions about St. Paul. "Isn't it true F. Scott Fitzgerald made his home here at one time? Was it *This Side of Paradise* that he wrote?" I worried about the impressions we would make. There were just the two of us, plus our large Malamute dog, and though sometimes our home seemed small for our needs in terms of office and studio space, it was still an entire house. I wondered what Aunt Lucy would think of two people having so much room. Uncle Tim, her brother, had sent letters complaining that the Chinese government, coping with peasants pouring from the countryside into Beijing, had appropriated half their house in order to shelter some new arrivals. A traditional structure built of four wings facing a garden courtyard, the house had been Yeh Yeh's legacy to Uncle Tim, his wife Dora, and Aunt Lucy to live in for the rest of their lives. Now, my uncle and his wife were left with only one wing, with Aunt Lucy occupying the one next to it. They were forced to share the courtyard and small kitchen with strangers who hung their wash on Yeh Yeh's plum tree and left rotting vegetable peelings all over. Uncle Tim had filed a petition to reclaim the house, but was told such matters took years to resolve. *And living at such close quarters with your Aunt Lucy is not easy,* Uncle Tim complained. *She finds fault with everything, and plays the same depressing Schubert songs over and over on her phonograph.*

We arrived home and began to unload the car. Maya, our dog, lumbered from her spot under the vibernum bush. Before I could stop her, she rose up and put her huge paws on Aunt Lucy's chest.

"Ai yah!" Aunt Lucy cried, as I grabbed Maya and pulled her away.

"Did she hurt you?"

"No." Laughing nervously, Aunt Lucy looked Maya up and down as she carefully edged away. Suddenly, I remembered an article I had read about how the Chinese had banned dogs, because they consumed too much food. Most dogs in China had, in fact, been eaten. No wonder Aunt Lucy looked at Maya so appraisingly. Maya was the size of a small cow.

While Fred showed Lucy around, I began making dinner. After waffling between serving Chinese or American food on my aunt's first night, I had finally decided on baked chicken, salad, rolls, and ice cream. The chicken went into the oven first. While I was tearing up the lettuce I heard Fred and Aunt Lucy wander into the alcove behind the kitchen, where Fred stored all his records, tapes, and stereo components. As I was slicing the tomatoes I heard Aunt Lucy exclaim, "Ah, I see you have *Winterreise!*"

Strains of Schubert began to sound throughout the house just as I was peeling off the paper from a tube of Pillsbury crescent rolls. Aunt Lucy watched as I rapped the tube against the counter, widening her eyes at the yeasty, muffled explosion and the sight of dough oozing through the slits of cardboard.

"It's like bread," I explained, rolling the triangles of dough, arranging them on a baking sheet. Aunt Lucy drew close, pushing her glasses up on her nose to see. I slid the baking sheet in the oven next to the pan of chicken. Aunt Lucy squatted to peer through the glass window of the door. Though in her seventies, she folded up with the elasticity of a six-year-old, and remained there the entire eight minutes it took the rolls to bake. She looked up at me twice, as if to confirm, like a child, that what she saw was actually happening. *"Hoo hoo hoo!"* she laughed. *"Hoo hoo hoo!"*

I laughed with relief. She seemed to be enjoying herself; I had made the right choices, so far.

We sat down to eat. Fred passed the butter.

"Ah!" Aunt Lucy exclaimed, sitting up in her chair. "It's been forty years since I had butter last, in Chicago!" She lopped off a chunk and spread it on her roll. Finishing that she reached for another roll, another chunk of butter. I pushed the basket of rolls toward her. Next she picked up a piece of chicken, nibbling at a drumstick gingerly at first, then, turning her head, gnawed at it with her incisors and molars, like a terrier. It was then that I realized she wore false teeth and that they didn't fit.

At the airport, I had had a mixed impression of my aunt. She stood about five feet tall, and though it was difficult to tell because her shirt and trousers were baggy and loose, seemed terribly thin. Her face was sallow, her hair greasy and so sparse that she appeared to have maybe twenty or thirty strands drawn back in a bun. At a distance, she looked like a little shabby old man. When we walked to the airport parking lot, she moved lightly, with surprising speed and vigor. There was something odd about her gait. When she got to the car, I heard her panting, as if the short distance had exhausted her. Not until days later did I notice that she walked on the balls of her feet, hardly letting her heels touch the ground. Later, when I mentioned this observation to my mother, she said it might be an indication of a neurological disorder, but did not elaborate. During that first dinner, I suspected something of that nature was going on when I looked under the table, annoyed with what I thought was Maya's tail thumping, but discovered that it was my aunt's foot kicking, kicking against the table leg.

The next morning, Aunt Lucy gave me a package wrapped in plain paper. "Your grandfather left this for you," she said. "He managed to save it from the burning. It's called *The Sound of Grass*."

It was a book of Yeh Yeh's poetry, written in Chinese. I had known that the Red Guards had seized all of Yeh Yeh's books and burned them in public. That he had somehow salvaged this one volume and given it to me made me feel indescribably honored and moved. I felt as though he had extended his hand across time and all that he suffered to touch me. My knees shook as I unwrapped it. Yeh Yeh's book was the size of a large paperback, bound with thick brown paper that had turned waxy with age. When I opened it, there was a faint cracking sound and brittle paper fragments fluttered out. I stared at the vertical lines of my grandfather's graceful calligraphy. Yeh Yeh was there, all right, in every stroke of the brush, but I couldn't read a word.

Aunt Lucy planned to stay with us for ten days before flying to Chicago to receive her award from the university. By now the number ten had stamped itself into my consciousness, as the Cultural Revolution had lasted ten years, from 1966 to 1976. Aunt Lucy said the Chinese now openly referred to the period as "The Ten Disastrous Years." I thought this was an extraordinary confession for the government to make, given its intractable nature. Still, simply because a movement had ended did not mean the suffering had. The enormity of human loss could not be summarized in the turn of a phrase, or a term of years. I couldn't stop pondering this, particularly in light of what happened to Aunt Lucy. I hardly dared hope that she would speak to me of those years, or that I could bring myself to ask her about them, as I feared bringing up all the pain and suffering again. Even so, I sensed that what happened then was crucial to my understanding of not only Aunt Lucy, but Yeh Yeh, and perhaps our entire family.

During Aunt Lucy's visit, I couldn't help but notice that our conversations always veered from personal matters.

"I had thought, after my Whitman project, of taking on Melville," she said one day as we sat alone together. "But then I decided he is rather long-winded. I think I much prefer the humor of Mark Twain. Perhaps he is the quintessential American, after Whitman, don't you think?"

I nodded, even though I thought I detected in her tone an undercurrent of fatalism, as though she knew she wouldn't live long enough to tackle Melville. She told me that, due to hypertension, her eyes had gotten to the point where she couldn't read more than an hour or two a day. She carried a vial of drops and dosed herself every few hours so that the medicine welled from her eyes. Each time she tilted her head back to put in the drops, I was reminded of what she had gone through. Reading was not only vital to her work, but was her life's passion. So, along with everything else, the Cultural

Revolution had robbed her of her eyes and ability to read, and because I loved reading, too, I identified closely with her loss.

Talk of scholarship prompted Aunt Lucy to speak of her university days in Chicago, how she met and married her husband, a fellow Chinese student, and how they both went home in 1952 when Mao Zedong summoned all Chinese back to help rebuild their country. She used the word, *patriot,* repeatedly.

"We love our country, you know," she said. Her English was melodious, refined, inflected with British tones. It was the English of missionary schools to which Chinese teachers had returned fresh from their study at Oxford. It gave her voice a certain authority, a particular academic air that seemed emotionally arid. It did not invite intimacy.

Still, I ventured closer. We were now approaching the story to which I was most drawn, but also most fearful. Reminding myself that it was she who had volunteered to speak of this period in her life, I gathered my courage. "Then, after you returned to China and began teaching again, you and your husband, and Yeh Yeh . . . ?"

I paused, waiting, hoping that she would pick up the thread I had tentatively pulled. There was a long silence.

"We were arrested by the Red Guards," Aunt Lucy said. She reached down, casually plucked a ball of lint from the sleeve of her sweater.

We had reached the edge of the chasm. I peered into it, trying to read Aunt Lucy's silence, wondering how to proceed. I sensed she had retreated to a place to which only she had rights. She continued to look down the front of her sweater, plucking at lint balls here and there, unself-conscious, like a cat grooming itself. Yet there was something in her action that conveyed the sense that what she withheld, she kept hidden from herself as well. I knew there was no going on.

"You can't give time back to a person," Fred said, when I told him of my dilemma.

"She only talks about her work," I said. "It's like she's lost all expectation for the other areas in her life. Doesn't she want anything? You'd think she'd look forward to some comfort at this stage in her life, good medical care, at least."

"Maybe she thinks what she has is good enough."

"How could that be? Look at her teeth! She can hardly chew, for heaven's sake. There has to be something I can do."

"You're doing fine," Fred said. "Besides, it's not your fault."

He gave me a meaningful look, but I ignored it. "We have so much," I said. "It wouldn't be any skin off our teeth . . ." I stopped, reluctant to share that I had been fantasizing about Aunt Lucy. If she came to live with us, she would have proper medical care, access to literary and academic resources. I realized there were obstacles, of course, her visa status, insurance matters. Still, over the next few days, I envisioned setting up a writing table in her room where she could work on her epic book on Herman Melville.

When I found out that Aunt Lucy loved eggs, which she said were almost impossible to get in China, I made her two soft-boiled eggs every morning. I also noticed that she had eaten up her ice cream that first night, scraping up every drop with her spoon, so I went out and bought three different kinds in quarts.

"Watch out," Fred warned, after watching Aunt Lucy spoon up a big bowl of double-fudge ice cream. "You're gonna make her fat."

"I know," I said, squirming. "But you can see how much she likes it. She's been deprived!"

I thought I saw her plump up a little. Her skin looked smoother, her hair thicker. She bathed nearly every night, drawing gallons of hot water into our claw-foot tub. As we sat downstairs listening to the waterfall, Fred rolled his eyes to the ceiling.

"You better go check. Maybe she's drowned."

I knew he was thinking of the heating bill as I was, I admit. "But they don't have hot water in Beijing!" I pleaded.

One cool evening, a week later, while Aunt Lucy was sitting in her bath, I went into her room to get a sweater, which I had stored in the closet. On the way out I saw the medicines she had laid out on the night table next to her bed. There were vials, tins of salve, boxes and bottles which were covered with pictures of snakes, dragons, tigers, antlered deer, bees. I picked up a box, sniffed it, thinking it smelled earthy and pungent, like something that had been buried in moss for a thousand years. I wondered which medications Aunt Lucy took for hypertension, which for insomnia. Every night we had woken to the sound of her pacing on the creaking floorboards. Now I noticed other items on the nightstand: pieces of string, rubber bands, a stained paper napkin. Every evening, at dinner, she took from her pocket the same paper napkin that I had laid beside her plate the day she arrived. I could hear my mother's voice: *The Chinese waste nothing.*

Beside the nightstand, on the floor, was the suitcase Aunt Lucy had brought from China. It was made of cheap black plastic, laid open to reveal the clothes she had left folded inside. There were two or three pairs of pants, a few shirts, all made of dark, coarsely woven cotton or wool, cut and sewn by an unskilled hand. I remember looking at her things, thinking, *Poor, poor.*

The next day I offered to take Aunt Lucy shopping, but she demurred. I was hardly surprised. My parents used to host Chinese dignitaries traveling through Washington, D.C., so I knew how Chinese guests were difficult. Not only did they conceal their needs and desires, but seemed to prefer risking death rather than inconvenience their hosts or make a request they could not fulfill. This would cause loss of face, which, in Chinese terms, was the worst offense imaginable. When I mentioned shopping the next day, Aunt Lucy refused again, which I took to be a matter of course, knowing the Chinese custom of refusing offers at least twice. When I did not mention shopping on the third day, she actually seemed disappointed and went about in low spirits the entire day. On the fourth day, when I offered to take her shopping, "just to look," she not only accepted right away, but gave me a reproachful look, as though I had been grossly negligent as a host. It was only then I realized how much she had wanted to shop from the beginning.

I took her to the store known at the time as Dayton's, so she could see what a modern American department store was like. At first she moved slowly down the brightly lit aisles, hardly looking left or right, holding her hands close to her chest as if afraid to touch anything. Dressed in her dark, shabby clothes, so unlike the white suburban women wearing denim and neatly pressed khaki, she seemed unaware of the other shoppers staring at her, as if a bedraggled crow had mistakenly gotten into an aviary of songbirds.

"Isn't this nice?" I said, pulling a scarf from its display. It was dark blue, with a discreet geometric pattern. On an impulse I blurted, "Let me buy it for you, Auntie."

She stared at the scarf, then backed away from the counter, shaking her head.

"Why not?"

But she had fled across the aisle into the coat section.

I debated whether to buy the scarf and surprise her with it later, but couldn't tell if she had not wanted to feel obligated to me for buying it for her, or whether she had simply not liked it. I decided against it.

Down-filled coats are the ticket in Minnesota, and moving through the racks of plump coats was difficult, like wading through a flotilla of inflatable mattresses. Finally, I saw Aunt Lucy trying to fend off the advances of a determined saleslady.

"Just try this on," the woman was saying, holding up a coat that looked as though it had been pumped with helium. She held it up to my aunt, guided her arm into the sleeve. Aunt Lucy resisted at first but then gave in, disappearing into the coat.

"There! What do you think?" the saleslady said, steering my aunt in front of a mirror. The coat was silver in color, corrugated in tire-like sections all over. A patch with the American flag was sewn to the collar on the back, in the way astronaut suits are designated. It made Aunt Lucy look like a dirigible on the way to the moon. She plucked helplessly at the belt mechanism holding her captive.

"I don't think so," she said, her voice sounding muffled from the depths of goose-down.

But she had gotten a taste of what it was to shop. Sensing this, the saleslady brought three more coats. Shrewdly assessing my aunt's preferences, she held up a dark gray coat, a navy-blue coat, and a black coat. This time my aunt tried them on willingly, even grabbing impatiently while the saleslady fumbled with the hanger.

"My aunt is from Beijing," I told the saleslady proudly.

"Isn't that nice!" she said, her eyes fixed on getting my aunt into the black coat.

"It does get cold in Beijing in the winter," my aunt muttered, more to herself than anyone. She stood in front of the three-way mirror. Her face was without expression, but she turned this way and that, giving the coat a thorough once-over.

"How much?" she asked, finally.

"This is one of our pre-winter specials. Only a hundred thirty-nine ninety-nine."

"Let me buy it for you, Auntie," I said.

"No!" she said.

I wasn't surprised at her rather sharp rejection. I was familiar, after all, with the Chinese custom of fighting over the bill. You see this in every Chinese restaurant. It is a matter of honor, a necessary ritual. I might honor the ritual, I thought, but in the end I would win.

"Let me buy the coat, Auntie," I said again, firmly.

"*No!*" she repeated, letting the coat fall to the floor. She began digging in her big black purse.

"Here," I said to the saleslady, handing her my Dayton's card.

"NO!" my aunt all but shouted, pushing the card away from the woman. Taking hold of my wrist with a grip that surprised me with its ferocity, Aunt Lucy looked me in the eye. "*I have the money,*" she said. Her eyes, looking tiny behind the thick lenses of her glasses, were intense. "They gave me all my back pay."

"Who's they? What back pay?"

"The Chinese government! After the Cultural Revolution, they tried to make up for what they did to me by returning all I would have earned during those years. So I am rich, you see!"

Reluctantly, I stood aside, watching her count out the traveler's checks she had bought during her first stop in California. Now I remembered my mother telling me that, prior to her arrest, Lucy earned a full professor's salary at the University of Beijing. At the time, it was one of the highest-paid jobs in China. Ten years' back pay was a considerable amount, even by Chinese standards. How ironic, my mother commented sadly. What was Lucy to do with all that money now? There was nothing to buy in China.

At home, she modeled her new coat for Fred, and, later that evening, as she got ready to take her bath, I asked if she ever thought of living in America.

"No," she said.

"But you can have anything you want here. You're free to go anywhere, do whatever you like."

She looked at me closely. "I am Chinese. My home is in China. It is *you* who must come to China!" The tone of her voice and the look in her eye made me shout inside, "*I will! I promise!*" I had never felt more sincere in my life. However Aunt Lucy must have seen the nature of my unpracticed heart, for the light in her face died away, and her eyes took on the look of the very old, the last of a species. "Too much longer and it will be too late," she said. Her voice sounded weary, and for an instant, there, in her eyes, I thought I saw Yeh Yeh.

I was glad that Aunt Lucy would have the chance to hear our orchestra rehearse and perform. At the very least, it solved the issue of how we were to occupy her during our working hours. The program that week included some of my favorite music; Rossini's *La Scala di Seta* Overture, Mozart's Piano Concerto no. 27 in B-flat, and *Music for Percussion, Strings, and Celeste,* by Bartok. Aunt Lucy came to all our rehearsals, which were painstaking and difficult. Afterward I waited for her reaction, but though she smiled, she said little. I was reluctant to ask her outright what she thought, because Chinese frown upon that as a way of fishing for compliments. I thought the rehearsals were generally going well, though tightness of ensemble continued to elude us in the Bartok, and we were having some difficulty meshing the complex rhythmic patterns from one section of the orchestra to the next. My colleagues and I grew increasingly frustrated and anxious as the week wore on.

On the evening of the performance, I helped Aunt Lucy find her seat in the first row of the balcony, then rushed backstage to change into my concert dress.

The Rossini begins with an extended, lyrical oboe solo that ends in a series of key-clacking runs. Oboists freely admit it is a nightmare. Our oboist outdid herself, spinning the phrases flawlessly, negotiating the thicket of runs without a hitch. Inspired, the rest of us joined her, and at the end I remembered thinking that the performance was particularly satisfying, not only for its technical polish, but buoyant spirit.

At the end of the piano concerto, the audience rose, calling out bravos. The faces in the front row shone with the joy that comes of receiving a gift far exceeding their expectations. I looked up into the balcony. Aunt Lucy was applauding politely.

During the intermission, musicians milled nervously backstage. Some practiced the difficult passages in the Bartok. The air was tense, as before a skirmish. I rosined my bow. Then the house lights dimmed once again, signaling the beginning of the second half of the concert.

The Bartok emerges like primitive life from a pale, eery dissonance. The entire first movement feels like the tentative, groping evolution of an early millenia. The second movement, in contrast, bursts forth in roiling exuberance. Making one's way through the changing rhythmic patterns is treacherous going, like struggling to keep one's footing on constantly shifting tectonic plates. In that evening's performance, I concentrated like mad, thrilled by the energy of the music and my furiously striving colleagues.

After the music ended, I walked offstage, still reeling from the jangle of harmony, stabbing rhythms, the sensation of the floor shaking underfoot. It was difficult to tell how it went. As we packed our instruments, Fred remarked that from his vantage point in the bass section it had been a good performance overall, in spite of a few minor mishaps. The spirit had been there.

We met Aunt Lucy in the foyer. I was still nervous, charged with the adrenalin of the performance. Perhaps it was this that made me forget about the Chinese taboo of fishing for compliments.

"Did you like the concert?" I asked.

"It was quite all right," she said, in a noncommittal tone.

"What did you think about the Bartok?"

"Hoo hoo!" she laughed, then paused, searching for words. "It's a strange piece. I don't think it suits me."

I felt Fred tugging my sleeve, but I plowed on.

"Wasn't the soloist in the Mozart wonderful?"

She was thoughtful. "He was competent," she said. Then, elevating her chin, as though surveying the horizon far beyond, intoned in her high-pitched British accent, "personally, I have always preferred William Kapell's renditions of Mozart."

Later that evening, when we were lying in bed, I said to Fred, "You know, Aunt Lucy's a snob."

He shrugged. "Maybe she just has her preferences."

Rigid opinions was more like it, I thought. Now I understood why my mother's voice took on that particular tone when she pronounced the word, *highbrow*.

During the last few days of Aunt Lucy's visit, I took her to several used bookstores, where we searched for early editions of Mark Twain. I looked through the stacks and brought her book after book, only to have her say that she had already read them. She informed me that, since the end of the Cultural Revolution, friends in Chicago had sent her so many books that her library in China was quite comprehensive. I was glad that her friends had been helpful, but I felt disappointed, as though they had usurped a role I had hoped to fulfill.

"I just don't get it," I said. Again, Fred and I were in bed, reading before going to sleep. "It's been more than a week, and I'm no closer to knowing her than before. I can't get through to her, and she doesn't reach out, either. It's weird—like she's untouchable, somehow. Also, I get the feeling she disapproves of the way we live."

"Naw," Fred said, turning a page of the latest *National Geographic* magazine he was reading. "The ice cream's nearly gone."

"But she's leaving the day after tomorrow, and I haven't found anything to give her!"

"What are you talking about?"

"I know this sounds corny, but I want to give her something that will commemorate her visit here, you know, mark the fact that we finally met. But nothing I've seen or thought of so far seems right. I know I'll never come up with anything comparable to Yeh Yeh's book."

"But that was Yeh Yeh's . . . your grandfather's gift to you."

"I know. That's the thing." I sighed, confused, trying to think of what I was struggling to say. Then, before I could stop it, I burst out, "Aunt Lucy's not like Yeh Yeh at all! He cared about me!" I heard the self-pity in my voice, but I couldn't help it. I really missed Yeh Yeh and wished with all my heart I had gone to see him, but it was too late.

Fred looked at me, then went back to his magazine. I was annoyed by his detachment, then remembered this was probably one of the reasons why we were together. Someone else, a Chinese man, for example, a probable proponent of traditional Confucian ideals regarding family, might have had strong opinions and expectations of me. Perhaps, since I encountered so few growing up, I assumed Chinese and other Asian men like my father, emerging from World War II and the Vietnam War, struggling to make inroads in still-suspicious American mainstream society, harbored secret complexes or fury that led them to adhere to rigid hierarchical and sexist principles. Compared to them, Fred, whose heritage is Swiss, thus explaining the neutrality flowing in his veins, appeared as open and refreshing as the sun. Over the years, I came to realize that what I viewed as his cultural and racial imperturbability was rooted not in passivity or indifference, but in his general acceptance and liking of people of all kinds. He loathed to judge, and this was what I found both lovable and maddening about him.

On the day before she was to leave, I took Aunt Lucy on a final shopping trip. She had mentioned she wanted to buy fabric to have made into shirts in China, stating proudly that it cost only a dollar fifty there. I took her to my favorite store on Grand Avenue. There, she ran her fingers along the bolts of cotton, wool, and silk, clearly impressed by the large selection. I browsed in another part of the store, secretly watching as she approached the section marked HOLIDAY FABRICS and paused before the bolts of shiny satins and sheer metallic weaves. She stared at them closely. From the way her body leaned forward, she seemed to will herself not to touch them. Several minutes later, she was still standing there when I returned, after having selected a length of wool for myself. Only now she had gotten to the end of the row and was inspecting a red-and-green taffeta plaid with gold metallic threads woven throughout. It was stunning fabric, perfect for Christmas festivity.

"That's pretty," I said, deliberately casual.

"Oh!" she said, startled, laughing nervously. She held her hand over her mouth, covering her false teeth.

I rolled the crisp fabric between my fingers. "Nine-fifty a yard. Not bad. It would only take a yard and a half to make a long-sleeved shirt." I hesitated, then took the plunge. "Please, Aunt Lucy, let me buy it for you."

For a moment I thought I saw her waver. She had not taken her eyes from the fabric the whole time. Then she seemed to gather herself. "We don't celebrate Christmas in China," she stated firmly. I felt my face grow hot. She moved away from the row.

Eventually, Aunt Lucy selected three pieces of cloth, all in shades of dark blue with subtle patterns. I thought they looked muted and dull, but said nothing. As the saleswoman measured and cut the material, I noticed Lucy slipping away. When I turned, I saw her standing back at the bolt of red-and-green taffeta plaid. The clash of her reason and desire was palpable.

"Will that be all?" the saleslady asked.

"Just a minute," I whispered.

Aunt Lucy reached out, touched the fabric, withdrew her finger quickly, as though singed, then turned and hurried back to the counter.

"Would you like anything else?" the woman behind the counter said to her.

"No," Aunt Lucy said.

The next morning, I slipped out of the house while Aunt Lucy ate her soft-boiled eggs. When I got back, she and Fred were standing out in the backyard, chatting. The air was crisp, smelling of dried leaves and apples. Suddenly, I realized we had not taken any pictures. Fred got the Polaroid and took a picture of Lucy and me standing together under our elm tree. Yellow leaves drifted down at our feet. Then we went back inside. I approached Aunt Lucy, bearing the only gift I had found to give her. I felt strangely shy and my hands shook, though I tried to act calm, as if it wasn't a big deal. When Aunt Lucy opened the brown paper bag my heart gave a little skip. Then she drew out a piece of the red-and-green taffeta plaid she had admired that I had rushed out during breakfast to buy. I didn't know what I hoped to see on her face, pleasure, some tiny acknowledgment. She looked puzzled.

"Thank you," she said, in a tone she might have used to comment on the weather, then went upstairs to finish packing.

We ended up being late, rushing madly to the airport. When we arrived at the terminal, we decided to save time by checking Aunt Lucy's bags at the curb. Fred went to park the car while I walked my aunt to the gate where her plane, bound for Chicago, waited. I was almost glad we had little time to say good-bye. The plane was already boarding.

"Have a safe trip," I said, giving her an awkward pat on the shoulder. She went up the jetway. I was surprised when she turned and gave a little wave. Then she disappeared.

I ran into Fred on his way into the airport.

"Let's go," I said.

He gave me a surprised look but went back out with me. We drove home in silence. The Polaroid picture lay on the kitchen table where we had left it. Now fully developed, I saw that Aunt Lucy hadn't gotten plumper or healthier-looking or anything. Other than her freshly washed hair, she hadn't changed a bit.

The rest of the day, I moped around downstairs. I took up Yeh Yeh's book of poetry, as I had every day of Aunt Lucy's visit, opening it carefully, staring at the Chinese script. The beautifully formed characters, full of rhythm and grace, remained undecipherable. I felt nothing of Yeh Yeh, nothing at all, only pain and emptiness and a strange yearning, like homesickness. It wasn't until late in the afternoon that I got up the energy to go into Aunt Lucy's room to change the sheets on her bed. As soon as I entered the room, I saw the brown bag. It was on her bed, neatly folded. Inside was the piece of red-and-green taffeta plaid.

4

AFTERSHOCK

AUNT LUCY'S REJECTION OF MY GIFT FELT LIKE A KICK IN THE STOMACH, AND for days afterward I nursed my hurt, sifting through memories of her visit for clues explaining her action. I couldn't believe she had meant to be mean. I brooded over her refusal of my offer to buy her a new coat, her pride in being able to afford things on her own. Perhaps the term *highbrow* meant responding to situations in purely intellectual terms, without regard to social niceties. Maybe Chinese manners were simply different. None of these explanations fully satisfied me. Had she always been that way? Except for her childlike delight in crescent rolls, butter, and ice cream, her every expression, even in terms of music, had been as muted as the fabric she had chosen for herself. Did she have feelings? Then I remembered that she had lost her mind during the Cultural Revolution and wondered if she had lost all her emotional senses, too. Had the Cultural Revolution stolen them along with her husband and ten years of freedom? How could I ever understand what that was like?

Fred helped put things in perspective.

"Don't take it personally," he said.

I finally decided that Aunt Lucy had judged the taffeta as too bright, too unseemly for wear in China, and that her decision to leave it behind had nothing to do with me. Still, hurt lingered. After all, during this rarest of visits I had hoped to know my aunt better, develop a relationship, a connection.

I told myself I couldn't lose what I never had, yet loss is what I felt and continued to feel for months after Aunt Lucy left.

Two years later, in the winter of 1984, Fred and I packed our bags to fly to
Washington, D.C., where we were to make our annual New Year's visit with
my mother. Taking one of our frequent breaks from classical music, we listened to AM radio playing Tina Turner's hit song "What's Love Got to Do
with It?" The night was so cold the moon looked brittle, and the tree outside our window cracked apart. After packing, I burrowed deep under our
down quilt and hefted the book I had been reading on and off ever since
Aunt Lucy's visit. It was called *The History of China.* I had taken it, along
with my mother's *Joy of Cooking,* from my parents' house when I left to set
up my first apartment in New York.

"Still reading that? Looks kinda out of date," Fred remarked, glancing
up from the latest *National Geographic,* where he was reading about Aus-
tralian marsupials.

I had turned to the frontispiece, which was a giant map of China depicting a landmass tinted robin's egg blue with patches of yellow and pink designating different regions. The pages smelled musty and creaked when I
turned them. Randomly, I flipped to a page to read:

> The Great Wall of China, a structure over four thousand miles long, be-
> tween sixteen to twenty-seven feet wide and standing between sixteen
> to thirty-three feet high, was built over a span of several hundred years
> beginning in 400 B.C. Intended to separate warring factions within the
> country and repel hostile forces without, its construction, due to harsh
> conditions and the enormity of the project, cost thousands of lives.

I digested the book's description of the geographical features affecting the
course of Chinese history.

"I had no idea how people were socked in by mountain ranges, deserts,
river valleys. Did you know how many distinct tribes there are? Can you
imagine how difficult it was to communicate from their remote locations?
And the natural disasters! You think Job had it rough . . . do you know how
many earthquakes struck China in the last century? How many fires, floods,
droughts, plagues . . . ?"

I glanced at Fred. His eyes, long glazed over, had returned to the pages of his magazine, immersing himself in the life of wombats.

I wondered how I had gone through school having learned so little about China. In our junior-high world history textbook there was a short paragraph on the Boxer Rebellion, but the explanation was so vague, with so little reference to China or the Chinese people, that I remained in the dark. Who or what were the boxers, and what role had they played? Were they boxers as in pugilists? Boxer shorts? Boxer dogs? Nothing made sense and I was too embarrassed to ask. When Neil Armstrong walked on the moon, a news anchor remarked that the pictures he took of the earth were so clear that you could see the Great Wall. I was surprised at the shiver of pride I felt at the fact that the only man-made structure visible at that distance was in *China*.

Even though *The History of China* was out of date and simplistic, I was fascinated by its lessons: that extreme conditions begat extreme measures and that the Chinese built structures not only to keep intruders out, but to preserve what they considered necessary for their survival. I was astounded by the extent to which different rulers struggled to unify disparate tribes into a collective consciousness, to forge one nation out of the vast, physically divided territory. Perhaps the history of China was no more complex or rife with catastrophic events than another country, but I thought it striking how determined Chinese rulers were to conceal her internal affairs from the rest of the world. Not only had they built the Great Wall to ensure her stature as the Forbidden Country, but they also constructed realms that were off-limits even to their own people: the Forbidden Palace, the Forbidden City within the capital itself. China became, like a giant nautilus, a body of endless secret chambers. Even with the invention of the telegraph, radio, television, and satellite, she continued to try to deflect the prying eyes of other nations. During Mao Zedong's Communist revolution of 1949, the message Western nations seemed to hear more than any other was that China's inner struggles were strictly a private matter.

"We gotta get up early tomorrow, you know." Fred's voice came muffled from beneath the quilt. He had turned off his reading light long ago.

"Just a little more," I said, turning a page.

He raised his head, turned the light back on. His face was sleepy, curious. "What gives? You never used to be interested in that stuff."

I shook my head.

"No, really," he said, tapping my book with his finger.

I sighed. "Well, *okay*. I got a letter from my aunt."

He sat up. "When?"

"Oh, weeks ago."

"*Weeks* ago? What did she say?"

I pulled out the bed stand drawer, took out the blue aerogram.

"Read it to me," Fred commanded, fluffing his pillow, settling back as if readying himself for a bedtime tale.

I carefully unfolded the tissue-like paper and read aloud:

Dear Sung Lien,

The news is that the government is returning our house to us, in which case the peasants will have to move out. Tim wants to build a bathroom, but I wish to enlarge my apartment. I am the oldest, after all. Everything has come about thanks to your father, who wrote a letter to the Chinese government supporting our claim. Apparently his letter, with its American stamp, carried more weight than the appeals we've made over the past ten years.

We saw your father just last week, when he stopped in Beijing on his way to Mongolia. He came for dinner, but did not stay, though we prepared a bed for him. We are sad that he preferred a hotel to his family home.

I feel tired. All I want is to read and listen to music. Today there was a recital on the BBC by Elizabeth Schwarzkopf, recorded in 1956. Her elocution was superb, even though her voice sounded a bit metallic.

My translation of *Leaves of Grass* is finally out. I would send you a copy, but there is no point since you don't read Chinese. I must close for now. When are you coming to visit us?—Aunt Lucy.

The furnace kicked on with a bang, causing the air ducts to heave and the walls to make cracking noises.

"Nice letter," Fred murmured, settling back to sleep.

"Except how it would be pointless to send me her book . . ."

"Well . . ." He raised his head from the covers. Looking at me his face took on an uneasy look, as though he sensed he was not going to sleep that night. "Well, it makes sense, kinda. What's the point in sending you a book you can't read?"

I squeezed a pillow to my chest. "You know that's not it. It's that she's so *disapproving.* Why should I go to China to visit, if I'm such a disappointment?" I knew I sounded like a four-year-old, but couldn't help it.

"So is that what this is all about?" Fred said, pointing to the book.

I grunted and yanked the covers so that the dog, who was sleeping at the foot of the bed, raised her head. Turning out the light I tried to go to sleep, but doubts continued to flicker in the darkness. In the two years since Aunt Lucy's visit, they had grown in number and now felt as weighty as moths banging against my face.

The next afternoon, my mother met us at National Airport in Washington, D.C. She wore the same navy-blue coat she'd had for years, dark slacks, sensible shoes. She seemed happy to see me and broke out laughing when Fred hugged her, covering up by saying his beard tickled her. I was glad the two of them got along so well.

Though Fred offered to drive, my mother insisted on taking the wheel. Having gotten her license as an adult, she drove with exaggerated caution, shifting her thumbs along the rim of the steering wheel as though pressing pastry in a pie pan.

When we got home I wandered through the house, testing the emotional atmosphere, recalling how reentry in this place was a touchy thing. Somehow the house seemed more open, light-filled, and then I noticed the additional window that my mother had installed in the living room. Going downstairs I saw the new baby grand piano she had bought for herself. Her sole personal extravagance, its lid was raised, like a wing, so that it looked poised for flight. Near it, laid out on a velvet cloth, were my mother's recorders. Like painting, playing the recorder had become a recent passion of hers. She had joined a renaissance group that performed regularly in the metropolitan area. The group wore clothes of the period, and my mother made her own costumes. I tried to picture her, a Chinese woman in her late sixties dressed in the frills and lace of the French Renaissance, but even in light of today's multicultural dictums, I had trouble imagining it.

On the sunny side of the room my mother had set up her painting area, a table cluttered with rolls of rice paper and jars of brushes. A half-finished painting lay curled atop the heap. Nearby lay a paintbrush on a plate, still wet, looking as though my mother had just applied a last-minute wash of color before rushing off to meet our plane.

My father's scientific awards hung on the opposite wall. Presented by different prestigious institutions, they laud his several geological discoveries. Framed in black, lettered in gold, the testimonials previously claimed the center of attention in the room. Now, with the addition of the piano, the recorders, the paints, they seemed to recede into the walls.

My mother made stir-fried spinach and *kung pao gi ding,* spicy chicken with peanuts, my favorite, for dinner. As I scooped rice from the steamer I noticed the new clock radio placed between the refrigerator and the sink. It was another subtle change in the house, another sign that my mother, though living alone, was taking care of herself.

After dinner, she exclaimed, "*Ai Yah!* I forgot! Lucy sent her book!" and went to fetch my aunt's translation of *Leaves of Grass.* When she handed it to me, I was surprised by its heft. The pages were many and thin, like those in a telephone book. The Chinese print seemed like the marks of a tiny bird that had streaked across an ink pad and then performed intricate maneuvers on paper. Yet there was dignity in the neat upright rows, beauty and rhythm in the characters. Turning the pages, I felt the years of Aunt Lucy's labor. I set the book down carefully, then followed my mother into the kitchen, where she was washing dishes. Fred had gone into the living room to watch the *McNeil-Lehrer Report.* I picked up a dishtowel.

"I got letter from Da Bobo and Da Mama," she said, using the Chinese designations for Uncle Tim and his wife, Dora. "Now they got their house back, they build a real bathroom with toilet and bathtub."

She paused, as though waiting for me to react, but the stupidity in my face set her off. "They do it for you!"

The all-too-familiar alarms went off in my head. "You mean, they're making a bathroom just for me?" I stammered. "But I'm not sure this is a good time for me to go to China."

My mother's eyes narrowed before she turned away. Picking up a pot she began to rinse it, hitting the side of the sink. *Bang, bang.*

"I mean, shouldn't I learn Mandarin first?" I added hurriedly. "Middlebury College has a course, but it takes all summer—besides, I don't know if I can get off work . . ."

Suddenly my mother, with hands still dripping soapsuds, reached over and switched on the radio next to the sink so that music exploded into the kitchen, drowning out my voice. It was the aria from the opera, *Tosca,* in which Tosca rebukes her arch enemy, Scarpia. Her voice, shrill with scorn and betrayal, spat static from the radio. I was shocked by my mother's abrupt act, the uncanny coincidence of Tosca's concomitant message. Though I recovered enough to turn the radio down so that Tosca's voice was reduced to the sound of a fly buzzing in a box, I could think of nothing to say in my own defense. My mother began rinsing the last of the dishes. I sensed that though she was still angry, she felt a certain satisfaction knowing that cosmic forces, expressed by the radio, aligned with her view of me. It was too much to withstand both my mother and cosmic forces, much less deal with my own ambivalence and self-contempt. I left the kitchen.

That night, I got out of bed and leafed through the photo albums of my mother's China trips. I had seen them all before, but this time I was looking for something different. I opened the album marked 1976. Here were pictures of Yeh Yeh and Aunt Lucy posing in the courtyard of the family home. Both looked dignified, important, commanding the eye of the viewer. Now, for the first time, I noticed two out-of-focus figures, a man and a woman, in the background. It was not likely they were the peasant neighbors, because they would not have dared venture so close to my grandfather. So who could they be but my Uncle Tim, Da Bobo, and Aunt Dora, Da Mama?

Since my correspondence had been solely with Yeh Yeh and Aunt Lucy, I realized I knew virtually nothing about my other relatives. "Kind of a black sheep," my mother had said, referring to Uncle Tim, fifteen months older than my father. Although he had the same opportunity to come to the United States after World War II, he chose to return to China. He married Dora rather late in life, after she divorced her first husband. I surmise that the divorce, still considered anathema in China, forced them into a kind of social underground. I wondered whether it affected their standing in the family. I was also curious as to how Uncle Tim eluded scrutiny and punishment during the Cultural Revolution, avoiding prison, unlike his father and sister.

Among the many photographs, there is only one of Da Bobo and Da Mama alone together. They are sitting on the landing of the family home. My uncle's head looks egg-shaped, his cheekbones so high that his eyes look like narrow crevices in a rock. His thinning, close-cropped hair and the proud, faraway look in his eyes give him the appearance of a warrior, like Geronimo.

My Aunt Dora looks plump with white skin. Her hair is kinky, poodle-like, the result of a modern Chinese permanent gone haywire. She wears heavy black glasses like Aunt Lucy. Both she and my uncle wear shoes that are scuffed, the soles detached, gaping like the mouths of fish.

What would it be like to meet them in China, I wondered. Already I had failed to establish a bond with Aunt Lucy, and she was the one with whom I thought I had the most in common. Still, there was something in Da Bobo's expression that made me pause. He had the look of a person who was not a dreamer but a pragmatist, a man to whom life was simple and clear, who didn't know the meaning of ambivalence, much less defeat. I had no doubt I could learn something from him.

The next day was New Year's Eve. It was also Saturday, the day of the week my father came to visit my mother. It was an arrangement they had worked out together, many years ago, when we children had finally left home. Now my father lived in a condominium forty minutes away. It was small and sparsely furnished, my mother said, appropriate for a man who had undertaken the life of an ascetic and practitioner of Zazen, a form of Zen meditation. He had given away most of his possessions and avoided all social activity except tennis, which he continued to play as an acceptable form of exercise. He no longer played the violin, saying it was hard on his arthritis. In its place, he had taken up the panpipe.

"He looks shabby," my mother declared. Her tone conveyed not only her skepticism for his new lifestyle, but a tinge of satisfaction, as though, to her way of thinking, my father, rather than having transcended the conventionality of their life together, had actually slipped a notch. The tone of her voice made me think again of the revolution that had overtaken their marriage. I doubted I would ever know the entire truth of it. I knew certain things about a few events, but most of it happened when I was far away and preoccupied with my own life, so the rest was conjecture. What I sensed was that their revolution, like most revolutions, was ongoing. It was not resolved and might never be. The tenor of it remained consistent with what had been for my family for as long as I can remember: what went on flowed deeply, silently, and was so painful that no one dared speak of it.

My father arrived in time for lunch. He was dressed in a strange get-up for an ascetic: an Adidas jogging suit and flat black Chinese slippers. He carried a briefcase and his twenty-six-pipe pan flute. He had lost weight, but looked fit. Age spots were beginning to appear on his face and hands. His eyes were developing a hooded look, but he still looked far younger than his sixty-five years. We hugged in a stiff embrace.

Over lunch, which was noodles and dumplings my mother had heated in the microwave, I asked my father about his meditation techniques. I asked him out of polite but sincere interest, knowing it was a sure bet for conversation, like asking a casual acquaintance about his favorite hobby. He talked about the latest books on Tibetan meditation techniques and his experiments with biofeedback, which was much in vogue in the mid-eighties as a tool for spiritual exploration and self-improvement. He spoke in the measured tones of a scientist. Underlying his voice of reason I heard the tremulous hum of a fanatic.

My father has had several obsessions that I can remember, but the one that stands out is his sausage-making. When I was about five years old, he and my mother spent days up to their elbows in a vat of ground pork, using chopsticks to stuff the meat into pig-intestine casing. It was a laborious, messy process, and I remember sausage everywhere, even bits of it clinging to my father's eyebrows. The stuffed links were then strung on racks hung from the basement ceiling. I remember bumping into the moist loops when I went there to fetch my bicycle. I began to think of them as much a part of the basement as wet laundry on a line, but one day they were gone and that was that. I don't remember if we ate them or if my father gave them away. His obsessions were characterized by the intensity of his involvement and their abrupt end.

"Did you know that Einstein used only a tenth of his brain?" my father asked. He was perspiring from the heat of the noodle broth and had taken off his glasses, which were steamed up. Now he was sweaty and squinting, looking not only fanatical but downright crazy. "The reason Einstein was absentminded," he went on, "was because his brain waves were in the beta state, where the waves are slower, where creativity takes place. Did you know beta can be achieved through meditation? Here, look at this graph."

He opened his briefcase and unfurled a roll of paper the length of a Lincoln Continental. It was a graph illustrating his experiment using a biofeedback machine. He explained how he attached the machine's electrodes to his temples to track his brain waves during meditation. I tried to imagine him sitting in the lotus position with wires sticking out of his head, thinking that,

1) my father was a mad scientist.
2) the only thing he and Einstein had in common was that they both played the violin badly.
3) even if he seemed a little looney, I admired him tremendously for his curious, unstoppable passions.

I glanced at my mother. She had partially covered her mouth with her hand, a gesture that half covered a smile and half revealed it. The half-covered smile let it be known that she listened to this Zen-science talk every Saturday, and though she thought it was mostly hocus-pocus deigned to tolerate it. Her half-revealed smile invited me to join in a conspiracy of her view. Suddenly ashamed for my parents, I looked down into my bowl of noodles. I realized I had been half smiling, too, but for a different reason. It didn't mean I was willing to enter her pact.

After lunch, we went into the living room, where my father took out his panpipe and gave a few blasts to warm up. Though I sat across the room, I gasped with the pain in my ears. Playing the panpipe takes skill to get the sound going, then prodigious amounts of breath to sustain the tones. Self-taught, as usual, my father initiated his sound by pursing his lips and spewing air with enough force to propel a nail through a board. Since the air in his lungs was all but expended from such force, the tone he produced lingered in the air no longer than the initial blast. Thus the notes he played did not flow smoothly from one to another but were sent into the atmosphere like sporadic, unrelated projectiles. The most astonishing thing about my father's playing was the fact that he was totally oblivious to the effect he had on everyone else in the room. Closing his eyes in bliss, he played "Danny Boy," as if it were the anthem to a spitting contest. While Fred and I went rigid with shock, my mother listened calmly and even hummed along. After a few tunes, she fetched her recorder and began to play harmony to my father's melody. She had been playing for a few years, and though she was far more skilled than my father (she had taken lessons from a professional), her tone burbled now and then when her fingers missed the holes or wavered when she encountered note values longer than her breath. My parents' duet was most amazing in that the tones of the panpipe completely obliterated those of the recorder. My mother's gentle song could be heard only when my father was inhaling in preparation for his next detonation of sound. I thought there was no equal in the whole of nature for the sheer dischord. But what sounded was not what mattered. What mattered was the look on the faces of my parents as they sat at opposite sides of the room playing together. Here there was simple joy, and, finally, perfect attunement. How they had achieved this peculiar state of grace at this stage in their lives I did not hope to discover. There was no doubt that it was theirs alone and that it had come about only through prolonged and painful struggle. I began to see similarities in the transformation of their marriage and the changes that had taken place in China. Unhappiness and suffering brought about drastic measures. Revolution was inevitable.

After about twenty minutes, they both ran out of breath and put their instruments away. We wiled away time talking about the newest tennis stars and what it took to hit a backhand approach shot. My father sat in the chair in the patch of sunlight streaming in from the window my mother had just added. Here he was strangely highlighted, made focal in a way he had never been when he lived in this house. When I looked at him, leaning back in the chair with his eyes closed, I was struck by how contented he looked.

At five o'clock, he announced he was taking us out to dinner. We drove to the Big Wong, a huge restaurant near Seven Corners. At this hour, the restaurant, strung with gaudy decorations in anticipation of the New Year's crowds arriving later, was practically empty. My father ordered steamed flounder, orange beef, braised eggplant, twice-cooked green beans. When it arrived, we began eating silently. Almost immediately he grimaced.

"The string beans are tough," he complained, pulling a fiber from his teeth. "Too much orange in the beef," he went on, flicking a piece of orange rind onto the side of his plate. I felt my muscles tensing. From the side of my eye I saw my mother shift disapprovingly in her seat. Again I felt myself on the pendulum swinging between my parents, balancing precariously over their rift. Throughout, Fred, true to his Swiss roots, retained his equilibrium, quietly cleaning his plate. I tried to learn something from his example, but finally the strain became too great. Before I could think better of it I blurted, "So you saw Aunt Lucy and Da Bobo and Da Mama in Beijing?"

My father, eating eggplant, nodded.

"How were they?"

"Fine."

"Aunt Lucy said you stayed for dinner."

He chewed guardedly.

"But you didn't stay?"

Suddenly he made a noise of annoyance and spat out a gob of gristle. I looked over at my mother. Her thumbs were clenched between her fingers.

"I went back to the hotel, because I was leaving early the next morning for the rare earth deposits in Mongolia," he said, in a voice that barely contained his agitation. Then he burst out, suddenly bitter, "Why should I bother them? It was a business trip!"

Across the table I saw a flurry of my mother's hands. *Settle for that,* they signaled.

I felt my father's accusing eyes on my face. "I wrote a letter to the government on their behalf! They're getting their house back, aren't they?"

"I'm . . . I'm sure they're very grateful," I stammered.

My father snatched his chopsticks, began to stab at the fish. Ignoring the unfinished dishes on the table, my mother signaled for the check.

Back home, we gathered in front of the television, where I flipped through the channels, settling on a public television program on the mating rituals of black-footed boobies. Even the manic head-bobbing of the boobies was preferable to the tense silence that had taken over the house. During the fund-raising break, my father abruptly stood up and put on his coat.

"Time to meditate," he announced.

I looked over at my mother. She did not react, but her stillness looked as though it were crafted with every ounce of her strength.

After my father left, my mother looked as though she had caught a blow to the side of her head. My dismay gave way to anger.

"Does he always do this?" I asked.

Her sagging face was her answer, but the set of her shoulders warned me against pity. For her sake I said nothing, but pondered the hole my father had left, trying to make sense of it. Like a pit dug in the earth, it was slowly filling with something that felt thicker than water. Grief, I thought.

We began to scurry about, covering up the hole.

"I'll make tea."

"How about some duets?"

My mother jumped up to get her recorder. Soon she and Fred were warbling together while I listened, marveling at her resiliency. Once again, she had abandoned pain, leaving behind only a faint wake where I remained, contemplating the swells. Such was the cost of revolution, I thought.

The next day, as Fred and I packed to go home to Minnesota, my father phoned to say good-bye. Our conversation was brief. I thought I detected a tiny note of regret that he had spent so little time with us, choosing this new peripheral role in our family. Of course, we did not speak of this directly. We wished each other a happy New Year.

Just as we were about to leave my mother's house for the airport, the postman arrived. The sight of the blue aerogram he delivered struck me like a bolt out of the sky. Since it had covered an incredible distance, it seemed to relay a momentous message. Good news or bad? My response was the same to all the other aerograms I had received, a mixture of wonder and dread that an object so fragile and light should contain messages of such great magnitude, as Yeh Yeh's dying wish and my Aunt Lucy's reflections on a waning life. Unlike the other aerograms, the return address in Chinese script, was in handwriting I didn't recognize. My hands shook as I handed it to my mother, certain that it contained news that something terrible had happened to Aunt Lucy. My mother tore open the letter. After reading the first few lines, she shouted.

"It's from Da Bobo and Da Mama! They're coming to America!"

5

MINNESOTA

Weeks later, when we still hadn't heard from Da Bobo and Da Mama, I called my mother.

"Sometime take long time," she said, sighing audibly over the phone. "Hard to tell. Sometime Chinese government don't let couples go. Too risky. Maybe husband, maybe wife, but not both."

"But how could they be a risk? They're both retired, aren't they? And they're only applying for visitors' visas, right?"

My mother sighed again. "We just try be patient."

It was just as well my aunt and uncle weren't coming right away. On the *CBS Evening News,* Dan Rather reported that Minnesotans were suffering the snowiest, most frigid February in ten years. The TV camera panned over a barren white landscape whipped by vicious winds, lingering on barely distinguishable humps of cars piled every which way on Highway 35W.

Having learned to adopt the Minnesota way of coping with winter, Fred and I obeyed Public Radio's warning about eighty-below windchill: *Exposed skin freezes in under thirty seconds! Avoid going out at all costs!* We stayed in and took stock of our cans of soup. Every so often we had to let the dog out. Maya bounded in the snow, snouting tunnels and cartwheeling in the drifts with Malamute joy, coming back looking droopy and depressed only when it was dark and we were hoarse from calling her name.

At the end of February, the orchestra went on a regional tour, traveling by bus to Brainerd, Bemidji, Morris, Virginia, and Alexandria to perform in community college auditoriums and high school gymnasiums. In locker rooms smelling of athletic socks and chlorine, the women musicians changed into formal black concert gowns, remarking that it seemed an unusual venue for Mozart. Meanwhile the men, formal coattails flapping, practiced shooting baskets in the gym.

After concerts we went back to our motel, which was usually situated on the side of a remote rural highway. Since everything was closed by nine o'clock, we retreated to our rooms to watch nature shows on geckos on cable TV or to peer out from behind skimpy motel curtains into the icy gloom. Here, up north, the air was colder, drier. Breathing it made you feel as if you had thistles sprouting in your nose. Sleep was impossible because of the snowmobiles zooming around in the motel parking lot. I thought of my relatives in Beijing, wondering how they were getting through the winter. I imagined them huddled around the charcoal heater, their faces turning bright red, then blue.

After we got home, I called my mother. "Any news?"

"No visas yet."

"Can't Dad write a letter?"

"He already write. No more we can do."

"What should I do with them when they come?"

My mother gave a mirthful snort. "That's easy. They like everything."

"You mean they're not like Aunt Lucy?"

"Oh, no. Not highbrows. They don't read. I mean, they read, but that's not all they do."

"Do they like music?"

My mother paused. "Well . . . yes. But not classical."

"What, then?"

She thought for a while. "Bing Crosby."

"Bing Crosby? I don't have any Bing Crosby. How do I get Bing Crosby?"

"Don't worry," she repeated, and hung up.

That spring it rained every day, and the news in May was to expect the biggest crop of mosquitoes ever. Each body of water, from the Mississippi River to the puddle beneath our rainspout, was a potential breeding ground. Though helicopters flew overhead dropping anti-mosquito agents, we could still hear the ominous drone of the pests breeding and multiplying. In June,

I noticed dark swarms forming at the bottom of Summit Avenue. The drone turned into a high-pitched roar, signaling that the mosquitoes were throttling through the air like squadrons of B-52s. The *Pioneer Press* was full of tips: *Avoid going out early in the morning or at dusk. Avoid shady areas. Take vitamin B. Eat garlic!*

One late afternoon in June, after our concert season had ended and Fred was trying to light our first barbeque of the summer, the telephone rang.

"They're coming!" my mother shouted. "Da Bobo and Da Mama! They got visas! They're coming!"

"When?" I said, feeling my heart beat fast.

"Can't say, these things very unpredictable. I call you later," my mother said, and hung up.

Two weeks later, she called to say my uncle and aunt had arrived in Washington, D.C., and were spending a week with her before coming to visit us. I had already sent her money for their plane tickets to Minnesota. The day before their arrival I looked up the word *mosquito* in my Chinese dictionary: *Winze*. The next day, on the way to the airport, we stopped to pick up a can of jungle-strength OFF and a tube of Benadryl.

I spotted them immediately when they emerged from the jetway. Da Mama spied me among the waiting crowd, and, pulling Da Bobo along by the hand, rushed forward, looking me up and down.

"You look just like your father!" she exclaimed.

My uncle's eyes glowed strangely, as though he recognized not only me, but my father, his runaway brother, in my face.

"Sung Lien," he said, his voice trembling strangely, "we have waited so long to see you." Then he put both his hands around mine. In that instant, I felt him not only bind the loose ends of the rift between him and his brother, but soothe the wavering heart I had inherited. It seemed to me, as I had dared hope, that my uncle turned out to be a man to whom politics and national allegiance mattered little in the face of family ties. Overwhelmed, I stood there mute until the moment grew awkward and I withdrew my hands. Only then was I able to mumble, "I'm so glad you're here, Da Bobo, Da Mama."

On the drive home, my uncle and aunt stared out from the back seat of the car exclaiming, "Look at the trees, the grass! Look how green everything is! Oh! Look! A bird! A squirrel!" It was hard to say who enjoyed the ride more, my relatives, in the euphoria of their new surroundings, or us, witnessing their delight. I was touched by their open admiration of what we so often took for granted—the smallest expanse of green grass, the overhead cover of trees—but was struck by the extent of their deprivation. I had heard that Beijing was a stark place, so denuded of greenery there were no longer any birds, but I had not experienced the true impact of such desolation. I felt the magnitude of what my uncle and aunt had sacrificed and endured by staying behind in China all these years. I felt, as I had with Aunt Lucy, an overwhelming urge to compensate them for what seemed the inequitable riches of my life here in America.

When we arrived at the house, Maya, who was now ten years old, rheumy-eyed, and gaseous, greeted my relatives. My aunt took Maya's grizzled head in her hands and cooed endearments in Chinese. Da Bobo patted her and shouted in her ear as though she was a post. My mother had warned me that my uncle had lost a good deal of his hearing a decade before but refused to wear a hearing aid because the ones in China fitted so poorly. She said you could always tell who the hard-of-hearing were in China. They were the ones who walked as though they balanced invisible trays on their heads, afraid of tipping the hearing aids from their ears.

Da Bobo and Da Mama went through the house, admiring the woodwork, the leaded windows. They seemed deeply intrigued and impressed by the bathroom. After asking my permission, Da Bobo flushed the toilet twice.

"Do you have washing machine? Vacuum cleaner?" Da Mama asked.

I showed her the laundry room in the basement and the closet of cleaning supplies. She stooped down to stroke the Hoover as though it was a precious pet.

We were eating American that night. Da Mama confided happily, as she helped me shape the hamburger meat into patties, "We glad to eat American food. When we stay with your mother, she only make Chinese food. She good cook, but we want try everything new."

She oohed and ahhed in wonder at the prepackaged meat, the soft hamburger buns, saying there were no such things in China, and jumped back at the whirring sound of the electric can opener as though bitten by a snake.

Outside, Fred had gotten the coals going. I warned Da Mama about the mosquitoes, but she insisted on watching the hamburgers cook. I realized I already liked her very much. She stood close to the grill, waving her hands to fan the smoke away from Fred. Dressed in a T-shirt, pleated polyester skirt, and white plastic sandals, she looked stocky and sturdy. I made a mental note to get her a pair of long pants, to protect against the mosquitoes.

My mother phoned later that evening.

"Everything's fine, Mom," I told her. "We're playing tennis tomorrow morning. Then we thought we'd take them to a movie."

"Which one?"

"Oh, I don't know. Something with lots of sex and violence."

"No! You can't! In China, they . . ."

"I was kidding, Mom."

Her silence on the other end conveyed she was not amused.

"You were right," I continued. "They're so easy. They want to do everything. They're totally different from Aunt Lucy."

"That's right! Now, about money . . ."

"I almost forgot. What do you think? Is five hundred enough?"

"That much?" Her voice sounded like a lid snapping shut on a box. "For two weeks? They won't spend."

"Then they can take the rest home. Aren't they on a fixed pension?"

"Too much, too much!"

At first I thought to reason with her, then exclaimed, "Why do we have to be so chintzy with them?"

"What you talking about?"

"It's like you're afraid we'll spoil them, or like they're trying to take advantage of us or something . . ."

"I never say that," she said, curtly. "They don't know anything. They think we're rich . . . we have be careful, that's all I say."

Neither of us dared to venture further into the tangle of our disagreement. After quick good-byes, we hung up.

The next day, I woke up to slapping sounds coming through our bedroom window. Though it was early, the morning already felt sticky and hot. I looked out to see Da Bobo and Da Mama in the yard doing what looked like tai chi exercises. Normally, tai chi is performed in slow, measured cadences, but Da Bobo and Da Mama were twirling, hopping from foot to foot in crazy jerking motions. Then I realized they were slapping mosquitoes biting their faces, arms, and legs. They had ignored my warning and were experiencing the viciousness of the Minnesota pests. Finally Da Bobo threw up his hands and ran back into the house. Da Mama persisted a little while longer before she gave up, too, and joined him.

After breakfast, we dug out extra tennis racquets from the hall closet. Da Bobo practiced his forehand swing in the kitchen.

"Good form," Fred commented.

"Da Bobo captain of Senior Tennis League in Beijing," Da Mama said.

"I play the big shots when they come to town," Da Bobo said, boasting cheerfully. "I arrange games for the Hong Kong chief of police, the city commissioner."

"Do you play for real?" I asked.

He laughed, getting my meaning. "I make it close. That way, everybody has a good time, nobody loses face."

"They give him things," Da Mama said, frowning. "Big TV, Mr. Coffee."

Da Bobo shrugged, as if to show that was just the way things worked in China.

The tennis courts were a short drive away on the corner of Osceola and Dunlop. While Da Bobo and Fred warmed up, I showed Da Mama—who insisted she did not play well enough to play games, but was happy enough to practice—the hitting wall, behind us. After I watched her hit a few balls, I went back to the courts.

It immediately became apparent that Da Bobo had been an ace tennis player at one time and at the age of sixty-eight had only lost a bit of his edge. He was tall for a Chinese, around five foot ten and was lean and hard-muscled. He ran well, if a bit stiffly, and stroked the ball cleanly with pace. We played Canadian doubles, beginning a rotation of Da Bobo and me against Fred. Right off, I sensed that my uncle was keen to win. He grunted when he served and scrambled to return Fred's volley. When he missed, he shouted *"Ai yah!"* and muttered fiercely to himself in Chinese. At the changeover, I looked over to see Da Mama patiently swatting the ball, holding her racquet like a frying pan so that she sent the ball over the wall every few strokes.

"Be careful, Da Mama!" I shouted.

She waved her racquet cheerfully, crying *"Wah! Wah!"* whenever she sent a ball into the street.

The morning grew steamy. I worried about Da Bobo, whose face had turned sweaty and red. I offered him water from our thermos, but he refused, crouching down, readying himself for Fred's serve. His short-cropped hair was soaked, so that his hard skull showed through. When he hit the ball, he grunted loudly, throwing his entire weight into the stroke, passing Fred cleanly.

Feigning collapse, Fred draped a towel over his head and claimed he'd had enough. Only then did Da Bobo ease himself on the bench and gulp water. His chest was heaving. I watched him anxiously. Da Mama came over and sat down on the bench next to him.

"You're a fool," she said quietly in Mandarin. "What are you trying to prove?"

I wracked my brains for a way to let them know that I understood what they were saying, that the privacy they assumed speaking Chinese was not assured. I was surprised how much I was able to understand from my childhood storehouse of Mandarin, even though I lacked the confidence to speak it. One phrase did occur to me, one that anyone even remotely Chinese would know, and I let it fly from my mouth:

"Wo men cher!"

My uncle and aunt gave me a startled look, then promptly stood up and began gathering their things. "Not bad," my uncle said. "Your mother said you didn't speak Chinese at all!"

As we walked to the car, Fred caught my arm. "What did you say?"

"Time to eat!" I said, beginning to laugh, unable to explain how wonderful it felt to have actually said something in Chinese.

After lunch, Da Bobo tugged Da Mama's sleeve, and they went up to their room. I noticed they did everything together, consulting and arguing over every decision. A minute later they returned carrying a cardboard tube about three feet long.

"We brought this for you, Sung Lien."

Surprised, I didn't know what to make of the tube until I tipped it and a scroll slipped out. Fred helped me unroll what turned out to be a painting nearly seven feet long, matted on fine silk brocade. Painted in broad strokes of blue and green in a dramatic, expressionistic style, it was a water scene depicting lotus blossoms in a pond. Unrolling it was like pouring out a cool stream of water.

"Lotus blossom your name," Da Mama prompted.

I thanked my uncle and aunt warmly while Fred got a hammer and positioned a nail in the dining room wall. After he hung the painting, we all stood back to admire it.

"We hope the painting will remind you of us, even though you live far away," Da Bobo said.

He put his hand on my shoulder. I looked into my uncle's severe and honorable face, struck anew by his irrefutable belief that we were of the same clan. Again I lowered my eyes, searching for words, but found none. I felt anointed, yet still unworthy. For reasons I couldn't explain, I was unable to believe wholeheartedly that mere birth sealed kinship. My uncle seemed to read my state of mind. Gently removing his hand, he looked back at the painting.

"It looks good there, doesn't it?" he said.

6

KINSHIP

ON OUR WAY HOME FROM PLAYING TENNIS THE NEXT MORNING, WE STOPPED at Napoleon's bakery on St. Clair Avenue to buy chocolate and almond croissants. In the back seat of the car, Da Bobo and Da Mama dissected them, layer by layer, discussing the richness of the butter and how the delicate texture of the pastry was firm to the tooth yet melted on the tongue. They concluded—"*Ai yah! Ai yah!*"—the croissants were incontrovertible proof that American technology had surpassed itself. The rustle of bakery tissue paper stilled as they noted (I watched them in the rearview mirror, craning their necks) that Napoleon's was within walking distance of our house.

Their discussion stirred my thoughts about the Chinese view of food. At the core was the persistent memory of a people enduring centuries of starvation under the rule of an indifferent imperial class whose only apparent woe was culinary boredom. Though the courts of the emperors cannot be forgiven for their neglect and abuse of the Chinese citizenry, they must be credited for the invention of the classic cuisine, created by master chefs who tweaked nature's larder for sparrows' tongues, swallows' nests, snake livers, and other delicacies to concoct dishes complex enough to alleviate imperial malaise. Hunger and finickiness had existed side by side, albeit uneasily, even violently, until the downfall of the ruling class, which may explain the Chinese approach to eating today: wolfing food as though starved, while at the same time offering exhaustive critiques of each morsel. Even Chinese babies learn the fine distinctions of color and texture, the critical balance between bitter and sweet. Once, in a dim sum restaurant, I saw a three-year-old lean over her plate, eject a dumpling from her mouth, and remark in a voice that was tiny but sharp, "Yuck! Too much ginger!"

Da Bobo and Da Mama left a trail of pastry flakes from the car to the bank across the street, where I took them to buy traveler's checks. The whole time they continued to discuss in Mandarin the sweet-but-not-cloying filling of the croissants, sounding as earnest as economists discussing the Federal Reserve. Before entering the bank, I asked Da Bobo if he thought five hundred was enough. He looked astounded.

"Five hundred?"

"Yes. For spending money."

"Too much, too much!" Da Mama exclaimed, shaking her head. "You already buy airplane ticket, already give too much."

Da Bobo's face reflected a clash of spontaneous myriad thoughts: Shock at the mere mention of such a sum then the rapid calculation of what that equaled in Chinese money. Close upon that was a rapid assessment of my motive and what was proper in our relationship as uncle and niece, foreigner and American, poor and rich, man and woman, guest and hostess. Despite my good intentions, I realized how naive I had been and how what I offered presented overwhelming complications.

"You don't have to spend it all," I said, trying for a light tone.

Still conflicted, Da Bobo followed me into the bank. At the teller window I wrote a check and asked for traveler's checks, trying to sound businesslike but feeling happy and proud, thinking that I was helping my relatives at last. While Da Bobo signed the checks, Da Mama plucked at his sleeve, plainly distressed with what was happening. The teller put the checks in a plastic wallet and handed it to me.

"Here," I said, passing the wallet to Da Bobo.

He hesitated. Again, I saw ambivalence skitter across his face.

"It's okay, Da Bobo."

He took hold of a corner of the wallet, and for a split second, I saw in his eyes an unmistakeable gleam. At this moment, he probably grasped more money than he had in his entire life. Almost immediately the gleam was replaced by a shadow that flitted over his pride and sense of propriety. Without looking at me he murmured "Thank you," and slipped the wallet into his pocket with a gesture so furtive it was as though we had concluded a shady deal. Da Mama followed us back to the house, her eye fixed on Da Bobo's back pocket looking convinced he had sold his soul to the devil.

That first week with my relatives went by in an eye blink. In the mornings, Fred and I wakened to the sound of the back door slamming, signaling their return from Napoleon's. The waxed bakery bags crackled as they piled croissants, doughnuts, cookies, and turnovers on the breakfast table. My uncle asked for coffee in lieu of green tea, declaring that since he was in America, he was going to *eat American*. He also requested three soft-boiled eggs. Throughout the week, I became aware of a certain quirk of my uncle's, which was that whatever his sister, Aunt Lucy, had experienced in America, he was determined to experience, too, only in greater measure. This applied not only to his wish to have three, rather than two boiled eggs, but to practically every other matter as well. When we went grocery shopping at the Rainbow Food Store, he headed straight to the refrigerated aisle of ice cream, where he opened the doors and thrust in his head.

"Cherry Granite," he read, moving his fingers along the row of icy cartons. He turned to me, skeptical. "Are there really rocks inside?"

"It's hard candy, Da Bobo. Granite's just a marketing name."

"Did Lucy ever have this?"

I thought for a moment. Lucy had run the gamut. "I don't remember," I said, fudging.

"We'll try it," he said. He picked two other flavors, added them to the cart.

Each morning, I watched Da Bobo spread extra butter on his croissants while he ranted about China's agricultural shortcomings.

"There are too many people in China, not enough room for cows!" he shouted, spewing pastry flakes in the air. "We don't have milk or cream!"

"But that's healthier," I said. "Most Americans are too fat."

"We don't have butter!" His eyes flashed, decrying this national disgrace.

I opened my mouth, thinking to point out our mountains of government-surplus cheese, the harmful effects of fat and cholesterol, but changed my mind. Instead, I considered how quickly my uncle had adopted the American sense of entitlement. He had only been in the country a few weeks, and already he was demanding what he did not have. Who was I to judge? In China, people went without hot running water or toilets.

One day, Da BoBo and Da Mama made dumplings for lunch. Da Mama showed Fred how to pleat the edges of dough over the filling to create the traditional crescent shape. Her slender fingers were well-practiced, creating dainty dumplings that were perfectly symmetrical and identical, while it was plain Fred's bass-player's hands were meant for bigger tasks. Da Mama's mission was futile, like trying to teach a bear to make crumpets. Though Fred tried, he mushed the filling, tore the dough, and ended up dropping several on the floor. Later, he complained he had trouble grasping the concept of pleats. Eventually, Da Bobo, Da Mama, and I filled three cookie trays with dumplings. Every second row or so, Fred added his tortured creation. Among the uniform rows, his were easy to spot.

"Hey, that one looks like a flying saucer," Da Bobo said.

"No, no, a gizzard!" Da Mama laughed, then clamped her hand over her mouth.

"I think they're cute," I said, handing Fred a towel to wipe his hands.

When the dumplings were boiled, Da Bobo fished around in the broth for one of Fred's unmistakeable designs. "You get to eat your own," he said. "Here. This one's a submarine. Eh, what's this? Da Mama, what do you say, a gall bladder? Ha Ha!"

"Tastes all the same to me," Fred said, slurping them happily.

It felt good, all of it, making dumplings together, laughing, eating. We sat shoulder to shoulder around the kitchen table, breathing in the steam from one another's soup. I couldn't help thinking how this contrasted with the tense silence that reigned over my parents' table. When he had eaten, Da Bobo put down his chopsticks.

"Sung Lien, you and Fred have a good life."

I looked up, surprised.

"In China, every day is the same," Da Bobo went on, sighing. "We buy food, cook. Sleep after lunch. In the afternoon, we shop for dinner. It sounds like an easy life, not bad for a retired couple with no children. But prices keep getting higher, and this worries us old pensioners."

Da Mama put her hand on Da Bobo's arm. It was a gesture that offered sympathy and pleaded for restraint at the same time. "Da Bobo retired English teacher, me retired nurse," she said, turning to me. "Together we get one hundred forty dollar a month. Today, young people in China, no education, drive taxi, earn *four* hundred dollar a month!"

"Thanks to the Great Cultural Revolution!" Da Bobo hooted.

"Shhh!" Da Mama hissed.

"No, why not say it?" Da Bobo cried, jabbing a finger in the air. "We're in America, we can say whatever we want! Mao Zedong got rid of education during the Cultural Revolution, so what does that leave us? A ruling class of stupid old big shots, a free-enterprise system where young hoodlums drive taxis, sell blue jeans on the street, make ten times more money than us pensioners . . ."

"Shhh! Shhh!" Da Mama begged. "Stop talking like a tough guy."

"Who's a tough guy?" Da Bobo demanded. He was about to say more, but, having caught Da Mama's final warning glance, reluctantly closed his mouth.

When Da Mama and Fred got up to clear the dishes, Da Bobo leaned over to me and whispered in a hoarse, conspiratorial voice, "The communists never scared me. *Never!*"

Later that night, after dinner, I asked Da Bobo and Da Mama how they passed the time in China.

"We sing with our friends!" Da Bobo answered. Unprompted, he began to sing, *"Blue Skies, nothing but blue skies . . ."* but stopped, staring in disbelief at the quizzical look on my face. "Don't you know this song? It's one of Bing Crosby's greatest hits." He raised his head, closed his eyes, and sang "Blue Skies" from beginning to end. Halfway through I thought I remembered the song, vaguely, from an old movie. Even if Da Bobo carried a pipe and wore a cardigan, he couldn't have resembled the famous crooner more closely, as he captured every nuance of his smooth, mellow voice, even the signature warble of his final cadence. When he finished the song Da Bobo opened his eyes and smiled that slow, knowing smile, winking lazily like Bing himself.

"Where did you hear 'Blue Skies,' Da Bobo?" I asked, after Fred and I applauded enthusiastically.

"All the great American movies and records came to China," Da Bobo said. He nudged me with his elbow. "Your father had a mad crush on Hedy Lamarr."

"My favorite is *Gone with the Wind,*" Da Mama offered. In a voice that was mostly a monotone, she began to crow the theme song, "Da DAH da da . . ."

"What time is it?" Da Bobo said, abruptly.

"Eight o'clock," Fred answered.

"Hurry! *Stagecoach* is on!"

He rushed into the living room. Seconds later, we heard the sounds of Western movie music, horses neighing.

"He like Bing Crosby, but he love John Wayne best," Da Mama said, wrinkling her nose.

At eleven o'clock, after Da Mama had gone to bed and Fred went upstairs to read, I joined my uncle in front of the television. I picked up the *TV Guide,* paged through it idly. "What's next, Da Bobo?"

"Gunfight at the OK Corral," he said, settling in with his second bowl of chocolate-mint-chip ice cream. "It's got Kirk Douglas and Burt Lancaster. Real tough guys."

He had tuned to the cable channel that showed old movies in a continuous stream. In between there were several infomercials promoting mail-order kitchen gadgets. Da Bobo wrote down the number to order a set of ninety-nine knives. "Good deal, better than in Hong Kong," he noted.

The movie began, unfolded rapidly. The Earp brothers and Doc Holliday were set to face the Clancy brothers at the OK Corral. Da Bobo had the volume cranked up so loud I was sure our next-door neighbors would hear the gunshots. Before the final gunfight, an infomercial broke in where a man in a chef's toque began to demonstrate a multi-blade vegetable cutter. I turned the volume down.

"Da Bobo," I began, but hesitated because he was leaning forward, mesmerized by the sight of the chef dicing carrots double time. I clicked the mute button on the remote.

"Da Bobo, can I ask you something?"

He turned from the television to look at me, his eyes patient, expectant. I felt myself looking beyond the dark edge into the chasm again, as I had with Aunt Lucy. And, as before, I felt stymied by the same uncertainties, doubting my right to broach a subject that was surely painful, if not forbidden. Da Bobo continued to search my face. I felt the frank and open expression in his eyes draw me closer and closer toward the chasm until, finally, I pitched forward.

"What happened to our family during the war and the Cultural Revolution?"

At that moment the movie returned to the screen. My uncle's eyes flickered there, then back to my face. "I'll tell you," he said. "But after the tough guys fight it out, okay?"

I handed him the remote. He pumped up the volume, repositioning himself on the edge of the couch.

The shootout between the good guys and the bad guys began. I looked away as bodies fell, as I have never been able to watch violence, even though staged. Besides, I knew how it would end. When the smoke cleared, the good would claim their victory. In any case, I was busy celebrating my own triumph, because after all these years, I had finally leaped the chasm. The only surprise was that it was Da Bobo, and not Yeh Yeh or Aunt Lucy, who waited for me on the other side.

7

DA BOBO

THE WESTERN SUNSET BARELY FADED BEFORE THE MANIACAL CHEF BLIPPED back on the screen and began shredding cabbage into confetti-like bits. I turned off the television, carried the empty ice cream bowls to rinse off in the kitchen. Da Bobo helped dry them. When the last one had been put away, he sniffed the scent of lilacs wafting in the open window.

"Let's go for a walk," he said.

I unhooked Maya's leash from the doorknob.

We went out the back door into the alley onto Fairview Avenue and turned north across Grand Avenue to Summit.

The largest and best known street in St. Paul, Summit Avenue is wide, divided by a broad grassy median. Mature shade trees grow here as well as carefully tended plots of canna, impatiens, silverleaf, and candytuft. Large Tudor and Victorian houses stand on generous lots on either side. Rumor has it that lilac hedges planted along the avenue date from the time when F. Scott Fitzgerald and Louis B. Hill, the lumber and railroad magnate, lived there.

Streetlights illuminated a night full of people, mostly MacAlester College students and joggers from the neighborhood. Occasionally a bicyclist glided by, reflectors winking on silently spinning wheels. Da Bobo and I passed couples sitting on benches along the median. Some talked, but most were content to listen quietly to the sounds of crickets and observe the swifts darting in the night. Da Bobo and I claimed a bench for ourselves. Maya flopped on the ground at our feet, sighing.

My uncle sat at an angle so that the streetlight shone behind his left shoulder, illuminating the crosshatch of lines at the corners of his eyes and mouth. I had not realized how deeply etched they were. For the first time, I thought he looked worn, old.

"Where should I begin?" he asked.

I had not thought of a starting point, but suddenly what I wanted to know became clear.

"Tell me about the time you and Dad first left China."

Da Bobo thought for a while, squinting, as though trying to squeeze memory from himself. "In 1944," he began, "the war was nearly over, though we didn't know it. Your mother and father had been married nearly two years. Your sister was just a year old. In Beijing, we heard that the American army was looking for English-speaking Chinese to teach Mandarin to American G.I.s going to China to fight the Japanese. Your father and I enlisted and were sent to the American base in Hawaii. Part of the deal was that we would receive the same benefits as American G.I.s, which meant that, after the war, we could study in the United States."

"How come you weren't in the Chinese army?"

He made a noise of disgust so loud that a man jogging by turned his head. "Which one? The Kuomintang? Mao's ragtag communist forces? China was a mess. We were not only overrun by the Japanese, but torn apart by warring factions within. We never knew who was in charge. Power seemed to change hands daily. Whole sections of railroad were destroyed, telegraph wires cut, so there was no transport, no communication. Schools, hospitals, government offices were shut down. People were starving. Some moved inland to escape the Japanese bombardment on the coast, while others tried to flee China altogether. Your Aunt Lucy managed to get to Chicago to continue her studies. Since there were no jobs in China and we had families to support, your father and I thought the American army seemed the best solution at the time."

Da Bobo paused, watching two teenagers saunter by before continuing, "We were in Honolulu only a few months when the war ended suddenly. We were told we had a few weeks on furlough to decide what to do. For some reason, I don't really remember now, we decided to go to New York.

Can you imagine? Two skinny Chinese guys in Hawaiian shirts landing in Manhattan, with only one cardboard suitcase between us.

"We went to Times Square, Radio City Music Hall. *Ai yah!* Now I remember . . . we saw a movie with Fred Astaire and Ginger Rogers!" Closing his eyes, Da Bobo raised his arms as if he held an imaginary partner, swaying gently side to side. Then, opening his eyes, he said, "It was there we got word from Lucy that she had applied for a scholarship for your father to study at the University of Chicago."

"Just my father? She didn't apply for you, too?"

Da Bobo shrugged. "I was never a good student. I could never sit still long enough to study. Your father, on the other hand, was always the serious one, the one with ambition. He knew it would be impossible to do graduate work in China, because Mao had already begun dismantling the education system. He had also begun rounding up intellectuals and artists because of their focus on Western culture."

Da Bobo watched as the couple on the bench nearby got up and strolled away. Then he continued, "Yeh Yeh wrote, urging us to come home, echoing Mao's call for all Chinese to return to help rebuild their country. Your grandfather believed that the educated could contribute to the cause, that it was important for us to show that we were as loyal and committed to China as the proletariat. He wanted us to prove that we were patriots, too."

"So, you decided to go back?"

"Yes, but not to prove anything to Mao Zedong!" Da Bobo exclaimed, his voice sounding suddenly bitter. "I went home for China's sake, but also because my parents were getting old. Yeh Yeh never complained, but I knew it was getting hard for him, as a scholar, with his background. I knew the communists were watching and harassing him. I went back because China was my home, not for some stupid political reason, not for some damned bloody revolution!"

I stared at my uncle, thinking that not even Geronimo in his finest hour could have looked more fierce.

"Why didn't the communists come for you, too, Da Bobo?"

"Oh they did, they did!" he said, kicking the dirt next to the dog, causing her to growl in her sleep. "But what could they accuse me of, eh? I didn't go to school in America or England, I didn't write any books! And I didn't resist or tell any lies. When they accused me of corruption, I freely

confessed to committing odious crimes against the state. After all, I had
gone to New York, to Radio City Music Hall—I had seen Ginger Rogers!"
Da Bobo's laugh sounded like a bark. "I knew the communists arrested people
for lesser reasons than seeing American movies, but I knew they wouldn't
take me, because I was the sole support of the family. Who would take care
of Yeh Yeh and Nai Nai then? No, I was never scared of the communists.
They were just a bunch of hoodlums."

He grew quiet. The night had grown still except for the hum of the
streetlights overhead.

"Did you try to convince my father to go back to China with you?" I
ventured.

"Sure! But your father is a stubborn man, he had made up his mind!
When Yeh Yeh heard of his decision to go to Chicago, he wrote another letter. He addressed it to your father only, so I knew it was serious. Your father
wouldn't show it to me at first, but I insisted on seeing it."

"What did it say?"

Da Bobo paused, rubbing his neck. "Yeh Yeh reminded your father that
your mother and sister waited for him back in China. He warned that things
were so unstable in China, especially in light of Mao's suspicion of the West,
that the borders might close, which meant that your father might not be
able to return, ever."

"So, even knowing this, my father decided to stay . . . ?"

Da Bobo watched a bicyclist pedal by, his tires gently crunching the grit
in the street.

"Of course, we did not approve of your father's decision, but we understood his nature. And then we had no way of predicting how things would
turn out between China and America. Fortunately, as it happened, China
stayed open, so your father was able to send for your mother and sister as
soon as he could, though it wasn't until three years later." My uncle paused,
before adding, "It's easy to say going to America was selfish on his part, but
it must not have been easy for him, a poor student living alone in a strange
country. No, in the end, your father behaved honorably."

Suddenly, like a pebble dislodged from a riverbank, a memory came
loose in my mind. I was in danger of failing high school chemistry, because I
couldn't solve the equations involving units called moles. I was so frustrated
that I cried over my homework every night.

"Stop crying!" my father ordered. He stood over the kitchen table where

I had spread my textbook, papers, and box of Kleenex. "This is baby stuff. When you add two moles to four moles, what else could you get but six? Use your brain!"

We glared at one another in mutual frustration. My crying had taken him away from watching *Mission: Impossible* in the next room. After watching me blow my nose, he said, "Look," in a tone that made me suspect he was softening. "I nearly failed German when I was studying for my graduate degree in Chicago. It was a required course, and if I didn't pass, I wouldn't get my degree. Without a degree I couldn't get a job, and without a job I couldn't send for your mother and sister back in China. Even with the help of a private tutor, I had a terrible time." He sighed heavily, as though the memory still weighed on him. "I couldn't get *der, die, das* straight, and the word order made no sense. Why put the action at the end of a sentence?" He hesitated, as though expecting ridicule and ignominy to rise up again from the past, then burst out, "I failed the exam twice! Only three attempts were allowed, so I was down to my last chance. Everything depended on it. Do you see how important it was?"

I managed to nod, though I was in a state of shock at my father's uncharacteristic verbosity, his confessional tone, how, of all people, he confided this most painful and humiliating memory to me.

"See, Mei Mei," he said, addressing me by my childhood name. "It's not just German, or chemistry, but life! It's never easy. It's always going to be hard!"

I remembered looking at my father's face, seeing how, behind the lenses of his glasses, his eyes looked like hard little rocks. The little empathy showing there was dimmed by the bright, reflective gleam of his near-failure, his intolerance for any similar result by me or anyone else in our family. But the sound of his voice conveyed that however bad I was at counting moles, he saw—no, expected—greater things from me, and that I should benefit from the lessons he learned, bitter or not. His acknowledgment made me feel proud but also strangely uncomfortable.

"I guess you passed," I said.

He ignored my adolescent sarcasm. I bent over my homework paper, feeling him watch my hesitating pencil.

"Forget about the moles!" he barked.

I began scribbling and did not stop until he went back to his television show.

Da Bobo slapped a mosquito on his arm. *"Wah!"*

"I guess we'd better get moving."

We walked back along Summit Avenue.

"Do you think Yeh Yeh ever forgave my father for not going back to China?" I asked.

Da Bobo walked a while without speaking. Then he said, "I think your grandfather grew to accept certain things. Especially after what happened in the fifties."

I stopped. "What about the fifties?"

"Didn't you know? Your father tried to go back to China. He was going to bring you all back."

Again I felt something shift inside, but instead of a single pebble, an entire shoal gave way. Now, suddenly, I remembered my mother telling me that my father had bought the steamship tickets back to China. That we had packed and gotten all our shots. I must have been three or four years old at the time, my brother a toddler. Just as we were about to leave, the Korean War broke out, and ties between the United States and China were severed. No travel was permitted to or from China. We were stranded.

"It wasn't his fault!" I said, looking at Da Bobo. "Didn't Yeh Yeh believe that he tried?"

Da BoBo said nothing. We reached Prior Avenue, turned south toward Grand, where he stopped abruptly. "What's that wonderful smell?"

I sniffed the air. "Honeysuckle."

"Kind of like jasmine. Maybe not as sweet."

We stood under a streetlight near an overgrown hedge. I broke off a honeysuckle flower, handed it to him. "If you bite off the end, like this, you can suck the nectar."

Da Bobo did as I showed him, then pulled the vine toward him, stuffed several flowers into his mouth, and chewed them whole. As we continued to walk, I tried to sort through his narrative. The restrictions imposed by the Korean War and the different paths taken by Da Bobo and my father accounted for why we hadn't heard from Yeh Yeh during the fifties, and why, in 1961, when the war was long over, his letters were addressed only to me or my sister or my mother. Still, it amazed me how the tissue-thin aerograms carried the weight of those years, conveying not only my grandfather's incontestable, enduring authority, but also, in their poignant omissions, his ongoing rebuke of my father. I wondered what role, if any, the thin blue vapor of Yeh Yeh's disapproval played in the silence suffocating my family.

I became aware of Da Bobo studying my face, as though he was trying to read my thoughts.

"During the Cultural Revolution," he said, walking slowly again, "when Yeh Yeh was nearly eighty years old, he was arrested by the Red Guards. They spat on him, put a dunce cap on his head, made him get down on his knees in public and recant for his study of Western theology. Then, in front of the entire neighborhood, they burned his books, his poetry, even his calligraphy . . . his entire life's work."

Da Bobo was so close I felt the impact of his breath, a mixture of honeysuckle and outrage, against my face.

"Only two of his scrolls remain. One is for you."

I stopped in my tracks. "What?"

"What's the matter? Are you cold?"

"No." But I had begun to shiver violently.

"We don't know how he managed to save them. But they are part of his legacy to you, your brother, and sister."

We reached our yard. Maya sniffed at the back gate, peering up with her old eyes as though wondering why we had stopped.

"Why didn't you come to see him, Sung Lien?"

Da Bobo's eyes struck me like arrowheads. Undeflected by time or sentimentality, they were blunt . . . not hurtful, but nevertheless true to their mark. I felt pinned, helpless before their gaze.

"You were the last one left to see him," he said. "He waited for you as long as he could."

"I know! I don't know!"

Heart pounding, face burning, I reached out, pushed the gate.

Da Bobo placed his hand on the top of the gate, checking its swing into our yard.

"Sung Lien . . ."

I waited, dreading his words.

"When are you coming to get the scroll Yeh Yeh left for you?"

Summoning all my courage, I looked in his face. His eyes were calm, mild.

"Next summer," I said, hearing how the words sounded weightless, transparent.

My uncle said nothing, but seemed to wait for something. His arm was stretched out in front of me, hand resting on the gate, a barrier. Its presence there seemed to convey that I could pass easily enough, but that, once through, there was no turning back.

"Next summer. I promise," I said.

He gave a satisfied grunt, swung the gate wide, and walked toward the house. In the darkness, his pale skull stood out as distinct as an ancient stone in a moonlit clearing, as clear and trustworthy a sign as I could dare follow.

Inside the house, Da Bobo went upstairs to the guest room, where Da Mama lay sleeping, while I went through turning out the lights. I paused before the scroll of my namesake in the dining room, thinking that, despite the slight incongruity of its framing within the Victorian woodwork of our house, it looked perfectly at home. And then, suddenly, I saw it not only as a thing of beauty but as a symbol of my uncle's pardon. He judged me no more than he had my father for having left his family for America. Realizing this, a great weight lifted from my heart, and I felt gratitude and joy at being relieved of the guilt I had taken on as my rightful bequest. I felt expectation and obligation, like ballast fixed to a balloon, float away, and prepared to soar, fulfilling my promise to go to China at last. As I stood there before my scroll, I became aware of a tiny but insistent tug of a final remaining snag. What was it? What kept me anchored to the ground? Doubt dropped over me again, like the darkness in our house, as I pondered what this final remnant might be.

8

BLACK SHEEP

ON THE LAST DAY BEFORE MY UNCLE AND AUNT RETURNED TO MY MOTHER'S house, we took a picnic to the Lake of the Isles in Minneapolis. Fred found a spot on a little peninsula jutting into the lake and, lolling on a blanket which we had spread on the ground, we ate cold chicken, potato salad, nectarines, and Oreo cookies. Surprisingly, there were no mosquitoes. The grass was soft and fragrant, and Canada geese paddled nearby in the shallow water. After we ate, Da Bobo sang "Blue Skies," softly, sighing happily when he finished.

"This feels just like England," he said.

"When were you in England, Da Bobo?" I asked, surprised.

"Oh, never. But this is how I imagined it."

The four of us lay on our backs sprawled out like spokes in a wheel, our heads nearly touching. We stared at the clouds.

"I wish you weren't going," I said.

Da Mama reached over and patted my arm. "We wish, too. But your mother wait for us. We keep her company."

Though they had known for a long time about my parents' separation, her voice sounded sad. It was significant that, when they first arrived in Washington, they stayed with my mother, not my father.

"We always like your mother," Da Mama said. "She good person, have good heart."

Suddenly Da Bobo raised himself up on his elbow. "Why don't you and Fred come to New York to see the U.S. Open with us?"

My mother had planned to take them up on the Metroliner during the last weekend in August. They were to stay with my brother and his wife on the Upper East Side and take the subway to catch the early matches of the tennis tournament.

I turned to Fred, who shrugged as if to say, *Why not?*

"We'll see, Da Bobo."

The next day, my uncle and aunt flew to Washington, D.C. That evening, I called my mother's house. "Here's Da Mama," my mother said, handing over the phone.

I could hear Da Mama crying even before she put the receiver to her ear. "We miss you!" she wailed.

"Come to New York!" Da Bobo shouted from the background.

Later that night, Fred looked up from the *Audubon Society* magazine he was reading. We both realized he had been humming "Blue Skies." "I keep seeing your uncle as Bing Crosby," he said. "I mean, your aunt and uncle are so different from Aunt Lucy. They're more open, more Westernized."

"Well, my mother did say Da Bobo was the black sheep in the family."

"Black sheep? I don't think so. He's real. And so's Da Mama."

And then it struck me how I had viewed Yeh Yeh, Aunt Lucy, and my father as representing the whole of the Chinese character, how I had swallowed the notion that all Chinese were Mandarins, intellectuals, and ascetics, as narrow a view as any other stereotype designating the Chinese as clever, industrious, or inscrutable. I was shocked to realize that I had, as a member of this first, transplanted generation, lost sight of the individual in my race, that I had actually pigeon-holed myself with my narrow focus. That being different together did not mean that we were all the same. And though I knew about the Chinese in Chinatown and the diversity of people immigrating from the different regions in China, including farmers, shopkeepers, and fishermen as well as scholars and scientists, it still came as a relief, a revelation, to know there were black sheep, ordinary people, in my own family. I was glad that, in Yeh Yeh's house, strains of Bing Crosby mingled with Schubert, and that, however incongruous it might have sounded, it also made for a place of infinite fascination and possibility. I wondered how I, with my own patchwork cultural vocabulary and outlook, might fit in.

Two weeks later, Fred pointed to an ad in the paper: Northwest Airlines was promoting a low, end-of-the-summer fare to LaGuardia.

"Da Bobo!" I yelled into the phone, minutes later. "We're coming to New York!"

Arriving at my brother's apartment in Manhattan, Da Bobo and Da Mama hugged us, saying how moved they were that we had flown out to see them again. My brother seemed unconcerned that so many people were crowded in his tiny apartment, though it turned out to be a good piece of luck that his wife was away at a conference in Boston that weekend. The apartment was in a good building, but it faced the street so that the windows rattled and the floor shook every time a bus rumbled by. The two small rooms looked even more cramped due to the futons rolled up against the wall, my relatives' luggage stacked all over.

I went to the bathroom to wash my hands and found laundry hanging over the tub, plastic traveling kits stacked on the floor. A strange sensation, like a faint tune that seems familiar yet hovers out of range, came over me. Then I remembered my mother's description of the basement room she and my father had shared when she first arrived in Chicago in 1949. It was so small and dark they could barely turn around. Overhead, they heard their neighbors ranting day and night. The image brought to mind a word that conveyed to me her enduring sense of shame and unease, something she had bequeathed to me as sure as life itself: Immigrant.

My mother came into the bathroom, startling me. Her proximity in the close space amplified the tension normally between us. During our last phone call, I sensed she wasn't exactly pleased by our spontaneous decision to come to New York; we had never come at the drop of a hat to visit her, after all. Instinctively, we sought space apart, she at the sink, I against the bathtub. She began to wash her hands. "How's it going?" I asked, trying to sound casual.

"Fine," she said.

She had arrived two days earlier with my aunt and uncle. Evidence of her pleasure at being reunited with my brother was visible throughout the apartment: special treats she had brought for him, his favorite coconut candy, a sweater she had knitted. She wore the new pearl earrings he had given her. Lately, as if to compensate for what he perceived as my father's abandonment of my mother, my brother had taken to buying her jewelry. In light of this latest proof of their closeness, I felt a sudden pang of resentment, like a ravenous hatchling forced to watch as my parent presented the worm to the other chick. And then, like the proverbial bolt out of the blue, I realized what that last remnant was, why I still hung back from going to China. It was because I knew I would have to go with my mother. The thought of spending a month or more with her, bound in the suffocating air of her silent but omnipotent disapproval, held me sure as a vise. There was no apparent way out, as I could not imagine going alone with my limited ability to speak Chinese, and the unwavering tradition in my family was that everyone went escorted by my mother. I was trapped, as sure as a cub in a snare, and there was no way I could see, short of chewing off my own foot, that I could free myself.

For the next three days, we watched the tennis matches at the U.S. Open, perched in the grand stadium among thousands of excited fans. Our seats were so high the court looked like a playing card, the tennis players like fleas jumping from side to side. From this height even the antics of John McEnroe seemed minute, insignificant. While spectators around us complained loudly about the nosebleed aspect of their seats, the exorbitant price of hot dogs, or chatted about the summer sales at Saks Fifth Avenue, vociferously intent on everything but the tennis below, I was struck by how little it affected my uncle and aunt. Even when a very large woman, hauling a sack of knishes and pickles, stepped on Da Mama's foot, bellowing "Excuse me!" as though it were Da Mama's fault, my relatives seemed impervious to the cacophony. While they cheered at the well-played points, they remained strikingly serene. *Like stones embedded in a stream,* I thought. Was it their age, their perspective, having gone through revolution and war? At what cost had they arrived at their present equilibrium, which seemed to have less to do with resignation or complacency but rather a keen sense and acceptance of their place in the raucous world?

Due to the brevity of our visit and the cramped quarters of my brother's apartment, time and space were compressed, made focal in an extraordinary way, so that one thing stood clear: My mother was by herself. Da Bobo and Da Mama, Fred and I, my brother and his wife—even though she was in Boston at the time—had each other, but my mother no longer had my father. This imbalance in the family scheme caused me to reflect anew on my brother's view that my mother had been shortchanged in her life.

Then it occurred to me that no one knew how she had felt when my father went on to America in 1945, leaving her and my sister behind in China. Though, as Da Bobo claimed, the entire family understood my father's character, no one knew how my mother had reacted to his decision, which meant separation and upheaval in her life for three long years. Had anyone ever asked for her point of view? In any case, it seemed that coming to America had failed to provide her with fair treatment, and if she couldn't count on my father or the U.S. government, then who could she count on but us children? Other than giving her things—my brother's domain—I struggled to think of a way I might tip the scales in my mother's life. Not so much out of pity, because my mother deserved more than that, but out of respect and simple fairness. Wasn't that why people came to America?

For the entire weekend I wracked my brains on how to accomplish this, as well as find a way to revise my mother's view of me so that she would realize that even though I was self-absorbed and unreliable like my father, I was not incorrigible. When the solution finally came to me, it was so obvious and simple that I laughed out loud.

The chance to reveal my plan came at the end of the weekend when I found myself alone with my mother, after dinner, when the others had left the apartment to buy ice cream. She and I cleared the dishes, piled them into the sink. I stood next to her, drying the dishes as she washed.

"I like Da Bobo and Da Mama a lot," I began, casually.

My mother said nothing, continued to scour a pan.

"Da Bobo says I should visit them in Beijing."

She rinsed the pan and began scrubbing the bowl in which she had mixed dumpling dough, frowning a little with concentration. When she finished, she took up the cutting board, the last item in the sink.

"He says Yeh Yeh left me a scroll," I went on. "He says I have to go to the house in Beijing to get it."

My mother held the cutting board above the water, watching a mass of soapsuds slide down the wood until it gathered in a shimmering glob at the edge. It continued to pulse there as water continued to run down the board, backing up against it, threatening to push it over.

"I could go in June, when the season ends, or August, when the summer music festivals are over." I was careful not to look at my mother, keeping my eyes on the mass of soapsuds that continued to gather and strain at the edge of the board.

"China is too hot in August," she declared, turning to face me. There, in her clear brown eyes, I saw an opening. It wavered, as though her pupils, wary of too bright a light, were poised to snap shut at any moment. I knew it was my last chance.

"Okay, June it is," I said. Then I hesitated, rolling the next words around in my mouth, testing their unfamiliar taste. "Will you go with me?"

We were both startled by a splash as the mass of suds, caving in from the pressure of the water above, dropped into the dirty gray water. My mother pulled the plug, and we watched the greasy water swirl down the drain.

"Sure," she said.

9

MANDARIN

I HAD MANY CONCERTS AND TEACHING OBLIGATIONS TO FULFILL OVER THE next several months and had also written part of a novel that had been accepted for publication but required completion. By the time I was finally free to plan a trip to China, it was 1986. Nearly two years had gone by since the time I had made the pact with my mother to go together.

During the interim I read books by Edgar Snow and Jonathan Yardley and studied a map from one of Fred's *National Geographic* magazines. It lay tightly folded within the pages but, when released, sprung across our dining room table like a giant fan. All of China, from below the icy white skullcap of Siberia to the rocky ridges of Tibet, was depicted on its glossy, pleated surface.

As soon as I began telling people I was going to China, all kinds of people appeared wanting to show me the way. Our neighbors, a retired insurance salesman and his wife, dropped by to share tales of their recent Silk Road Tour, bringing snapshots of the Great Wall, the Forbidden City, the terra-cotta warriors of Xi'an, and two stuffed panda bears the size of toddlers. At the forefront of the photos was their guide, a young Chinese woman in a blue uniform carrying their tour group banner and megaphone. The harried, distracted expression on her face reminded me of an overworked sheepdog.

"A tour's the way to go," my neighbor said. "We didn't have to do a thing. The people were friendly and the food was pretty good."

"*I* thought the food was way too salty," his wife interjected, grimacing. "And we couldn't get a decent cup of coffee anywhere. Still, we figure we got our money's worth."

And then, in the fall of 1986, we had an unexpected visit from an old friend we had not seen in over a decade. Evan called from the airport, saying he had just flown in from China to visit the Zen Center in Minneapolis before flying on to his parents' home in New York. We invited him to dinner, to which he responded by insisting he would bring the meal himself. The last Fred and I had heard of him was the shocking news, via the musicians' grapevine, that he had abruptly quit his position in a large orchestra, sold his precious Italian cello, and gone to India to study with a famous guru, the same one who had taught the Beatles. No one had heard from him since; everyone assumed he had dropped off the face of the earth.

Evan arrived at our house by bus. When he took off his raggedy coat, I thought he had been in a terrible accident, because he was swathed in bandages. Then I realized he was wearing a garment of a single piece of gauze that wrapped him from his neck to his ankles. His face was hollow, gaunt, his expression gentle and passive to the extreme, giving him the look of a starving saint, or idiot. He carried two paper bags, one of which he handed over, explaining that it contained our supper. His voice was so soft I had to strain to hear, and he spoke with a peculiar accent that made me immediately skeptical and irritated because it didn't sound like Evan but somebody he was trying to invent. I missed the Evan we knew back in our student days, a big guy then, with a voice that boomed, especially when he drank too much cheap wine and burst into stentorian renditions of Bruckner's Seventh Symphony.

"I am a vegetarian now," he pronounced, intoning "I am," and "it is" as though he was a holy prophet, or a character from *Star Trek*. And he needn't have proclaimed his vegetarianism, it was obvious. He must have lost eighty pounds, and his skin had the transparency of a paramecium.

We put the food on the table: rice, tofu, a pale gruel of legumes and seeds that looked to have been regurgitated by a canary. I served the food and observed Evan as he closed his eyes to give the blessing. His eyelids, thin as parchment, fluttered with a kind of fervor, and his voice, murmuring and vaporous, made me strangely agitated. I found myself wishing that Evan's bandages would fall off, that he would get roaring drunk and tell his stories of growing up in the crazy household of a dyspeptic Jewish father and hand-wringing Irish Catholic mother. Instead, he told us how he had begun his quest in India, where he had gotten sick right away with amoebic dysentery. After recovering, he decided that India did not hold what he sought, and traveled on to Burma, then China. It was only in China that he found his true self and peace at last.

"The Chinese live simply," he said, crossing his legs, revealing his tattered black Chinese shoes. "They are poor, but rich in spirit."

"So you think Communism is a good thing?" Fred said.

Evan looked at him, and for an instant I thought I saw a flicker in the eye of our feisty old friend.

"It is not the system that matters, but the people," he said, evenly.

"People aren't so different. Nobody likes starving," Fred said.

I gave his foot a little kick under the table. He glanced at me sharply, and I saw that he was just as irked with our friend as I, just as hopeful that Evan would drop his holy hermit act and return as his old self.

"You have to go there to understand," Evan said.

His tone, with its slightly wounded but forgiving resonance, conveying his willingness to overlook our pagan ignorance and intolerance, reminded me of my brother's after his return from China. At least, in time, my brother emerged from his zombie-like state, so I held out some hope for Evan that he would snap out of it as well. It crossed my mind to offer him a Coke, thinking it might speed the process, wondering at the same time how it was that China had this radical effect on people, causing them to reject, with missionary zeal, physical comfort and psychological-emotional satiety, all those things Americans strive for. Perhaps it was as simple a matter as the rice diet, where white begets white, leeching even the most robust appetites. I remembered my brother's explanation, following his second can of Coke: *When you're someplace where no one has anything, you feel embarrassed, no, ashamed, for the weirdest things, like having athletic ability, for having B.O., for even feeling hungry. Second to giving them whatever you have* (which he did, handing over all his clothes) *all you feel like doing is try to show them you're no more deserving, that you're no different.*

Now that he was back home, my brother seemed to realize that it was one thing to become aware of the terrible imbalances in the world, but quite another to nullify himself, to try to make things right by becoming someone he was not. My guess was that Evan had made this same mistake, and that, for all that he had embraced in China, he could not have strayed completely from his hard-wired American-ness. He had amassed the largest collection of jazz tapes of anyone we knew (this was pre–compact disc days) and held out for the day when the Boston Red Sox would win the World Series. I wondered how long it would take him to revert to this true self, as my brother had done. He seemed to sense I was thinking this. At least, he was watching me closely. He seemed to be appraising everything in our house, sizing up the number of square feet, our plush velvet sofa, our succulent houseplants, with an air that reminded me of those infinitely polite, coat-and-tie people who tap on your door and press literature into your hands proclaiming the imminent end of the world.

Nevertheless, when Evan talked of where he had been in China, naming several cities and provinces, my heart sank, because I heard that his command of the Mandarin language was masterful, even elegant. It pained me, somehow, this spectacle of a white man who so calmly and competently rolled my family's language from the tip of his tongue.

"Where did you learn to speak Mandarin?" I blurted.

"From a tutor in Beijing. His daughter wanted to learn to play the cello, so I traded lessons. After a year, I developed my own course in Mandarin to teach to American businessmen there. That is how I supported myself. Here." He took a shoe box from the second bag he had brought. "When you told me you were going to China, I brought you these."

Inside the shoe box were hundreds of small white cards printed with English and Chinese phrases. I picked one out, read it aloud: "*Da.* Big. Example: Jackie Gleason is a big man. *Jackie Gleason sher egah da ren.*"

"Lemme see," Fred said, taking the box and flipping through some cards. "Here's one on baseball. And John Travolta! How come John Travolta?"

"*Saturday Night Fever.* The Chinese are big on disco."

"Evan, you shouldn't," I said. "Is this the only set you have?"

He waved his hand. "One of the businessmen let me use his computer so I've got them all on disk. I can print up as many sets as I need. In fact, I'm taking a few when I go back."

"You're going back?"

Evan nodded. Suddenly he coughed, a dry, hacking sound.

"That sounds pretty nasty," Fred said.

"Bronchitis. Most everyone gets it in Beijing, especially in the winter, with all the coal burning. Had this for months, on and off." Evan hacked again, his ribs sounding as if they were cracking apart. When he looked up his eyes were streaming.

"Aren't you cold?" Fred said. "Let me get you a sweater."

Evan shook his head, clearing his throat. "I'm fine. Maybe just a little tired. It's a long flight."

"Evan, can I ask you something?" I said.

He nodded.

"Why are you going back?"

He shrugged. "I told you. Life is simple there. I don't mean that it's easy, it isn't. But the people . . ." he paused, squinting at the air in front of him, searching for words. ". . . there's something that comes from suffering. I don't mean the kind that comes of intermittent war, as horrible as that is. I mean *perpetual* suffering, the kind that gets passed from generation to generation, dynasty to dynasty. It's like people who experience chronic, debilitating pain, yet are still somehow able to find meaning and contentment in life . . . for whom the smallest act, the smallest exchange, counts for more. There's something incredibly rich about that. I really can't explain it. You'll see when you go."

I noticed he had begun contracting his words. Was he coming around? "Got any advice?" I said.

Evan thought for a moment. "Bring toilet paper. And plenty of the pink stuff."

"Pink stuff?"

"Pepto Bismol." He was about to say something else, but hesitated.

"What?" I said.

"Don't make a big deal out of this, but try not to go off the beaten path. Be careful not to draw attention to yourself. Pay attention to who's around you."

There was something in his voice that made my stomach tighten.

"What are you saying?"

He shook his head. "It could be me, but I think something's brewing. It's been eight years since the end of the Cultural Revolution and the Chinese people are daring to speak out that it was a big mistake. They're still suffering from the aftereffects. Students, in particular, are resentful of today's policies, speaking out against oppression. Naturally this makes the government edgy."

"How come we don't hear about this?" Fred asked.

"The last thing the Chinese government wants is to air its dirty laundry. That's why tourists aren't allowed to go anywhere on their own, where they might find dissent, incriminating evidence." Again, Evan hesitated, a look of uncertainty on his face.

"What? Tell us!"

"Well, remember this is an unusual circumstance. I can't see why this would happen to you." He took a deep breath. "I met this guy on a train going from Shanghai to Beijing. American. He looked in bad shape, thin, dirty. Didn't look like anyone had roughed him up, but he was clearly shaken. Said he was a journalism student. Told me he had gone off on his own, poking around in some backwater village, trying to get Chinese peasants to talk about how they thought they were being treated by the government. Next thing he knows, he's grabbed by some guys in uniform, detained for a couple days, asked all kinds of questions. He said he thought he was a goner for sure. No one knew where he was, he had no way of reaching anybody. Finally he told his captors his father was a big shot in D.C. and if he were hurt or disappeared there'd be trouble. He was released a few days after."

"Wow. That's kind of scary. Who was he? Was he the son of somebody famous?"

Evan shrugged. "Terry somebody. Never got his last name. Don't know if what he told me was true. But he sure looked like he wasn't going to mind anybody's business but his own from then on."

We were quiet for a while. I noticed how Evan had reverted to his former way of speaking, how political foment brought out his old self, which had an activist bent and was intrigued by social unrest. I was troubled by his story and how it might have bearing on my upcoming trip.

"Did someone rat on him?" I asked. "How did the officials find him?"

Evan held up his hands, indicating it was anybody's guess. "During the Cultural Revolution, things were so touchy that anyone was a potential target for suspicion. No one felt safe saying anything in public. People were spying everywhere, pointing fingers. Neighbors, family members, turned on one another. It was a kind of mass hysteria. There's probably still some of that around."

I had heard of guilt by association, how relatives of those indicted were also implicated. A shiver ran through me as I thought of Yeh Yeh and Aunt Lucy and what they had gone through during the Cultural Revolution. Would I be viewed with suspicion, simply because I was their granddaughter and niece? Would the fact that I was American-born stigmatize me further?

Doubts raced through my mind. Maybe I ought to postpone my trip to China until things simmered down there.

Evan seemed to read my mind, "Don't worry," he said. "I'm sure you'll be fine. I can't see you doing anything stupid."

His words were anything but reassuring. Sensing my state of mind, Fred went out of the room, returning shortly with a bottle of wine and glasses. "Hey Ev, remember this?"

Our friend laughed when he saw the label. "Seems like forever since I had any of that."

"Come on. The fumes will do you good."

But Evan put his hand over his glass and watched, smiling, as we raised our glasses and drank to his return. The look in his eye was different now, not saintly as before, but tired, content, like a patient on the mend after a long illness.

We pressed him to stay the night, but he insisted on returning to the Zen Center in Minneapolis, explaining that he intended to meditate there early the next morning. He left town, the day after, and we didn't hear from him again until four years later, when he sent us a card from Munich saying he had gone back to playing the cello, married a German woman, and had a job in the Bavarian State Radio Orchestra. He sounded happy and fulfilled. He didn't mention China.

In the weeks following Evan's visit, despite lingering fear of going on my trip based on his story about the young American, I resolved to plunge ahead. I went through the cards in Evan's shoe box, thinking to study his Chinese language system. By learning Mandarin I hoped to gain confidence in going to China, but it didn't take me long to decide that his system was too idiosyncratic. I learned how to say "play ball," and "where can I buy sheet music," and some other phrases before I realized they were the words of a man loony with homesickness. Realizing this, I called the Chinese Community Center in St. Paul and asked for the name of a tutor in Mandarin. By this time, it was the end of February, and I was beginning to feel the pressure of having only three months to prepare for my trip.

The center gave me the name of Mrs. Dorothy Fang, who was originally from Shanghai but had lived in Minnesota for more than thirty years. Her husband, an engineer, had recently retired from Honeywell. Our first lesson took place on a snowy Tuesday evening. Mrs. Fang was about sixty years old, four and a half feet tall, and wore a gray Eddie Bauer coat which made her look soft and round, like a mole. Her hair was dyed blue-black, her eyebrows plucked in the shape of crescent moons, giving her the look of permanent surprise assumed by so many of my mother's Chinese friends. Hers was the classic dowager look, only slightly modified to Minnesota standards by her sweater, which was embroidered with mallards, and her white Sorel boots. It was a hard image to bring off, a Mandarin in Minnesota, but Mrs. Fang managed it.

I put the kettle on, and we made small talk while we waited for the water to boil. Fred poked his head in the room to say a brief hello. He was gone in a second, but Mrs. Fang reacted as though she had seen a ghost. She did not jump or scream, but emitted a cool atmosphere all around her, as though she had turned to ice. I had observed this phenomenon before, when my parents or their friends encountered people outside their clan. The response was not so much a deliberate act on their part, but more the result of a spontaneous chemical reaction that took place during the clash of unlike elements. I knew there was nothing essentially harmful about Mrs. Fang's reaction, but there was still something about her that made me hold my breath.

Mrs. Fang herself rapidly regained her composure. She said she was sure I would be a good student because I had spoken Chinese when I was young. Her voice was soft, refined, her smile radiating confidence. I felt somewhat reassured. I was eager to get on with my lesson.

We moved to the dining room table, where Mrs. Fang laid out notebooks, a tape recorder, pencils, and a hand mirror. She began the lesson by pronouncing the four major tones in the Mandarin language: a sustained high tone, a tone that went from low to high, a tone that went from high to low, and a short, sharp tone that began high and ended lower. I was struck by the change in Mrs. Fang's voice, how it sounded pinched and nasal, as though she stored her Chinese in her nose. Released into the air it had a nagging, fretful quality to it, as though it scolded her for keeping it captive there. She had sounded so normal, or, rather, Minnesotan, before. She could have said "ice hockey" and "eelpout," and I wouldn't have blinked. Now she sounded strangled, as though she reeled from the strain of reining in her Mandarin. Mrs. Fang fixed her eyes on me.

"Say '*ma*,' "she ordered.

I obeyed, parroting what she said exactly, I thought.

Mrs. Fang explained that the word *Ma,* pronounced in the long high tone, meant *mother.* However, pronounced in the tone that went from low to high, it meant *horse.* And in the short tone, *to beat.*

"The right tone is very important," she said. "Wrong tone, and you say you beat your mother. Ha ha!" Her laughter sounded too well-practiced, humorless, which made me suspect she had told me her one patented joke. Next, she instructed me to repeat an example of a primary sound.

"Rui," she said. *"Fish.* Like this." She raised her lips from her teeth, the better for me to obsevre, rolling her tongue lengthwise so that it looked like a kind of moist hors d'oeuvre. She held the hand mirror to my face so I could try to duplicate the act. I stared at my tongue, waggled it around.

"Yee," I said, grimacing. "Sorry."

"Try again," she said.

I tried twisting my tongue the other way. *"Ree,"* I said. "Oops."

"That's a hard one," she said, clucking her tongue. "Let's try another." I tried several more, but what came out of my mouth is indescribable. It was like playing horribly out of tune, yet not knowing how to correct it. I knew how to manage my fingers on the fingerboard of my violin, but manipulating my tongue into these intricate, contortionist maneuvers, and scooping, bending, and squeezing those sounds in my larynx was beyond me. At first Mrs. Fang smiled patiently, waving her hand like a magic wand in encouragement, but after an hour, when I mewled and yawped like a cat trapped in a tree, she began to heave weighty sighs.

I had heard these sighs before, from my mother and her Chinese friends in the days when they sat around the kitchen table talking about their children. Their sighs expressed the burden of coping with the abandonment of Chinese ways, like interracial dating, SAT scores below fourteen hundred. The sighs hung heavy in the air, conveying disappointment and resignation like suppressed keening.

During a break in the lesson, I poured fresh tea and brought out a plate of Pepperidge Farm cookies, thinking this might placate Mrs. Fang.

Suddenly she asked, "Do you have children?"

"No."

She lowered her eyes, nodding discreetly, as though to indicate she was modern, after all, but at the same time letting loose another sigh, this one louder than all the others. In the next instant, she seemed to decide something, straightening her shoulders and assuming a stoic expression like all those brave and self-sacrificing souls who had perished in one of innumerable hopeless endeavors peppering China's tragic history. It was clear she was not about to give up without a struggle. Indeed, she seemed more resolved than ever to take me on as a personal challenge, a nut she was determined to crack.

The next visit, she brought pictures of her grandchildren, two girls and a boy. One of the girls, who was seven, played the violin and had already soloed with the Minnesota Civic Symphony. Her parents, a cardiologist and an architect, were determined that their children were given every opportunity to compete successfully amongst their peers. Mrs. Fang pushed the picture of her two-year-old grandson toward me. He was chubby, staring out of his bunting with eyes that were already serious and accomplished.

"Not too late for you," Mrs. Fang said, in that tone of admonition that sounded all too familiar. She wore gold and jade rings that loosely circled her bony, arthritic fingers. During stressful moments of our lessons, while she waited for me to mispronounce a word, for example, she twirled these rings with her thumbs so fast they sang. Her thumbs reminded me of my mother's tightly clasped fists, which escalated the already high state of tension in our lessons. The final straw came when, once again, Mrs. Fang brought her mirror close to my face, insisting that it would help me to watch the errant writhing of my tongue.

"No, listen, *rui,*" she insisted, repeating that dreaded Chinese word for fish. For her that seemed to be the key, the one word I could not possibly go to China without being able to pronounce.

"*Wee,*" I said, feeling my tongue flipping like a minnow on a hook.

We both winced. Mrs. Fang reconnoitered, saying we would return to fish later. Methodically she spread out her homemade vocabulary cards. We went through the numbers, a few conversational phrases. I learned the words for *airport, train, tickets. Today, tomorrow, yesterday.* As I repeated the words I felt pleasure in the rise and fall of the tones, the way the language imitated the sounds of nature, how simple yet ingenious words or phrases were constructed. The Chinese word for *owl,* for example, is put together from *mao, tow, ing,* meaning, literally, "cat-head bird." I laughed out loud saying it, thinking, *What a wonderful language! (Just don't make me say fish.)* But, sure enough, Mrs. Fang wheeled, circling craftily with the stealth of a raptor.

"Owls have heads like cats," she said, her eyes narrowing, "and cats like to eat . . . ?" she took out a piece of paper, and with a flourish drew a gigantic fish—a shark, actually—with a scythe-like dorsal fin. She looked at me with an exaggerated smile, her head bobbing, her eyes popping with encouragement, as though I were a child. *All she has to do is thrust the mirror in my face and that would be the end of it,* I thought, but she remained frozen, her eyes fixed on me with that look of expectation. Looking into her pupils I thought I saw, glinting beyond the veneer of cajoling benevolence, the ambition of her entire generation, its vicarious aims, and suddenly I understood why children clam up and pretend they've never been born. After a moment or two, when I had still said nothing, the light in Mrs. Fang's eyes darkened.

"Go ahead. Say *fish,*" she said.

Mute as a cornered but stubbornly defiant six-year-old, I faced her implicit accusation that by not saying *fish* I rejected the key to my ancestral world, avoided coming to terms with my cultural identity, and therefore embraced condemnation to a life of cultural purgatory. *It was easy for her to say* fish, I thought, *she had been born over there, and still embodied whatever that meant. But China doesn't exist anymore!* I wanted to shout. My inherited culture, if indeed it had been mine to begin with, had been uprooted, wiped out, disseminated so that all that remained were mere fragments drifting in outer pockets of the world, in the hearts and souls of people like Mrs. Fang. My so-called homeland had been culturally purged to the point that all that remained was a hulking bureaucracy the main purpose of which was to sustain its creaking, bloated self. Even if Mrs. Fang was correct, that language was indeed the key to whatever remained of this world, her manner and use of it was imperial, uncompromising, like the very system that had imploded it. Suddenly, maybe because there was something in her tenacious, expectant attitude that reminded me of my mother, I searched desperately for a way to tell her that it was her system, not her, to which I objected. But I saw from the way she looked at me that I had balked too long; she had given up on me. Much later, I realized that rather than feeling like a failure I felt tremendous relief. Even though I was still unclear and inchoate about my reasons for going to China—other than seeing my relatives and retrieving my grandfather's scroll—I finally realized my reasons didn't have to line up with Mrs. Fang's. Even though I looked Chinese, I was not like her. So, regardless of the failure of the lessons, I learned something more about myself, and if it was only knowing who I wasn't, it was still more than I knew before.

After Mrs. Fang left, I plugged along on my own, reciting numbers and phrases out loud, trying not to put too much pressure on myself for getting the tones right. Weeks went by. I made my own cards and taped them up around the house. One day, Fred caught me standing in front of the bathroom mirror.

"What's the matter?" he said. "Got a toothache?"

"Shhh!" I looked back in the mirror, rolled up my tongue like it was paper around tobacco. "*Wree. Rui. Rui.* I did it! *Rui rui rui!*"

"What the hell does that mean?" Fred said.

"Fish!" I shouted.

In New York, when I had told Da Bobo I was coming to Beijing, his whole face lit up, but then instantly fell dark. "We'll have to build a bathroom," he said, in tones that sounded doomed, fatalistic, as though he had been called to build an extension of the Great Wall. I thought I might have misread this, but then I saw him glance at Da Mama with a helpless look of resignation, which she confirmed with a shrug of her shoulders, as though she, too, like the wife of Job, glimpsed a swarm of locusts on the not-too-distant horizon. I insisted that building a bathroom wasn't necessary, that what worked for them worked for me, but Da Bobo set his jaw.

"Well," my brother replied, when I called him for his take. "It's not like they have Home Depot over there, you know." His voice tolled dual tones of knowing and doom. "They have no organized labor force, and raw materials are scarce. What do you think they're gonna make a bathroom out of, chopsticks?"

Throughout the winter, my uncle's letters seemed to bear out my brother's prognostications:

Dear Sung Lien,

The workmen promise they will be done with the bathroom by the time you and your mother come, but I haven't seen them in two days. When they do show up, they stand around scratching their heads. One of them fell into the hole they dug and couldn't get out. They demand I give them lunch, cigarettes, beer, but still they fall asleep on the job. I hate hiring through the back door, but there is no other way.

I do not mean to burden you with our problems. Thank you for sending us

the Bing Crosby tapes. Please stay with us for a month, at least. There is so much to see and do. You must get the full flavor of your homeland!
Love, Da Bobo and Da Mama.

P.S. As for what to bring—we don't need anything, but if it will fit in your suitcase, please bring a box of microwave cake mix. A hot-shot tennis player from Hong Kong gave me a microwave oven!

Almost in tandem, Aunt Lucy's letters arrived, providing her own view of things:

Dear Sung Lien,
Thank you for the tape of Hermann Prey singing Schubert. Although I prefer the timbre of Fisher-Dieskau's voice, Prey's interpretation is not without its merits. All is difficult to enjoy, however, due to the continual uproar over the bathroom. The laborers seem to be making a game out of gouging your uncle, showing up late, then lolling about, gossiping and napping. Then they have the gall to clamor for snacks and tips! Even though your uncle shouts and threatens (they are going at it even as I write), they know they have him over a barrel. Such is the way things work here in China, not like your capitalist system where incentives lead to competition and superior production. I shall never forget the service I received while shopping in America. I am reminded of it daily when I wear the down coat I bought in Minnesota.

Thank you for asking about my eyes. I visited an apothecary who prescribed new medicines for me, so I remain hopeful.

I wait patiently for the day of your arrival. I do not mind that you bring along a tape recorder to tape our talks, but please do not expect much, as I am afraid my memory is not what it used to be. Until then, Aunt Lucy.

It was Fred who suggested I buy a microcassette recorder to tape my talks with Aunt Lucy. I hoped to document through her the history of my family, back to the days when Yeh Yeh was a boy. The cassettes were the size of credit cards, and I bought enough so that if Aunt Lucy were to recite the entire works of Charles Dickens, I would get it all.

Throughout the winter, I filled my suitcase with items I thought of bringing to China: a tennis-ball holder for Da Bobo, a pretty slip for Da Mama, plain traveling clothes that I planned to rinse out overnight. Even though I kept rearranging, taking out, and adding items, it felt wrong, somehow, incomplete. Something was missing.

"What do I need to bring?" I asked my mother over the phone.

"Toilet paper," she said, in between gasps. She was out of breath, having answered the phone after playing two sets of tennis. "And don't forget Pepto Bismol."

"Right," I said, recalling our friend Evan's admonition. I forced from my mind residual anxiety left by his account of his young American traveling companion and his brush with Chinese authorities. "How about bug spray? Are mosquitoes bad there?"

"Terrible. Last year encephalitis break out. Oh! I almost forgot. A bad cousin probably write to you."

"A bad cousin?"

"Black sheep. From your father's side. Adopted son. He grow up during the Cultural Revolution, so he has no education. I don't know how he got my name, but he wrote, ask me to sponsor him here. I said no, because I already sponsor your cousin Shi Shi. But he wrote back . . . demand this, demand that. Sound very bad."

"Why would he write to me?"

"He the kind who ask anyone for money, or sponsorship. He think we're rich, we owe him. That's what they think of us. Anyway, look out, he's trouble."

My mother heaved another sigh.

"What?"

"It's not fair to us here legally, pay taxes! Few black sheep is all it take. Pretty soon people say all Chinese this, all Chinese that!"

Her voice was strident, the way it sounded whenever she complained about people who didn't play by the rules. It was hard for her, being a model citizen, bad enough that people cheated. But to her, if they were Chinese, that made it worse. She had higher expectations of clan members, especially in a country where you're different and know you're being watched. If the speed limit was 15 mph, that's what you drove, keeping the speedometer needle smack on the line. And if someone gave you too much change, you returned it promptly. Though I teased my mother about her scrupulousness, I realize I'd inherited something like it, a predisposition that remained unaffected by boundaries of time or space. It didn't matter how long ago you'd come from China, or how your life turned out in America, the appearance of a black sheep still stirred the clan consciousness to a red state of alert.

"Mom, what does 'back door' mean?"

"Oh." She made a sound of disgust. "That's when you bribe people to do things for you. When you can't do things legally because of crooked officials or stupid rules, you find people, pay them under table to get what you want."

"Like what lobbyists do here, right?"

"What?"

"Never mind. I think I get it."

My mother's warning turned out to be timely, because not long after our phone call I received an aerogram, postmarked from a city in the western province of China, which read:

Dear Cousin Sung Lien,

I am your cousin Chih Piao and I am write to ask you sponsor me in United States. I want come to learn business to make money. If you cannot sponsor me, please send:

- 2 mens suits, one dark, one light
- 4 white shirts
- 2 pairs Adidas sports shoes
- 2 watches, digital, waterproof
- Elvis Presley tapes
- Walkman (Sony)
- $1,000 in traveler's checks.

Please send to return address.

Signed, your cousin,
Chih Piao.

The signature was crudely scrawled, as though by a child. I was impressed and appalled by this so-called cousin's grasp of English, his brand-name savvy, his gall! Following my mother's advice, I threw the letter away, though for days afterward, felt troubling aftershocks to my conscience.

In May, the orchestra went to play in Carnegie Hall and the Kennedy Center in Washington, D.C. My mother met us at the airport in Washington and drove us back to her house. Our concert was not until the next evening, so we had plenty of free time. As always, the Virginia countryside was beautiful this time of year, with azaleas, forsythia, tulips, and jonquils flowering along the road to my mother's house.

After dinner, my mother brought out our itinerary in China, a large sheet of paper filled with diagrams and dates and arrows pointing every which way. It looked like the master plan for a bank heist.

"This is what Da Bobo suggested," she said. "We stay in Shanghai for a few days, visit relatives, then take train to Beijing where we stay with Da Bobo, Da Mama, and Aunt Lucy. From there we fly to Xi'an . . ."

"Fly?" I interrupted. "I thought you said we weren't going to fly . . ."

"Oh, Chinese planes much better now," she said.

"But I've read that planes crash in China every month," Fred interjected, avoiding my eyes. "And those are only the ones we hear about. They're dilapidated Soviet crates from World War Two whose maintenance records have vanished."

"Isn't there a train from Beijing to Xi'an?" I pleaded.

"Too far," my mother said, her lips beginning to compress.

I felt a stab of annoyance at my mother's intractability which prevented me from paying full attention to the rest of her description of our itinerary.

". . . and that bring us back to Shanghai," she concluded. "Five weeks."

"Five weeks! Whew! That's a long time!" Fred said.

I looked at him and saw that it wasn't that I was going to be away from home that concerned him so much as the fact that my mother and I would be together. He knew our history of misunderstandings and probably sensed how my red flags were up because of her disregard for my fear of flying. Had she always been this inflexible, I wondered. Or was she, at sixty-eight years of age, more set in her ways? Though I knew she meant to respect Da Bobo's suggestions and that logistical limitations were a fact of life in China, this latest exchange reminded me all too well of how my mother and I had always struggled to communicate.

Was it because English was not her first language? Was it because my brother and I, both born in America, thoughtlessly teased her when she confused her pronouns, referring to my brother as "she" and me as "he"? The Chinese language makes no distinction for gender, denoting all subjects as *"ta,"* whether they be he, she, or it. I believed other grammatical insecurities caused my mother to simplify and truncate her speech so that she often came across as brusque or defensive. I was embarrassed when I thought others perceived my mother as angry or rude. I have to admit that sometimes I myself had trouble telling. I would try to apologize for her, which I think made her furious, though she denied it. Only her silence and her clenched thumbs gave her away.

"I think I've got a plan," I said. This was later, after we had all retired for the night. "I've decided, that for five weeks, I will simply defer to my mother at all times."

"Oh sure, right," Fred said, rolling his eyes.

"No, I mean it. How else am I going to make it? We'll be on her turf, there'd be no point in arguing. I don't want to set myself up for her disapproving silences. Anyway, I don't know Chinese well enough. I'll be depending on her for everything."

"That's what I mean. You're not exactly good at being dependent."

"It'll be a good test," I insisted.

Being a wise man, he said nothing more.

Earlier that evening, my mother brought out the suitcase she was bringing to China, the same she had carried on all her previous trips. It was the size of a hatbox, battered but sturdy, its every inch embodying Chinese character. Inside, my mother had packed two pairs of slacks, two shirts, a plastic poncho, two pairs of underwear, her toothbrush, a bottle of Pepto Bismol, and a tin of aspirin. I was impressed by the readiness of the bag, as though my mother was prepared to go to China at any moment, in the way expectant mothers rushed off to the hospital, or dissidents fled marauding authorities. I thought of my own bulging suitcase at home, disheveled from so much rummaging and indecision. Fred was right. It was hard to imagine two more disparate souls. How would my mother and I manage for five long weeks together?

I had the rest of May to prepare myself for the trip, and by the time June arrived, felt reasonably ready. The only thing left was the final packing. After pushing things around in my suitcase for the umpteenth time, I thought I heard a voice and whirled around, believing that someone had placed a hand on my shoulder. The voice, though I had never heard it before, seemed familiar. *Sung Lien!* it intoned, and in that instant I knew it was my grandfather. Though he was nowhere in sight, he sounded vexed, as though my letters filled with split infinitives lay before him. I realized that, in my self-absorbed anxiety, I had forgotten to consult my wizard, my most powerful guide. I took his letter, which I carried in my viola case, and put that along with the photo of him with the sock on his head in my suitcase. As if those were the final, missing pieces of my trip, things suddenly leapt and arranged themselves into place like iron filings drawn by a magnet. I was packed in no time at all. My grandfather's presence faded as though, with the completion of this task, his job was done. Viewing my suitcase, which now had plenty of room to spare, I had no way of knowing how Yeh Yeh's letter and picture would serve me as touchstone, compass, and, indeed, as lightning rod in the weeks to come.

On the day I was to leave, Fred drove me to the airport, where I was to join my mother on the continuation of her flight from Washington, D.C., to Shanghai. The plane arrived on time, and my mother got off during the hour-long layover to stretch her legs in the airport.

"Well, I'll hold down the fort," Fred said, as we watched her walk through the terminal.

We both hated good-byes.

"Don't forget Maya's heartworm pills."

"Got everything? Ticket, passport, visa?"

We kissed. My mother returned. We talked idly, anxious for the waiting to be over. Finally the call for boarding sounded over the loudspeakers.

"Bye," I said once again, grabbing Fred by the hand.

"Ow!" he gasped.

"Come on!" my mother urged.

I couldn't let go.

"You'll be fine," Fred said. "You'll have a great trip."

People were moving past us. I managed to let go of Fred and hurried after my mother. Just before entering the jetway, I turned one last time. Fred was waving. I followed my mother, who was entering the long curved ramp to the plane, focusing on her hair, which was springy and stiff from her new perm. *Don't think, just follow,* I thought to myself. Suddenly, she turned. A flicker of surprise crossed her face, and I saw that she hadn't truly believed that I was going to China with her, that she had expected me to come up with yet another excuse, even at this late hour. Seeing I was on her heels seemed to convince her at last. She wheeled around. "Here we go!" she exclaimed. As I followed her through the door of the plane, I thought I had never heard her sound so happy.

PART TWO

River of Years

10

SHANGHAI

AT ELEVEN O'CLOCK IN THE NIGHT, AFTER CROSSING THE PACIFIC OCEAN, the luminous horizon of Japan, several time zones and other indefinable dimensions which my mind and body struggled to breach, our plane arrived in Shanghai. The DC-10 landed, jouncing along a runway that stretched like an endless washboard, after which a rickety metal stairway was brought in order for us to descend to the cracked, stained tarmac. Clumps of tall weeds, illuminated by the faint light of the air tower, grew in widespread fissures in the concrete, giving the airfield a forlorn, neglected aspect, like that of an ancient abandoned city reclaimed by jungle habitat. The air was hot, muggy, and filled with the sound of feverish nocturnal insects. The smell was fecund, primieval, and bacterial. I felt as if we had flown not only halfway around the world, but back several centuries in time as well.

My mother and I crossed the runway to the terminal, picking our way past piles of rubbish reeking of rotten fruit and urine. At first the terminal seemed deserted, an empty hangar rather than a reception area for international travelers. Phosphorescent lights cast a weak, greenish glow, illuminating great scabs of paint peeling from the walls. A stinging, sulfurous smell hung in the air, and swirls of mist snaked through the pallid light like giant smoke rings. As we got closer, I saw a few indistinct figures moving about before this shadowy scrim.

I was shaking all over. I told myself it was because I had been traveling for fourteen straight hours, and that my body was sending urgent messages that I had abandoned it somewhere over the Pacific Ocean. Deep inside, I knew it was because I had arrived in China. Though I had been careful not to nurse expectations, I was overwhelmed by the feeling of promise; that what was to come would likely be nothing I had ever imagined. In spite of the smoky air, I inhaled deeply, bent down, and touched the ground. I told myself I was not going to miss a thing.

We went along with the other passengers to the customs area, which was divided into three lines, one for American tourists, another for returning Chinese citizens, a third for overseas Chinese. I hesitated, confused, scanning for the line that described me, who was none of these. A little evil chime, *imposter,* began to clang in my head. Where was the line for unspecified hybrids such as myself? Finally, an impatient guard, dressed in the dark green, red-trimmed uniform that I later learned was the official garb of the communist army, brusquely directed my mother and me to the third line. While the Americans in the large tour group were quickly processed and whisked to buses waiting outside the terminal, my mother and I were scrutinized by a skeptical-looking official who kept referring to a book of regulations the size of a telephone directory. I tried to look innocent as my mother answered the official's questions, but something about me must have alerted him, because he made an abrupt gesture for me to open my suitcase. Rummaging there, he took out Yeh Yeh's photograph, then the letter, and scrutinized them, and me, looking back and forth several times. Then he took out an official-looking log and began to write. I became aware of my heart pounding, my palms sweating. If I had managed to look innocent before, I was surely now the picture of guilt, whatever that was. Finally, the official took my passport and stamped it, slowly, with exaggerated reluctance. It was clear he felt admitting me into his country was a mistake.

One of his comrades, noting his actions, was approaching, making me certain that I was to be arrested and thrown into a Chinese jail for the rest of my life. Just at that moment, three civilians rushed up and began speaking to the officials in a strange dialect. They addressed my mother, who, though surprised, responded in a cordial tone. Whatever they said seemed to mollify the officials, who allowed them to take our suitcases and lead us to the opposite end of the terminal, where a dilapidated bus waited. We boarded the bus, squeezing among what seemed like an entire village of Chinese and their belongings, collapsing finally in the middle of a family clutching bags stuffed with pots and pans and two or three sleeping babies.

Reaching over the bags, I tried to fan away thick diesel fumes emitted by the idling bus engine. I noticed my mother's growing agitation and realized that the three men who carried our luggage were nowhere in sight. Her expression conveyed that we might be in a great deal of trouble. Before we could investigate the whereabouts of the men and our bags, the bus ground its gears with a horrendous screech and lurched away from the curb with a blast of diesel exhaust.

The night air was dense with fog so that the feeble lights of the bus barely penetrated a path twenty feet in front of it. Still, I was able to make out the sign: SHANGHAI. It was a small sign by the side of the road, but I felt a powerful shiver at the sight of it. The bus driver ground the gears once more, and the bus slowly groaned its way along the airport road and onto what looked like the main thoroughfare into the city.

Overloaded and moving with agonizing slowness, the bus seemed an easy target to what hurtled out of the murky darkness toward it at terrifying speeds. One vehicle with lights locked directly onto those of our bus, advanced at manic speed until, at the very last moment, our driver swerved, with much cursing and hauling at the steering wheel. In the flash of the near-collision, amid a din of frantic honking, I glimpsed the pale faces of Chinese children bouncing atop a heap piled in the back of the retreating lorry. The sharp, unmistakeable stench of pig shit poured in through our open window from the lorry's wake, leaving no doubt as to what the children were deposited on.

Other vehicles zoomed by, following what I now perceived was the Chinese law of the road, which is to say, no law, only fleeting, marginal gaps which the most opportunistic vehicles seized with incessant, angry honking and gunning of engines. These were mostly diesel trucks of every type, from recognizable German-made ones to metal Frankensteins bolted together from parts of this or that, their steel plates, hinges, and pipes clattering as they swerved wildly from one side of the road to the other. Less likely daredevils plied the road as well, like the farmer who peddled his bicycle at a fantastic rate, his scrawny white legs a blur as he vied for space among the trucks. Not only did he carry a huge straw basket, the size of a Volkswagen, filled with leafy vegetables, but at least four children who clung to various parts of his body, blinking in the passing glare of lights like dazed opossums. Straddling the handlebars of his bicycle was a woman who clutched another babe in her arms. Despite his load, the man remained perfectly balanced as he pedaled, as poised beneath his death-defying pyramid as the sturdiest member of the Flying Wallendas.

Dizzy and nauseated from jet lag, steamy heat, and the hot sweaty bodies around me, I continued to worry about the disappearance of the three men and our bags. Glancing again at my mother, I saw that she seemed lost in her own thoughts or had dropped off to sleep. I couldn't believe that she could sleep in the face of this likely disaster. As a seasoned international traveler, I had dealt with lost bags, canceled connections, and other perils, but here I felt helpless. I didn't know Chinese well enough to ask about our bags and was reluctant to make a fuss among all these strangers. I was forced to rely on my mother, and despite my resolve to defer to her on all accounts during our trip, I felt frustrated. I reminded myself that she had returned to China several times since it re-opened in 1972, and that she surely knew the ropes. Still, I found it hard to accept that she could just doze off like that.

As the bus bumped through the steamy night, I stared groggily out the moisture-beaded window, imagining that I peered through the porthole of a bathysphere submerged twenty fathoms in the ocean. Lights twinkled in the dark and advanced slowly, then rapidly, revealing sights as strange and won-derful as undiscovered species from the deep. A beautiful young woman ap-peared, drawing alongside our bus on her bicycle. She wore a dress made of translucent material that fluttered daintily about her knees. Wearing opaque white anklets, high-heeled platform shoes made of shiny plastic, she pedaled efficiently, looking fresh and dewy in the sodden night. *Where was she headed?* I wondered. A moment later, as though she suddenly realized the lateness of the hour, now well past 1 A.M., she kicked into gear and sped off. I pressed close to the glass to watch her as she darted away, still luminescent, in the darkness.

My mother dozed so that her body sagged against me, her drooping head occasionally bumping my shoulder. She was so close that I smelled the acrid scent of her new perm. Strange feelings rushed through me. When I was a toddler, my mother cautioned me to stay close, particularly when we went to strange places, so I used to take hold of her hand, grasping her little finger in my fist. Once, in a department store, I mindlessly let go. Moments later, when I realized I was no longer attached, I reached up, thinking to take hold of her finger again, but grabbed a stranger's hand instead. This lady shrieked and shook me off like a rat.

The instant I realized I was lost, I began to bawl and did not let up even when the woman alerted department store people to look for my mother. After what seemed like hours, my mother finally found me. The sense of security I got from feeling the bones and sinews of her finger immediately relieved the terror I had felt at being lost and alone. Yet, even as I grew older and got over my childish terrors, I never forgot that moment of overwhelming anguish when I was separated from my mother.

I thought of it again as her sleep-heavy body jounced against mine on the bus to Shanghai, because the weight of her shoulder, the scrape of the rough skin of her elbow, brought home the realization that one day I would lose her forever, and however sad this was, I knew there might be even greater separation between people than death. Because my mother and I, though now physically in the same space, the same country, her country, remained worlds apart. We were like other mothers and daughters of immigrant families continually facing the schism between one generation rooted in the customs and mores of another country as well as the terrible memories of revolution and war, and the first generation born in America. Being born in America, I was beneficiary to all the entitlements, including learning English at a young age, grasping the key to fluency in American culture, social niceties, and nuance. My parents, though English-speaking, retained accents as well as the unmistakeable air of immigration, and lacking the all-important birthright, remained essentially foreigners, both in how they viewed themselves and how they were viewed by other Americans. I saw they were less willing or able to adapt to American ways, or abandon their old-fashioned Chinese ways. I saw them as stuck, treading water, especially my mother because she aspired to be a medical doctor and had to settle for being a laboratory technician due to prohibitive rules regarding her transcripts from China and because she was too busy raising children.

At a certain point in our lives, when I became a teenager, I exchanged leads with my mother, explaining American ways to her and speaking for her even though I felt uncomfortable about the reversal of our roles as mother and daughter. I sensed her wounded pride even as she reluctantly went along. The air between us grew awkward, confused, forming a palpable gap. It got so language, any language, failed us. We stopped talking. Silence became the way between us.

Now that we were in China, back in the place where my mother had been born, where she was fluent, at home, and where I had already acquiesced to her lead, I wondered if the natural order of our roles as mother and daughter would be restored. Except now I was a thirty-eight-year-old adult. Now I was to taste what she had stomached for all those years. Though nervous, I also felt curiously hopeful. Maybe we would grow to understand one another better. Perhaps grow close. At least learn to talk. It surprised me to think that these, of all things, might be the true aim of our trip.

The bus pulled over to the side of the road at seemingly random points that were regular stops. Passengers got off and were greeted by friends and relatives who had been waiting in the dark. As the crowd thinned, we discovered our three men sitting at the front of the bus, our bags tucked between their legs. Again I wondered who they were. They had seemed not so much pleased to see us but relieved and had been almost painfully deferential to my mother, who was clearly a generation older.

Finally, when it was nearly two o'clock, we arrived in Shanghai. The city was quiet, dormant under the greenish pall of streetlights. We got off the bus with the three men and hailed a cab. During the short drive to the hotel, I managed to piece together that they were nephews of my mother's sister-in-law, or something like that. They apologized on this woman's behalf, explaining that she had not been able to welcome us herself due to ill health. Instead, she had asked her nephews to meet us, which required them to take time off from their factory jobs fifty miles outside of Shanghai. It was an elaborate and taxing arrangement, I thought, but one which I learned was typical, indicative of the importance of propriety in Chinese relationships.

Our hotel looked as though it was still under construction, with pieces of lumber, coils of wire, and spilled concrete mix lying around the entrance. Before our three chaperones left, they handed small envelopes to my mother and me. My mother put hers in her purse without looking at it. She offered to pay the cab fare to wherever the three men were going, but they declined, saying they would take a bus to the train station. They seemed in a hurry. Perhaps they felt relieved to be done with their task or anxious about missing another day's work. Before we had finished thanking them, they were gone.

We went into the hotel, where a band of listless Chinese musicians played "Staying Alive," by the Bee Gees. The saxophonist seemed to doze as he played, while the drummer swished his drums with the bored look of a dishwasher scrubbing a pot. The lobby reeked of insecticide and room deodorizer.

Behind the reception desk an elderly man, his face wreathed in smiles, rose, holding out his arms to me. "Yeh Yeh!" I gasped, astonished. My mother gave me a look as though I had lost my mind. When I turned to look again I saw a young Shanghai woman—plainly sleepy though chic in a Western way with an upswept hairdo and red lipstick—pushing a hotel registration card at my mother. "Please to sign here," she said, yawning. My jet-lagged imagination must have been playing tricks, I thought, because Yeh Yeh was no longer there, risen from the dead to welcome me to China.

While my mother signed the register, I opened the envelope handed to me by the nephews. Two pieces of paper slipped out, fluttering in opposite directions like butterflies. I picked up the first paper, recognizing the handwriting immediately. *Welcome to China*, it read. *Love, Da Bobo and Da Mama*. Then I retrieved the other piece, which had landed several feet away. The writing was minute, upright; I knew it well. *At last*. It was signed, *Aunt Lucy*.

SHREWIN

THE NEXT MORNING, THE HOTEL WAITER SERVED MY MOTHER AND ME THE Chinese version of American breakfast: fried eggs floating in oil, limp toast, salty orange drink, and Nescafé the color of silt. While we ate, my mother coached me on the names of the people we were meeting that day. At the top of the list was Shrewin, her sister-in-law's son-in-law, who had escorted her on all her prior visits to Shanghai.

"Say *Shray wen,*" my mother said, lifting her upper lip à la Mrs. Fang. She explained that Shrewin was married to Biring, the daughter of my mother's sister-in-law, whom I was to call Auntie Aifong. Auntie Aifong was the widow of my mother's second oldest brother, Henry. Head spinning with these convoluted but important details, I practiced saying Auntie Ai-fong's name aloud between bites of soggy toast. Then, out of nowhere, Shrewin himself appeared at our table. He bowed and shook my mother's hand in a manner that seemed polite and disinterested at the same time. In his mid-fifties, he was stocky, balding, with a flat, shiny face, and had crooked teeth that poked from the sides of his mouth like tusks. His eyes bulged and were oddly filmy, as though they swam in oily tears. Looped over his arm was a clear plastic bag filled with numerous small packages.

"Can she speak Chinese?" he said to my mother in Shanghai dialect, pointing to me.

"Only very poorly," my mother said.

"I speak a little," I piped up, in Mandarin. "I understand more than I speak."

Shrewin looked at me incredulously, as though I was a poodle that had spoken.

"Does he speak English?" I whispered to my mother.

"No," Shrewin said, shaking his head firmly.

He came with us to our room, which contained two narrow beds covered with panda-print spreads. On a side table there was a vase of plastic orchids and a thermos of boiled water, something I would see throughout my travels in China. Shrewin went through the room, fiddling with the controls of the air conditioner, flicking on the television. *Bonanza* exploded on the screen: Hoss Cartwright galloped across the Ponderosa ranch whooping in poorly dubbed Mandarin. Shrewin watched, unimpressed, then wandered into the bathroom. I thought him extremely presumptuous and gave my mother a questioning look, but she turned away, looking both resigned and resentful, clearly not wanting to talk about it. I sensed that an oft-repeated ritual that she had tired of long ago was again underway.

We listened to Shrewin running the shower, pulling the shower door back and forth, flushing the toilet. I had heard that modern plumbing was nonexistent for most people living in Shanghai, so I guessed he was merely curious about the conveniences of our hotel. I felt pity for his deprivation as well as a vague sense of violation. It occurred to me that my mother had not actually invited him to our room nor had he asked. There was nothing solicitous about his manner; he had simply come, as though it was his due. When he emerged from the bathroom, my mother opened her suitcase and presented him with a carton of Marlboros. I was shocked at this, as my mother is vehemently opposed to smoking. The sight of cigarettes in her hand was as improbable as if she had pulled out a gun. Shrewin did not seem surprised, but accepted the cigarettes as a matter of course, as though he had been expecting it. From his plastic bag, he handed my mother a jar of Chinese cold cream and a yellow pincushion that looked like all the others she had at home. To me, he gave a tiny ceramic doll with a mispainted face, its eyes peering cross-eyed from the top of its head like a planaria worm. At the end of this exchange, Shrewin and my mother offered polite thanks that sounded hollow and perfunctory.

Then my mother said, "Did you get the tickets?"

Shrewin's face turned greenish white. Stuttering, he began a lengthy explanation in Shanghai dialect. Though I couldn't understand all that he said, I could tell by the way he shrugged his shoulders and how my mother's face grew tight that the news wasn't good. At the end of his report, there was a long silence, broken only by Little Joe, the youngest *Bonanza* boy, shouting Chinese expletives from the television. Abruptly, Shrewin switched off the set and headed for the door.

We followed him out of the hotel, stopping short of the front awning as there was a torrential downpour. Shrewin moved off to one side, beyond earshot, and stared into the pouring rain.

"What was that all about?" I asked my mother.

"He didn't get our train tickets to Beijing," she said. Her sigh came out as a slow hiss. "I was afraid of this."

I glanced over at Shrewin, who had tucked my mother's Marlboros protectively under his jacket. He had lit one of his own cheap Chinese cigarettes and was squinting through the smoke. Hunched against the rain that swirled beneath the awning, he had a furtive look.

"Can we trust him?" I said.

I regretted my words instantly, as they sounded not only melodramatic, but implied that my mother's previous experiences with the man counted for little. However, as time passed under the rain-soaked awning and my mother kept silent, I realized she was thinking the exact same thing.

According to Da Bobo's plan, we had to be in Beijing in three days, because he had planned excursions from there that depended on our timely arrival. The train ride itself took nearly twenty-four hours, and the fact that we didn't have tickets lent the matter greater urgency. Although I hadn't experienced the inefficient and frustrating Chinese bureaucracy first-hand, I certainly knew of its notoriety. Hardly an auspicious beginning to our trip. I looked over at Shrewin, who stood with his back to us, watching the bicycle traffic splash by. He seemed to have forgotten about us.

"Can't we call a travel agent?" I whispered to my mother.

She shook her head irritably, like a horse flicking off a fly. "That not good way to see China. We have to join other foreign tourists, cost us three times as much."

Better than going nowhere, I thought.

"Back door only way," she muttered, stealing a quick glance at Shrewin. "His contact say train tickets impossible to get these days."

"Why?"

She hadn't appeared to have heard. "I always have tickets before," she said, mumbling more to herself than anyone. "No. It's something else."

Suddenly, I understood. "It's not that there aren't tickets. He just wants more money, right?"

My mother said nothing, but looked grim.

I glanced at Shrewin again. Now he looked downright shifty, like Peter Lorre in a Humphrey Bogart movie.

"I didn't know you brought cigarettes," I said. I had meant to convey wonder, admiration, but my mother, the most scrupulous of people, looked pained.

"What are we going to do now?"

She said nothing, only withdrew into the collar of her poncho against the rain, hunkering down like a sodden duck on her eggs. I couldn't be sure, but it looked like she had entered a kind of waiting game with Shrewin. Either she had to cough up more money, or he had to produce the tickets. Each kept their cards close. I realized there was nothing I could do but trust my mother and, more important, not badger her with questions. Still, I couldn't help but wonder how she would handle Shrewin. I sensed she weighed the advantage of her age and Shrewin's deference to her against his inclination to even out the economic disparity between us, and that she struggled against giving in to the Chinese way of going through back doors, which she despised.

While the standoff continued, I watched scores of bicyclists, all wearing identical green plastic ponchos, slog by in the rain. The hooded, faceless riders moved in both directions, churning the fine yellow mud beneath their wheels, swerving in undulating waves like schools of fish. They moved as though in a single, telepathic consciousness, avoiding accidents, which seemed miraculous in view of their overwhelming numbers. Everyone seemed to be going somewhere but us. What if Aunt Lucy, like my grandfather, died before I got there? What if she had a stroke, caved in from the stress of waiting for me? I turned to my mother, resolved to convince her to find a travel agent, but she must have seen the scheme in my face and turned away. Stung by her rebuff, I felt myself slide toward the childhood trough of whinery, then remembered my vow to Fred that I would follow my mother's lead in China. Even so, I was unable to shake my frustration. How ironic, I thought, that I had finally made it all the way to China, yet was still unable to reach Yeh Yeh's house.

After a while, when I was convinced the entire morning had lapsed in the course of this tense waiting game, I glanced at my watch and saw it was only eleven o'clock. The rain had let up. The sun was breaking through the clouds, causing thick banks of mist to rise up from the street. Shrewin flicked what must have been his tenth cigarette into the muck and approached my mother. They spoke briefly in terse tones, then she beckoned to me.

"Let's go."

Shrewin took off, setting a fast pace under sycamore-like trees that grew along both sides of the street. Though the rain had stopped, heavy drops continued to sprinkle down from the branches that formed a thick arbor overhead. All along the street people emerged from doorways and alleys. Ignoring the thick mud, they set up crates, oil drums, and wheelbarrows and piled watermelons, cucumbers, and spiny, mysterious fruit to sell. Women hauled portable sewing machines to the curb, setting up business. I watched one cut a piece of cloth, measure it by holding it up to the shoulders of her customer, and sew with mind-boggling speed, hauling the fabric beneath the needle of her tiny machine while pumping madly with her mud-caked foot. In no time she held up the finished garment, a sensible-looking shirt that the customer examined and then stuffed into her string bag, handing over a limp piece of paper and some coins—$1.50, the price indicated by the sign hanging from the seamstress's neck. The woman was cutting another shirt when Shrewin yanked on my sleeve. Jerking his head impatiently, indicating that I follow, he moved off at a brisk trot. My mother followed him closely. Neither looked left or right. Though the street was packed with people and I found myself bumping and bumped on all sides, Shrewin found ways to slip through, like a snake in the grass, my mother nearly in tandem. From her brisk air of certainty it was clear she knew the way, from her previous trips here with my brother, my sister and her family, as well as on her own. It was all I could do to keep up with the two of them. I felt myself growing hot, agitated, and exhorted myself to shake off the jet lag and stay alert or I would surely be lost. There was so much to see that I was not able to, at this pace, yet I knew if I took my eyes off Shrewin's bald spot, or my mother's crisp perm, I was a dead duck. Still, I managed to snatch glimpses of the astonishing diversity of faces that streamed by, of beautiful women like the bicycle princess I had seen the night before, toothless old pensioners, peasants with faces leathery as goatskin. Rushing along, I smelled rank sweat, wet clothes, the sulfurous stench of the mud, felt feet tramping against mine and hard bodies pushing, pushing.

Somewhere along the way I managed to steal a glance at a side street, glimpsing a woman, a child slung on her hips, emerge from a dark hole in the alleyway to throw out a pan of water. Behind her spread a network of narrow dark lanes winding in all directions, like a rabbit warren that twisted deep into the heart of the city. I paused here thinking to explore, as I sensed this was where the real life of Shanghai might be, but then I heard Shrewin bawling my name: *"Sung Lien!"* Even from the huge crowd, I picked out his face from its scowl of disapproval. The moment he caught my eye he turned and was on his way again, deep into the thickest throng of people.

I turned from the lane and hurried after him, stepping on the backs of people's legs, murmuring *"dway bu chi"* (sorry!), feeling bitterness rise in my throat with each misstep. I could barely keep sight of Shrewin's head as it bobbed farther and farther in the distance. Fighting panic, I was beginning to hate him. All prior sympathies I had for my less fortunate relatives and, indeed, for all poor Chinese people, no matter what they had suffered throughout the ages, fell away. Doubt filled me the way it must have overtaken missionaries facing torture and death at the hands of those they would save. No intentions, however well meaning, seemed relevant here now. Scrambling desperately, I could only watch as Shrewin disappeared into the crowd. *He doesn't give a shit,* I thought.

I caught up with Shrewin and my mother at the mouth of a large boulevard where two opposing seas of bicycles ran up against each other with a furious clanging of bells and shouting. Buses and electric trolley cars tethered to overhead lines wallowed along, spewing sparks and thick black diesel fumes. Here, Shrewin and my mother turned into a smaller side street. Following them, I was immediately struck by an intense, savory smell and the sight of a man cooking dumplings over a makeshift oil-drum stove. He made two kinds, one where the dough was sealed shut, the other formed with vents in the top, like mini-volcanoes. Both had the sheen of freshly risen dough, the tantalizing aroma of roasted meat, shrimp, and mushrooms. I pointed to one of the miniature volcanoes. The vendor wrapped it in a piece of newspaper that he tore from a sheaf at his belt, and handed it to me. Just as I was about to bite into it, something hard and furious knocked it from my hand. "Hey!" I shouted, wincing from shock and pain, looking up to see Shrewin's red face inches from mine.

"No good!" he spat, pointing to the dumpling which now lay broken in the street. In brusque tones he explained to my mother that there was a hepatitis epidemic currently raging in Shanghai. Street food was deemed taboo, because dumplings, lying around unsold and re-heated for days, were a prime host to bacteria. I realized I was indebted to Shrewin and tried to thank him, but he turned away and moved briskly down the street. I was half glad. Though he might have saved me from getting seriously ill, my hand throbbed painfully from his blow, and the last thing I wanted was to feel obligated to him for anything. Reluctantly, I hurried after my mother and our host's rapidly retreating head.

When we finally caught up to him at the end of the street, Shrewin motioned us into a restaurant there. It was lunchtime, and it seemed everyone in the city was there, lined a dozen or so deep behind people eating at the counter. Though I was hungry, I was glad to wait in line, as that gave me a chance to observe the goings-on. Customers bought tickets from a man at the door, exchanging them for dumplings served at the counter. Those seated there ate with assembly-line efficiency, oblivious to those standing behind them, breathing down their necks.

While Shrewin stood in line to buy our tickets, I sneaked to the kitchen door to watch the cooks work. A man stirred the dough in a huge vat, using an oar-like paddle. Another cut the mixed dough into sections, then rolled them into long thin tubes. These he slung in the air to a woman who deftly cut them into quarter-inch slices. She scooped the slices onto large tree stumps where two women, using wooden pins, rolled them into perfectly shaped rounds. The rounds were then flipped to men sitting next to a mound of chopped pork the size of a prize Iowa hog, who scooped meat onto them. These were then folded and pleated by a final team of cooks working so quickly that the finished dumplings appeared from their hands like coins from the hands of conjurers. Finally, the dumplings were placed in bamboo steamers and set on an enormous iron stove to cook. Throughout, waiters rushed in and out, flinging empty steamers into the concrete sinks, grabbing fresh hot ones from the stove, shouting, "More! More! Faster! Faster!"

A loud commotion broke out. I turned to see Shrewin scuffling with another customer. His arm was thrust out, blocking the man from taking a seat. Looking up with a face red from exertion and sweat, Shrewin gestured furiously for my mother to take a seat. She moved quickly, pulled me along to take the seat next to her. Though I hated butting in line, taking advantage of the fact that we were foreigners, I saw there was no arguing with both of them, so I sat down. I braced myself for complaints from the others waiting in line, but there were none. The man who had contested Shrewin's claim moved silently to another line.

Steaming baskets were slapped at our places. When I lifted the lid of one, steam infused with the smell of pork fat and dried mushrooms fogged my glasses. Six dumplings the size of Ping-Pong balls nestled on bright green leaves. My mother peeled off the leaves, explaining they kept the dumplings from sticking to the bamboo. All around us men frantically gobbled dumplings, acting like oxygen-starved fish gulping bubbles. Famished, I bit into the chewy dumpling dough, felt the squirt of pork juice and crunch of bamboo shoots and green onion in my mouth. As soon as my basket was empty, a waiter whisked it away, slapped another in its place. By the time I finished my third basket, I was stuffed. By now the line of customers snaked out through the open door of the restaurant into the street. All looked like workers, pale and slight, dressed in dark pants and white nylon shirts. *What do they do? Where do they work?* I wondered. I wished I could talk to them, ask them about their lives, but, beyond issues of language and gender— my mother and I were the only women there—no one seemed open to conversation, only eating. The man next to me attacked his dumplings as though he were competing in a pie-eating contest. After watching him devour his fifth basket, I looked up to discover Shrewin still standing in line. I was astonished, as I had expected him to take a seat near my mother and me, but he waited among the others, the expression on his face heavy and resigned, as though he was used to moving nowhere. For the first time I began to understand how he viewed our relationship. Though he was a relative, albeit distant, and our host, he was still Chinese, we American, and, as such, from different castes.

By the time Shrewin reached the counter and ate his dumplings, my mother and I had long finished. We followed him into the street where he picked his teeth with a toothpick he pulled from his shirt pocket. Then he began walking again, obviously intent on resuming the tour he had devised for us. Now, at least, thanks perhaps to the heat of the day and the rich meal, he set a more leisurely pace.

By this time Shanghai had undergone an amazing transformation. The streets had dried beneath the midday sun and were nearly empty of people, as they had gone home to take their customary *xiu shi,* or afternoon nap. Only buses continued to lumber up and down the avenues, spewing diesel fumes and bleating government regulations from megaphones set above the driver's cab. Recorded in a high-pitched, female voice that shrilled like an angry doll, they scolded: "Clear the path! Step to the rear! No spitting!"

My mother plodded along stoically, limping a little, wiping the sweat that poured down her face with a handkerchief. All the dashing and dodging before had taken its toll on her arthritic knee. Her expression was stony, so I knew she was trying to ignore it. Because of this I held back from pestering her with questions as to where we were going, though I was dying to know. It was hard for me to follow along, trusting and clueless like a dog, especially after someone like Shrewin, who again strode far ahead as though we didn't exist. There were so many things I wanted to know, like what neighborhood we were in, what dialect the few people in the street were speaking. It sounded different from Mandarin, more like the swishing of raw silk, "*Shhh . . . Shhh . . . Shhh.*"

A thick yellow haze filled with the sulfurous, stinging smell I had first noticed upon arriving in China hovered over the city. My mother coughed into her handkerchief, and I began to feel a strange cramping sensation in my chest, as though tiny crabs pinched my lungs.

After trudging through the baking streets, passing shuttered doorways and windows behind which I imagined cool, dark rooms, we arrived at the gates of a temple. Before approaching the entry kiosk, well beyond the view of the drowsy attendant there, my mother slipped Shrewin some money.

"Do we have to bribe him just to get in?" I asked, after he had gone to buy tickets, realizing, too late, the accusatory tone in my voice.

"If I show guard our money," she explained, "he know we're foreigners, and charge us three times more for ticket. But if Shrewin pay with Chinese money, then we pay what everyone else pay. That's why I gave him foreign money to buy for us, not Chinese money."

Earlier that morning, my mother and I had changed our traveler's checks for Chinese money at the hotel cashier. We were given foreign exchange certificates, crisp pink, blue, and green bills that looked like Monopoly money. These were differentiated from the *renmenbi,* or people's money, which the indigenous population used as currency. I gave most of my certificates to my mother, since she would be handling our transactions. She had already given Shrewin the money, some of which I assumed he used to pay for lunch, so I wondered about this latest installment. When he went to stand in line at the temple kiosk, I saw him count the money in a manner that looked stealthy, well-practiced. Unexpectedly, he looked up and caught me observing him. He seemed startled, but covered quickly by turning his face and coughing.

Not fast enough, I thought. *Extortionist!* But then it occurred to me: *What choice did I have?*

After we passed through the gates of the temple grounds, Shrewin walked over to a tree and, plopping down, covered his face with a sheet of old newsprint he had picked up from the ground. My mother and I walked along a path toward a man-made lake, reeling from the waves of heat that radiated from the pale crushed rock. We reached a low-lying bridge beneath a willow tree where we sat and watched multicolored carp roiling at the surface, begging for food. As soon as I sat down, I felt crushingly drowsy. Trying to make conversation with my mother seemed too much of an effort. In any case, she appeared to be lost in her own thoughts, having taken off her shoes and dangled her legs from the bridge.

Seeing her there reminded me of when she had come to bring me back from camp, how we had swung side by side in the swings with nothing to say to each other, only this time there wasn't tension between us, only an acute feeling of malaise that neither had the will to stir. She dipped her toes in the water, swishing so that the carp darted away. The look of concentration and pain on her face had disappeared so that she looked relaxed, young. I was surprised by this, the notion that she had been young at one time. I had always thought of her as my mother, a grown-up, not someone who had had a childhood or a life that had been distinct and separate from my own.

Who had she been, besides my mother? Now I took deliberate note of her, the finely wrinkled skin on the backs of her hands, her little jowls, her brittle, graying hair, at the way she carefully stretched her leg to ease the stiffness in her knee. The very act of looking at her in this way seemed to speed a process that was already taking place between us, which was the more I tried to see her, the more she seemed to slip away. I felt a stab of fear as I realized my mother was growing old before my very eyes.

"You should go see temple," she said, pointing across the lake.

I squinted. The temple sat on a small hill, looking solitary and distant.

"Go ahead," she urged, fanning herself. "I stay here. The water feel nice."

I hesitated. "You'll be all right?"

"Go! That the most famous temple in Shanghai. It tell you about China."

She sighed heavily, whether exasperated or exhausted, I couldn't tell. Maybe she wanted to be alone. I got up, started to walk down the path. Turning to look at my mother once more, I saw that she had lain down and put her handkerchief over her face. The gravel burnt like hot coals beneath my sandals. The stones were uneven, piled deep so that my ankles turned with each step. I wished I had worn a hat. The sun was blinding, and my head was aching, pounding. I trudged along for several minutes, struggling along the stones, thinking that the temple looked no closer. By now I really didn't care about seeing it, as sight-seeing wasn't the real reason I had come to China. I had come to see Yeh Yeh's house. And now it struck me that not only was I more than a thousand miles away, but had no way of getting there. *"No tickets to Beijing."* It had sounded so final. My mother had seemed resigned at the news, but I couldn't believe she would give up so easily. Surely there must be another way, though neither she nor Shrewin gave any evidence of pursuing it. That was what was most annoying. Nothing seemed to be happening. In America, I would be on the phone, calling agents, demanding service. No tickets, what bullshit. But of course I knew I was being unreasonable. I was in China. What did I know?

Finally, I reached the temple. It was deserted except for a young couple lolling on the grass under a tree, talking in lazy voices. The only other sounds were of sparrows squabbling over crumbs on the path, water lapping the edge of the lake. I stared at the temple, a painted wooden structure reaching up into the sky. It stood among a growth of evergreen trees, towering over an arrangement of volcanic rock lying in the water. The whole of this was reflected in the glass-like surface of the lake, so that horizon and water merged to create a seamless image that looked symmetrical and immutable. This was antiquity, I thought, where all dimensions had lost their edges, where there was no sense of time passing. Here, earth and sky were one, and a century was as long as a day. I imagined myself like the image spread in the water, as much a part of the past as the future, as much memory as expectation or hope.

I felt the sun burning the top of my head, a sign that it was time to go back. Every twenty paces or so, as I retraced my steps back toward the stone bridge, I turned to look back at the temple. It seemed to call to me, urging me not to leave. The farther I walked, the wider my perspective grew, so that the temple and its grounds shrank beneath the skyline of the city. I could see the dark yellow fog of pollution spreading over all Shanghai, hanging like a dirty halo. Though the sight of the temple receded with each step, its power continued to trail me like a great anchor dragging. As I slogged forward, I sensed myself approaching the present, which continued, simultaneously, to stretch beyond my reach. I felt the heavy pressure of the past bearing down. Rather than merging seamlessly with the present in the way the horizon had joined with the sky on the surface of the lake, there was the sense of impending collision, of rupture. Instinctively I sought safety.

I reached the spot where I had left my mother napping. She had placed her purse on the ground and laid her head on it. Her arm was flung out, as if in her sleep she had tried to catch her handkerchief that had fluttered a few feet away. Her face sagged on her purse and her mouth was slack. She looked so still that I became afraid. Then I saw her breathe, her side going gently up and down.

When I was small, afraid of the dark, I used to go into my parents' room to stand next to my mother's side of the bed. Though asleep, she always sensed me waiting there and would wake up to ask me what was wrong. The sound of her voice immediately chased my fears. Now, watching her sleep, a voice suddenly sounded inside me: *Remember this.* Past and present converged, and despite willing with all my might that things might stop, stay as they were, time continued to pass. My mother must have sensed me standing there, because she opened her eyes.

"What's the matter?" she said, sounding groggy, blinking to clear the sleep from her eyes. The outline of her purse was etched on her face in an angry-looking welt. "Did you see the temple?"

"Yes."

"What do you think?"

"It was . . . just like you said."

"So, you learn something about China?"

I nodded, but didn't say anything. How could I explain what I had learned?

She sat up, shaded her eyes, looking around, probably for Shrewin, but he was nowhere in sight. Now she seemed fully awake.

"I had a dream," she said. "I used to have all the time, but not have it in a long time. Did I ever tell you about my bomb?"

"Your bomb?"

"It was during World War Two. My college had moved west to Hunan. One day . . ."

"Wait a minute," I interrupted, confused. "What do you mean, your college moved?"

"The Japanese bomb us, so my college pack up . . . books, laboratory equipment, chalkboards, everything . . . we move."

"How? By train?"

"By train, bus, truck, donkey cart, whatever we find. I pack clothes, say good-bye to parents, take train west." She paused, bemused at the look of disbelief on my face. "See, China was falling apart, not only because of Japanese, but because communists and nationalists fight each other. We don't know who to believe, who to trust. All we know is it important to keep colleges going, because as long as they go on, we have believe in something. That the most important thing. Otherwise life totally hopeless."

My mother's voice quavered strangely. She plucked up a few stray leaves that lay in the grass, then went on. "My college arrive in Hunan Province and set up class in few empty building in small town there. We near mountains, near caves in foothills. We use caves as bomb shelters."

She took a deep breath before continuing.

"One day, when we have class, air raid siren go off. My classmates and I start running to caves. Nobody scared, because siren sound all the time, mostly false alarm. Still, caves far away and no road to get there, so everybody cross fields and gullies on foot. I run and run, zigzag across open area, then I realize I carry my biology books. I think, Stupid! Why make myself heavy with books? But books most valuable things I have, I just grab them by instinct when siren go off. Then I hear planes. It sound like there are many, always getting closer. Everyone scream and run faster. Lucky I was hurdler on track and field team, so not so hard for me, but some of my friends fall behind, and I run a little slower so we don't lose each other. But planes get closer and closer, and we hear bombs go off, shake the ground.

"The caves still far away. I remember our professor tell us about sound bombs make . . . high pitch, whistle sound. He say if you hear that, you fall on ground, curl up, cover your head with arm. I hear that sound behind me. Suddenly I see no classmate near me, that we get separated somehow. I was in shallow hole in ground, and I climb up to see where are my friends, but then I hear sound. It whistle from way up high and drop lower in pitch when it get to ground. It sound like it right on top of me. I fall on ground and curl around my books and wait. I know I'm going to die. I thought what a shame I bring my books, because they going to be ruined.

"Then something drop, make ground shake. I wait for explosion, but nothing happen. I hear ticking sound. I think, Strange! Why clock here in middle of nowhere? I look up. At first I see nothing, but then ten feet away, I see bomb. It three feet long, gray, shaped like fish. It had nose buried in dirt. It still ticking. I don't know how long I stay there, wait for it to go off, but suddenly I saw one of my friend jump up and down on a hill close by. She cover with dirt, her hair wild like crazy. She scream, *'Run! Run!'*

"Somehow I get up, but my legs, they don't move. My friend keep screaming at me, then she turn and run. Finally I make my feet go. I know bomb can still explode. I run twenty feet away, then thirty, before I realize bomb is bad, don't work. Then I run faster than I ever run in my life.

"I run all the way to caves. My classmates all there, hug each other, cry. When they see me they shout, 'Wan Rui! Why you just wait there? What if bomb go off?' But I can't explain. I still in shock. 'Look,' someone say, point at me, laugh, like I am class dunce. 'She carry her books!' Everyone laugh and laugh. It was miracle all of us make it, that no one get more than scratch. Later, when we back in town, my classmates still tease me. 'Wan Rui, she so fast she win race with bomb!' The next day, one of my professors, who heard about it, say, 'You had a lucky bomb.' So from that day everybody call it my bomb."

My mother flipped a willow leaf in my direction. "Just think, if that bomb go off, you wouldn't be here."

I couldn't stop shaking my head. "What an amazing story. How come you never told me?"

My mother stood up, brushed her slacks. "It was long time ago." Then she shaded her eyes, scanned the area. "Every time I come back to China, I remember something. Strange, huh? My bomb not even happen here, in Shanghai."

I could only stare at my mother, still stunned by her story. What other stories, previously forgotten, might be triggered for her on this trip?

She picked up her handkerchief, wiped her face. "Whew, it's hot," she said. "Where's that Shrewin?"

12

SIX FLOORS UP

AT THREE O'CLOCK, PEOPLE BEGAN TO DRIFT ONTO THE TEMPLE GROUNDS, A sign that *xiu shi* was over. Shrewin reappeared and, after conferring briefly with my mother, took off again at breakneck speed. After following him for twenty minutes or so, we reached an old section of the city where a group of apartment buildings leaned against one another like trees in an ancient grove. The sooty tenements sagged atop crumbling concrete, their exposed network of stairways looking like cracked vertebrae. Shattered tiles and glass crunched underfoot as we crossed the courtyard. The area was cool and dank, resonant with the sound of crying babies, tinny radios, a lone bird chirping. Pale faces gazed down at us from the windows above. A man in a tattered undershirt spat into the courtyard, his gob of spittle dispersing into a fine mist overhead.

Shrewin led us past a jumble of parked bicycles into a foyer, where I was nearly knocked flat by the smell of human waste and cleaning fluid. The stairwell was crammed with mattresses, crates, empty bottles, and boxes, all of which were covered with a thick layer of grime, as though they had been there for centuries.

As we went up the rickety stairs, suspicious residents peeped out, slammed doors. Four doors, indicating separate apartments, abutted each landing. After climbing six flights, when my heart was pounding and I knew my mother's knee was throbbing, Shrewin stopped and opened a door that looked like all the others.

Inside, the room was about twelve feet by fifteen, divided in half by a mattress folded over a metal frame. On one side were piles of clothes, books, newspapers, an old television, radio, and electric fan. On the other side there was a small folding table at which an old woman presided. She said nothing, but merely regarded us as though she had been expecting us for an eternity as the bearers of bad news. Another woman, a slightly younger version of the older one, came forward to greet us. She was thin, sallow-faced, bent over as though someone had scooped her out, and she smelled of mothballs. Shrewin arranged folding chairs around the old woman, who I assumed to be Auntie Aifong. After we were seated, she welcomed us and asked for news from the United States, speaking in a voice that sounded sprinkly and dry, like flour falling from a sifter. My mother relayed greetings from Aifong's sons and daughters, who had emigrated to America several years before. I caught a few words here and there, but finally gave up on the Shanghai dialect. It was all I could do not to stare at Auntie Aifong. She was the saddest-looking person I had ever seen. Appearing as if she had been born wearing widow's weeds, Auntie had a stiff, hard face that seemed carved from pine. Despite the stultifying heat she wore a black sweater, black wool trousers, and a black shawl. On the wall behind her hung a portrait of her dead husband, Henry, my mother's older brother. I recognized him because of his resemblance to my mother, particularly the Lin family jowls. In the picture he looked to be around fifty years old with the warm, kindly eyes of a family doctor. As the president of Shanghai University, he had been arrested by the communists, dying in prison in 1958. Beneath his picture, on a dresser, were snapshots of his and Auntie Aifong's other sons, daughters, and grandchildren, who were now living in California.

Auntie Aifong signaled Biring to serve drinks. I offered to help and followed her to the far end of the room, which ended in a narrow balcony crowded with plants and jars of food. Next to the balcony was an alcove in which there was a single cot. Black clothing hung from pegs above, so I guessed this was where Auntie Aifong slept. Beneath the cot was an insulated case, from which Biring took out bottles of orange soda. Following her back to the table, I realized I was already feeling oppressed and trapped in the claustrophobic apartment. I couldn't imagine what it was like for the three adults living there. While my mother and Auntie Aifong engaged in conversation, Shrewin lit a cigarette and began to pace from the table to the balcony and back. There was something compulsive and desperate about his movement, like a bear shuffling about its zoo enclosure, a far cry from the person who had boldly explored our hotel room earlier. I felt a pang of empathy for him.

I managed to glean from the conversation between Auntie Aifong and my mother that her family had reached a crossroads. Shrewin and Biring's son was still searching for a job in California. However uncertain his future, he already enjoyed a better life than the one he had left behind in Shanghai and had been urging his parents to follow. Meanwhile, Auntie Aifong, Shrewin, and Biring had put their names on a waiting list for a new apartment. Located in a recently developed neighborhood far from the center of Shanghai, the new place had two bedrooms, a living room, kitchen, and toilet. The family's quandary was whether to remain on the list, which meant waiting for at least a year or apply to go to California. Daunting obstacles loomed in either case. The government often took years to approve visas, and there was no guarantee it would allow all three to leave. Applying for the visas might jeopardize their chances of securing the new apartment. Finally, the cost of airfare to the U.S. for the three of them was more than their pensions combined. Auntie Aifong's sorrowful look darkened as she described their dilemma. I found myself wondering what kind of resources they might have. As a war widow, Auntie must draw a pension of some kind, and, according to my mother, Biring had taught English in the past, so she probably drew retirement pay. It remained unclear whether Shrewin worked or not. If he did, he could not be earning much. In any case, their situation seemed hopeless. Now I began to understand the darting look in Shrewin's eye whenever my mother opened her purse.

Biring rose, saying it was time to make dinner. I offered to help, glad for an excuse to escape the apartment. As we went down the six floors, eyes peered from doors on every landing, noting our passage. It gave me a creepy feeling. *Spies,* I thought, recalling my friend Evan's story. Wide cracks gaped in the floorboards and wooden walls so that murmuring and noises of ordinary life within the apartments became public. There were no secrets here, for sure.

The kitchen, a narrow, dark room with a single grimy window, was on the first floor. It was equipped with a sink two feet square, two grimy gas burners, and a work area the size of a place mat. Out of nowhere, Biring produced an enamel pan containing three slender eggplants, a knob of gingerroot, cloves of garlic. From the sink she lifted a pot of water in which a fish had been soaking, and a bowl of hollow-stemmed vegetables. Standing on tiptoes she took bottles of soy sauce, oil, vinegar, and a jar of sugar from the window ledge. She rinsed rice under the cold water faucet, set it to cook on one of the burners. As she cleaned the fish, scales flew in the air. Following the trajectory of one I saw it land on the rim of the toilet, which I had not noticed before, as it was situated behind the stove. Suddenly a man poked his head in the room and pointed to the toilet. Rinsing her hands, Biring beckoned me to follow her out of the room. The neighbor went in, closed the door.

"Very crowded here," Biring said, tucking a loose strand of hair behind her ear. She had a thin nose, narrow lips. Her English was tentative, but well-pronounced and clear.

"How many people share this kitchen?" I said.

"Fourteen. Four families. Most Shanghai like this. That's why we apply for new apartment. Everyone want to leave."

There was the sound of the toilet flushing. The neighbor, looking embarrassed, came out, and shuffled up the stairs.

"Sorry," Biring said. "Only three toilets in building. This one is for families on first and second floor. We're lucky ours on our floor."

We went back in the kitchen-bathroom, where I watched her chop the eggplant and sauté it quickly in hot oil. Droplets of grease rose in the air, settling on the dusty fur of the electrical wires exposed in the ceiling.

"Your mother say you're a writer, too," Biring said. She had finished the eggplant dish and was chopping the hollow-stemmed vegetables. Her arms were wiry, strong.

"Yes. I write fiction. Mostly lies," I joked.

"I was English major," Biring said. "But I don't get to practice much now. Very few people speak English. Very few books "

"I'd be glad to send you some," I said.

She shook her head. "My son in California send me books."

"What do you like to read?"

She thought for a moment. "*Mommie Dearest*. Joan Crawford very popular in China."

Biring tossed the hollow-stemmed vegetables into the hot oil, added soy sauce, sugar, and sesame seeds. The dish was done in less than a minute. She took out a metal tray, piled it with plates, chopsticks, the eggplant dish, and bowl of hollow vegetables.

"Please, can you bring up? I come soon with fish and rice."

I took the heavy tray and began to climb the six flights, trying to picture Biring climbing up and down for each meal, three times a day, every day. There was no refrigerator in their apartment, at least that I could see, so I assumed she shopped before each meal. When I reached each landing, I paused to rest the heavy tray on my knee, ignoring the sound of doors opening and closing softly. Finally, I reached the apartment on the sixth floor. After Shrewin set the places, Biring arrived, carrying a tray with a large bowl of rice and the fish, which she had steamed with slivers of scallion and a light sauce of black beans. I was amazed how she had managed to produce this elegant feast in that tiny kitchen.

After the meal, Biring collected the plates, and I helped her carry them back down the stairs. She rinsed the dishes in the cold water sink and stacked them beneath the counter. A tired-looking woman carrying a potful of vegetables squeezed into the kitchen just as we left. Returning to the apartment, we found Shrewin pacing back and forth, smoking, while my mother and Auntie Aifong spoke to one another in hushed tones.

From what I could gather, they talked about Uncle Henry, how Auntie Aifong still could not believe the turn their lives had taken. She related, in a voice that trembled with fresh pain and outrage, how the communists had broken into their home in the middle of the night and dragged my uncle away with such brutal speed that he had not been able to say good-bye. Auntie never saw him again. When she began to speak of the present political landscape and its knotted, ineffective bureaucracy, she ranged beyond the bounds of my meager vocabulary so that I tugged on my mother's sleeve for a translation. She obliged at first, offering a brief summary after every few phrases or so, but after a while, whether she was exhausted by the effort or was absorbed by Auntie Aifong's narrative, she ignored me. I listened, muddling along as best I could, catching a word here and there. Then I realized that Auntie's painful story needed no translation. Each line on her face spoke a thousand words.

Biring, noting my efforts, tried politely to talk to me in English. After a few awkward exchanges, it became clear she tired of dredging her rusty store of words. All this time, Shrewin continued to smoke like a chimney, pacing back and forth from the balcony.

Suddenly, three loud knocks sounded at the door. Auntie Aifong's head jerked. I saw the whites of her eyes, the tendons popping in her neck, and felt a sharp shift in the atmosphere. Everyone froze. After what seemed an eternity, it came again: *bang, bang, bang.* Finally, reluctantly, Shrewin removed the cigarette from his mouth, went to the door, and opened it. A uniformed man stood there. I felt a stab of fear. Somebody must have ratted on us. The uniform looked like the same ones worn by the airport officials who had scrutinized my passport and my grandfather's photo and poem. I was sure they determined that my passport was bogus, and that Yeh Yeh's picture and poem proved that whatever identity I claimed was nullified or, at the very least, tainted by my association to him, a notorious revolutionary. Whatever plans I had to search for an identity of my own, independent of family history and connections, would be viewed as subversive, because in China only the government defined and meted out identities. I would be charged with piracy, treason, thrown into jail to rot. That was why the man in the uniform had been sent. No reason to involve my mother, I thought. I stepped forward to surrender myself.

But the stranger walked past me and greeted Auntie Aifong and my mother with a respectful bow. He was young, in his twenties, extremely thin, with a sharp, smart face that had the look of the feral underfed. Now I noticed that his jacket uniform was unbuttoned and that the undershirt he wore underneath was stained. He wore pomade in his hair and a cheap gold-tone watch that slipped up and down his bony wrist. Shrewin introduced him as our contact, and my dread gave way to a flood of relief and curiosity, because here I was face-to-face with the back-door messenger himself.

My mother reacted differently, straightening her back and squeezing her thumbs, clearly assuming her battle station.

Shrewin explained that the contact worked for the railroad and thus had firsthand knowledge of the ticket situation. He offered the young man a cigarette from a pack of Marlboros, lit it for him, then invited him to explain the latest development.

The contact drew deeply on the cigarette, obviously enjoying it, then tilted his head and let the smoke out from the side of his mouth. He had refused the chair Biring offered him and stood in an exaggeratedly casual pose, balancing his weight loosely on one hip. He squinted through the smoke, and with the cigarette still in his mouth so that it flopped up and down as he spoke, he addressed my mother in speech that sounded like a coarse version of Shanghai dialect.

There were no train tickets to Beijing, he explained. Travel was unexpectedly heavy this time of year. To make matters worse, the government had commandeered blocks of seats for military bigwigs who were traveling to an important, top-secret meeting in the capital. He drew on his cigarette, let the news sink in. My heart dropped like a stone. Auntie Aifong nodded mournfully, as though she had expected as much all along.

"What about plane tickets?" my mother inquired.

The contact tossed his head, shaking a hank of hair that had fallen into his eyes. Now, with his swagger, the insolent curl of his lip, and the glossy hair, I realized he reminded me of Elvis Presley.

No plane tickets, either, Elvis declared. The Shanghai-Beijing route was sold out. But other routes were possible. Were we interested in a flight to Xi'an, maybe?

My mother gave no indication that she heard, only sat motionless, inscrutable, her head sunk between her shoulders like a turtle. Several moments passed. The stranger continued to smoke, watching her, then glanced at Shrewin with what looked like a flicker of uncertainty. It was then I wondered if my mother was employing a strategy of some kind. Elvis gave my mother a second wary glance, then moved to the balcony, his shoes tapping loudly across the worn wooden floor. Earlier that afternoon I had observed gangs of young men with taps on their shoes clicking and scraping along the stone-paved lanes unaware that the fad had passed in America long ago. These youths seemed permanently at leisure, strolling aimlessly or gathered at street corners, chatting indolently, smoking Chinese cigarettes. Their expressions were all of ironic detachment and boredom. They wore identical communist uniforms and were ostensibly "at work," yet it was impossible to ascertain what they did. Every once in a while when a nonuniformed person—a vendor or student—passed, they stopped to jeer and spit derisively at his feet. Angry words were exchanged, so it was clear there was tension between the government and nongovernment factions. Occasionally, when the squabbling became especially heated, men wearing military uniforms would appear, at which point everyone scattered. I noticed I wasn't the only one made nervous by such confrontations. Most people on the street gave all uniformed men wide berth.

We waited while Elvis conferred with Shrewin on the balcony. From the corner of my eye, I saw Shrewin shake his head, at which point Elvis's voice rose, sounding petulant and demanding. Shrewin replied sharply, slamming his fist into the palm of his hand. Throughout, my mother serenely maintained her turtle pose. Her eyes were half closed, but I glimpsed the faint glitter of her eyes, which told me she was tuned in to every word that passed between the two men. Their discussion went on for some time, punctuated by taps and scrapes of Elvis's shoes as he moved about the balcony. Finally, they returned to the table. Elvis cleared his throat. He was sorry there were no train tickets to Beijing, he said, but it was not his fault.

"Still, there are many abundant opportunities here," he went on in English, which, though heavily accented, was fluent. "Especially for someone on her first trip."

He looked pointedly at me, acknowledging me for the first time. Then I realized that, during their balcony tête à tête, Shrewin had filled him in on my newcomer status, and the two had discussed me with calculated interest, like two doctors conferring over a patient under anesthetic. Now, addressing me, Elvis continued, "There's West Lake, Hangzhou, and Suzhou. These are very beautiful and romantic places, very popular with American tourists." He flashed a dazzling smile. So that was how he saw me, I thought, just another American tourist, a sucker with a handbag. *I might as well be from South Dakota,* I thought. Didn't the fact that I was Chinese, or at least looked Chinese, count for anything? My mother, on the other hand, didn't appear the least bit fazed by his suggestion. Turning to me she said, mildly, "You know, your father's family is from Suzhou. We have distant relatives in Hangzhou, as well."

"You mean, we're giving up on Beijing?" I yelped.

She pinched me under the table. I was shocked, but then realized that her painful signal meant for me to shut up and take notes. We were in a drama under her direction, and now we were entering the final act.

Elvis offered, in a smooth tone, that he could get us train tickets to Suzhou and Hangzhou, a pleasant, two-day excursion, the day after.

There was a long silence. My mother looked so disinterested she seemed asleep. Then Elvis sighed heavily. "I will try to get tickets to Beijing in another day or so," he said. "Perhaps I will have better luck then."

At that, my mother opened her purse. The snick of its clasp seemed to dispel all the suspense in the air. She withdrew a wad of bills the size of a small paperback and gave it to Shrewin, who handed it, along with a fresh pack of Marlboros, to Elvis. This apparently signaled the conclusion of the deal. Biring jumped up, offered Elvis an orange soda, which he refused with a grimace, acting as though she had offered him a snakebite. Glancing at his watch, he declared he had another appointment. He shook hands with Shrewin, my mother, bowed to Auntie Aifong and Biring.

"Day after tomorrow," he said, sounding businesslike. My mother nodded. Shrewin walked Elvis to the door. As he made his way down the stairs,
I thought the rapid *click-click, click-click* of his taps had a satisfied, jaunty
sound.

I turned to my mother, trying to read her face. She looked noncommittal,
but I thought I detected a cloudy look in her eyes. It was a look I knew well
from my childhood, the one she wore after she and my father fought, after
she had spent the evening paying bills, or when she had come home late after work selling curtains. It was a look that said, *Don't ask.* Something about
it always made me want to crawl into her lap and put my arms around her,
but the set of her body, the way she crossed her arms, invariably stopped
me. *Why did she think we didn't already know?* I wondered. Even my sister
and brother concurred that seeing that look was no less frightening than
what she thought she was sparing us.

We bid Auntie Aifong and Biring good night. Shrewin accompanied my
mother and me down the stairwell. On the street, the night air was cool.
Vendors were putting out the last embers of their oil-drum fires. Children
squatted in a circle beneath the faint light of a street lamp, whispering childish incantations over lightning bugs they had captured.

I wondered what my mother and Shrewin thought of one another following this latest strenuous negotiation, but both walked along without
speaking, preoccupied with their own private thoughts. We arrived at the
hotel, where Shrewin turned back to go home. My mother and I rode the elevator to our room, and after we closed the door I asked her if we had won
the war.

Sighing, she dropped her purse on the bed, pulled off her shoes. "Everybody got his share," she said.

"So Shrewin and Elvis got their commissions?"

"Elvis?"

"Our contact, I mean."

She shrugged.

"And we did all right?"

"We just go to Hangzhou and Suzhou before Beijing, not after, like Da
Bobo plan. We find out about tickets to Beijing when we get back."

My mother lay on her bed, not moving, her eyes on the ceiling. Now I realized that the evening's drama, with its posturing and suspense, had exhausted her, even with her vast experience. Suddenly I felt ashamed for my

preoccupation with money, with winning and losing. The amount my mother had paid Elvis for his services was maybe twenty dollars at most. And the few extra bucks and two cartons of cigarettes for Shrewin would go toward his family's relocation fund. As distasteful as bribery was as a way of doing business, I conceded there was little to complain about.

"We'll have to tell Aunt Lucy, Da Bobo, and Da Mama about the delay," I said.

"Later, in morning," my mother replied wearily.

I hated nagging, but anxious words flew from my heart. "So, do you think we'll get tickets to Beijing?"

She sighed, confirming that I had reached the end of her patience. *What is she keeping from me?* I wondered. I thought of her ability to diagnose diseases in people and wondered if she could see the future as well. If she could, she wasn't saying. I would simply have to wait, let time play itself out, go along without struggling. That's what being in China meant, I thought. I got up, took a shower. The water was cool, salty-tasting as it washed away the soot of the city. Standing under the rushing water, I began to think that my first day in China hadn't been so bad after all, despite rushing around in the heat, Shrewin knocking the dumpling out of my hand, seeing the way my relatives lived in their cramped apartment, getting gouged by Elvis. *Even though we might have been arrested,* I thought, suddenly remembering that moment of paralyzing fear when I saw the uniform. Surely, I was in the clear. If they viewed me as a suspicious element, they would have stopped me by now. But maybe they waited for proof of my true intentions, maybe they only bided their time. As I turned the water off and dried myself with a skimpy Chinese towel, I told myself to stop being paranoid, that I had only imagined the airport guard's untoward scrutiny, his suspicion. Yet there was no mistaking his double-take at the sight of my grandfather's photo and letter, his narrow-eyed stare at me. Then I looked over at my mother and remembered her tack—just wait, and let time unfold. *Don't struggle.* I told myself that though our journey to Beijing was delayed, I was excited about going to Hangzhou and Suzhou. After all, these were family places, as well. Eventually, somehow, we would get to Beijing. Fate would not deny me, when I had come so far. Surely, by going to America, my parents had negotiated a different karmic path for me, and by returning to China, however late, I had sealed the bargain, appeased Fate. Surely.

13

WIDGETS

THE NEXT MORNING, MY MOTHER AND I WENT DOWN TO MEET SHREWIN, who was to take us to the oldest teahouse in Shanghai. In addition to the torrent of bicycle riders, the street was filled with people hammering metal, winding string, and sorting knobs, buttons, and nails into trays. Officials toiled at makeshift, child-sized desks tallying numbers in ledgers the size of Oxford dictionaries. Vendors bawled singsong choruses selling roasted nuts, dumplings. The overall din was deafening, nonsensical, like a gigantic factory that madly churned out widgets. I couldn't help wondering how the government oversaw it all. It seemed a stupendous, if not an overwhelming and hopeless task. Everyone toiled at something, but what? If there was any ostensible product or meaning, I couldn't fathom it. It occurred to me that occupation in itself had value, that thousands of people simply couldn't remain idle. Yet what did it all mean? Perhaps, because of the sheer number of people, doing for doing's sake served a necessary purpose in China. In contrast to the American view of work, as a vital extension of personal identity, if not at the very core of it, the Chinese viewed work or busyness as a vital element of its national identity. Might this have explained, in part, the driving force behind the building of the Great Wall? Perhaps undergirding the official view that the wall was necessary to keep out invaders was the fact that building it ensured the occupation of hundreds of thousands of laborers, serving to unify national purpose. If so, then what role did the individual have in light of such a policy?

Such questions as these reminded me of a conversation I had had with my father, at a time when I was still struggling with what career I would choose, before I had made any distinctions between career and identity. It took place on a Saturday afternoon at my mother's house, after my father had stopped to catch his breath following a particularly strenuous bout with his panpipe. At this particular moment, he looked utterly happy and fulfilled, and it struck me that had he followed his heart and soul he would have become a poet, musician, or philosopher, rather than a scientist. When I asked him how he had chosen his career, he threw back his head and laughed, as though he found my question preposterous, not only because of its nature, but how late it had been posed in his life.

"The Chinese government needed scientists to explore for minerals and natural energy sources," he said, after recovering himself. "So they made me a geologist."

"You mean you had no choice? Wasn't that hard?"

He paused, as though reflecting back to his youth, then shrugged. "In those days you became what the government told you to be. In any case, I got used to geology. I enjoyed collecting samples, looking at mineral crystals."

I was struck by his acceptance at the turn his life had taken. His attitude reminded me of Aunt Lucy's when she described her experience during the Cultural Revolution. I was impressed and appalled how these two intense, strong-willed people gave in to the will of the Chinese government, yet looked back years later with a transcendent sense of detachment, as though choice was an irrelevant concept. Perhaps I was naive to think otherwise, that this was simply how it was for people living under a totalitarian regime. Still, it was inconceivable to me, with my American point of view, that self-determination and personal independence lay at the very core of our national identity. While Americans were prepared to live or die by their right to choose, defining patriotism in large part as the defense of this idea, the Chinese view of patriotism was that of deferring individual preference toward the greater good of the whole. Despite the gap between the two perspectives, I sensed that when China completed the modernization of her infrastructure, raised her standard of living, and emerged as a major power in the world economic marketplace, the Chinese people would see themselves reflected more clearly in the mirror of the West. Then, perhaps, they might perceive the bold face of the individual, and, whether good or bad, demand to make similar choices. It was already happening, in fact, by the evidence of the burgeoning entrepreneurial movement in the major Chinese cities, which the Chinese government continued to monitor with extreme caution. What threatened a totalitarian regime more than the heightened consciousness and ambition of the individual? In our family, this revolution had already taken place. My father had chosen to come to America rather than return to China, enabling his American-born children to fulfill his embrace of self-determination. Yet what were we to learn, as we groped through the dense thicket of our own choices, from the example of his and my aunt's lives, where choice had been illusionary or moot? I was dumbfounded by the possibility that choice didn't matter, as this contradicted everything I had believed up to that point, yet I also found it strangely liberating. The notion that who or what I chose to be might not matter swept away the bewildering, choked paths, the shutters and impediments confounding me. But then, if life was not for one to choose, what was I to do with my passion for playing music, writing, art, and discovery?

I was relieved to abandon these thoughts when we arrived at the oldest teahouse in Shanghai, situated in the middle of a man-made lake and reached by crossing an elaborate bridge of wooden planks bound by sisal rope. The teahouse was built of varnished snakewood, made up of many separate but connected chambers. As we wound through one chamber after another, moving deeper and deeper into the heart of the place, I felt as though I burrowed in a Chinese puzzle box with intricately carved layers nested one within the other. The interior was cool, open, and airy, so that refreshing breezes fanned through. The ceiling was so high I could barely see the characters inscribed on the roof beams. We sat at a table high above the lake and ordered tea. The only others present were a few old men wearing rusty black skullcaps who drank tea, read newspapers, dozed, or stared with a faraway look. They seemed unaware of us and were unperturbed by the sparrows that flitted and swooped about their heads. They conveyed an extraordinary stillness, as if they had been extracted from another century and placed throughout the teahouse, like antique figurines. Occasionally a breeze lifted the frayed sleeves of their jackets, carrying the smell of rotted silk, tung oil.

I felt calm here. Perhaps it was because I knew we were headed to Suzhou and Hangzhou the next day and that having a definite plan alleviated my anxiety about the immediate future. Not reaching Yeh Yeh's house seemed less fraught, merely postponed, delayed gratification rather than catastrophic loss. Earlier that morning, my mother had asked the hotel clerk to wire Da Bobo to explain our delay. The clerk wrote her message on a piece of paper and handed her a receipt, promising that the wire would be sent. There were no fax machines or computers in sight, so I wondered how he would do this, imagining that, as soon as we left, he would strap our message onto the leg of a pigeon and heave it into the air. My mother's expression, as she tucked the receipt in her purse, was neutral, as though she neither trusted nor doubted that our message would get through. She had done what she could, and the rest was up to the forces that governed China. For the first time I began to see the overriding practicality of this view. My need to badger her with questions receded, and I began to feel an odd sense of joy surrendering my need to know. *We had shot an arrow into the sky.* . . .

I watched the sparrows spiral about the dark interior of the teahouse, imagining that they trailed tendrils of time after them. Then I heard a tiny clink and saw an old man nearby set down his teacup. Strands of gray whiskers hung from either side of his mouth like wisps of smoke. He turned his face, revealing one eye missing. In its place was a dusky hole, like the worn sole of a shoe. He regarded me with his other eye with calm disinterest. Then he turned away, bending his head toward the flimsy newspaper spread on the table before him. Not once, in the considerable time that we spent there, did he turn the page. I found myself thinking it was hardly strange in a place such as this, where time and stillness had different properties. For the first time in my life, I felt content doing, thinking nothing.

When we left the teahouse, *xiu shi* was over and Shanghai had regained the volatility of a nuclear reactor. Shrewin pushed us onto a bus packed with people whose loudspeaker scolded "Step to the rear! Hurry up! Don't spit!" the entire way to the Bund. Here, we passed the waterfront with its rows of massive buildings with romanesque porticos. Built by German, French, and Dutch companies, the Bund had transformed Shanghai into the busiest and richest port in the world. I hung onto a worn leather strap, gawking out the window as the bus yawed through traffic. Then I noticed an elderly woman seated nearby staring at me.

"*Weiguoren,*" she muttered contemptuously to no one in particular. *Foreigner.*

"How does she know I'm foreign?" I wondered aloud as we got off the bus near our hotel. Shrewin snorted as though the answer was painfully obvious to him. I assumed it was my height—I was at least a head taller than the Chinese in the street—or my wire-rimmed glasses, unlike the thick black plastic frames most natives wore, but I wasn't sure. I made a mental note to ask my mother about this at a later date.

That evening, my mother and I took Shrewin and his family out to dinner. We asked them to select a fine restaurant and met them at an address where a huge tank, swarming with live fish, shrimp, crabs, and lobsters, dominated the entrance. The tables were covered with elegant white cloth, the places set with china and linen. My mother ordered a sumptuous meal: shrimp with peas, pork riblets lacquered in honey, spicy chicken with peanuts, twice-fried string beans, and a whole steamed fish with black bean sauce.

As I ate the delicious meal, I couldn't help noticing the occupants at the next table, an old man whose companion was a much younger, astonishingly beautiful woman. She was what the Chinese call a classic Shanghai beauty, with a pale, oval face, narrow nose, and eyes that were arresting not so much for their size or shape but their expression, which was demure and perfectly discreet. She couldn't have been more than eighteen years old. Wearing a silvery green silk *cheongsam*, she sat with her spine and neck gracefully arched, like a fiddlehead fern. I couldn't help staring, as she was the most beautiful human being I had ever seen. She looked indescribably rare, cultivated, like a priceless species of orchid.

In contrast, her male escort looked ancient, decrepit. Heavy black dye failed to conceal the white roots of his hair, reminding me of Da Mama's caustic remark about the obsession of the aging ruling class for immortality. His bilious face and hands were speckled all over with age spots. The green uniform he wore was encrusted with medals, signaling that he was a big shot. When the waiter brought lobster, a whole plate of crabs, and a bottle of champagne to their table, the old bigwig cracked the lobster claw with his big yellow teeth, letting bits fly, chomping like a horse. Throughout the meal, he said nothing to his radiant partner, seeming to accept her presence as part of the gratifying atmosphere to which he was entitled. I didn't think she would eat, but she did, opening her mouth only wide enough to admit one tiny morsel at a time, tilting her narrow head like an angelfish nibbling coral.

My relatives said little to distract me from this intriguing scene. The news from America had been discussed and nothing unusual had happened in the household since the day before. Auntie Aifong, looking wan and out of her element, ate only a bite here and there. Biring remarked blandly about the high quality of the rice, while Shrewin gobbled his food like a dog.

Something, a slight movement, drew my attention to the fish tank at the front of the restaurant. At first I thought there was an exotic species of green and red fish swimming in the water, but after looking closely I realized there were two men passing back and forth in the street on the other side of the tank, wearing the khaki and red uniform of the communist army. There was something stealthy and alarming about them, especially when they paused to survey the patrons inside the open-door restaurant. Even while seated on the other side of the tank, I sensed their probing eyes and froze, like a flounder trying to assume the coloration of the sand at the bottom of the tank. Still, I felt their hungry assessment of me, as though I might be the likeliest candidate for dinner. After a few moments, during which I was sure they would see through my camouflage and scoop me up in a net, the two men moved on.

Directly after they left, a young couple arrived, making a conspicuous stir. Both were young and handsome. The man wore an elegant Western-style suit of midnight blue with a fine cotton shirt, pale silk tie, and studs. The woman, whose hair was cut in a chic, contemporary style, wore a simple black sheath and an enormous diamond on her finger. Shortly after they were seated by the maitre d', who greeted them effusively by name, the young man casually dropped a wad of foreign exchange certificates on the table and lit a Marlboro with what looked like a solid gold lighter. He and his companion sipped cocktails and chatted easily in Shanghai dialect. Though the dialect was still foreign to me, I recognized the tone of easy money. The two were clearly Shanghai's new entrepreneurs, most likely in computer software, insurance, or real estate. They were having the best time of anyone in the restaurant by far.

Just as we were finishing our meal, I saw the big shot pull out a cigarette. Simultaneously, as he raised it to his lips, his beautiful companion held out a light. Her timing was exquisite. From where she had produced the silver lighter, I don't know. She held it until he had lit his cigarette, then placed it on the table, covering it with her palm. Mr. Bigwig made another gesture, and again, from nowhere, she produced a small jeweled case, from which she withdrew an ivory toothpick for him. Her movements were fluid, effort-less, those of an artist of the highest order.

I could have stayed all evening, watching the performance of this celestial fern princess, but my mother and I had to get up early the next morning to catch the train to Suzhou. We walked back to Auntie Aifong's, politely declining Biring's offer of watermelon, as we simply could not be accessory to her going up and down those six flights of stairs again. Then, as before, Shrewin walked us back to our hotel, turning on his heel to head home as soon as we arrived. Before I went to bed, I jotted a few notes in my journal, writing of the two mysterious men and the beautiful courtesan. The sight of the fern princess remained clear in my mind. Though I could not understand or sympathize with her role, I thought what a relief, what a gift it was that some artists and their art had escaped the axe of the Cultural Revolution.

14

SUZHOU

THE NEXT MORNING SHREWIN BROUGHT A PEDICAB, A CRUDE WOODEN BOX attached to an oversized tricycle, with its driver, a skinny old man who couldn't have weighed more than ninety pounds soaking wet. I couldn't imagine he could propel the three of us plus our overnight bags, but Shrewin gestured impatiently for my mother and me to climb in the cab, heaved himself onto the horizontal bar in front, and ordered the old man to get going. The driver gave a determined grunt and a hop, and slowly, pumping his skinny, ropey legs with all his might, got us rolling.

Immediately we were engulfed on all sides by bicyclists who rang their bells furiously, swerving to avoid us. Our driver seemed oblivious to all but the road directly beneath him, panting and groaning as he labored so that I was sure he would have a heart attack. I resisted the impulse to get out and walk, lightening his load, but it was too dangerous. *Why hadn't Shrewin hired a taxi?* I wondered. Even though it cost three times as much, it was still relatively cheap given the exchange rate and would have gotten us to the station by now. Was Shrewin skimping on the cash my mother had given him so that he could have more for himself, or was he simply following the Chinese mandate: Never pay for more when you can do with less? At least he was providing the poor old man with work. I only hoped he survived to receive his payment.

We arrived at the central train station, which was blocked by swirling crowds of people and vehicles. After Shrewin paid the driver, we carved a path into the terminal. Here the cavernous building was packed with humanity, from solitary men squatting on rags to entire families gathered with their belongings. Minority women wearing fantastic dresses embroidered with beads and mirrors sat cross-legged on the floor, breast-feeding infants bundled in felt. Muslims, distinctive in their black, hooded robes and look of mournful solemnity, huddled in separate enclaves. People looked exhausted, resigned, as though they had waited months with no hope of movement.

Overhead, speakers blared sporadic, garbled announcements. Shrewin pointed to doors on the opposite side of the terminal and began to pick his way through the human undergrowth. My mother and I followed as best we could, trying to avoid the tangle of bodies and belongings. We managed to make it halfway across when the loudspeaker suddenly bleated with an alarming tone of urgency. In an instant hundreds of people, making up an entire side of the room, rose up with a dull roar and began to pour across the floor in the opposite direction of where we were headed. Though I braced myself, I was caught and swept along in the hurtling wave of bodies. Fighting panic, I struggled for footing and to keep sight of Shrewin, whose familiar bald head receded steadily across the room. Then something struck me in the back of the knees so that I lost my balance, toppling. I was sure I would fall and be crushed, but there were so many people that I rolled shoulder and hip along a solid wave of bodies until, miraculously, I slipped into an opening, where I regained my footing. I looked everywhere for my mother, who had been right behind me, but she was nowhere in sight. The space where she had been was now filled with panic-stricken strangers who continued to run up against me. Finally I made it across the room, joining Shrewin, who waited at the doors. As soon as he spotted me, his face lit up, but then immediately resumed its scowl when he saw that my mother wasn't with me. Together we anxiously scanned the swirling mob, afraid that we had lost her. Dire scenarios with probable headlines ran through my mind: *Mother Lost in Mob! Daughter Stranded at Train Station!* Then, suddenly, out of nowhere, my mother magically appeared, like a bottle bobbing to the surface of the ocean. Before we could celebrate our reunion, the loudspeaker blared again, and Shrewin, whose quick reflexes impressed me more and more, hustled us through the doors. Here the crowd surged toward the train tracks, where a locomotive marked SUZHOU waited. Shrewin trotted along the length of the train until he reached the car corresponding to the number printed on our tickets, and motioned for my mother and me to climb on after him. Though marked first class, designating that it was reserved for foreigners and high-ranking Chinese officials, the car was already filled with peasants, bundles of hay, and crates of live chickens. Moving halfway down the aisle we located our seats, which were occupied by laborers who looked as though they had just gotten off work. Bare-chested, wearing greasy pants rolled to the knee, they reeked of sweat and exhaustion and looked as though they weren't about to move from their seats even if someone shot them dead. Shrewin studied our tickets again.

"Excuse me, but these are our seats," he said to the three men, in Shanghai dialect.

Several seconds passed. Then the man in the middle dug in his pocket and produced ticket stubs. They matched the numbers above the seat. Now what? Shrewin showed our tickets to the men, who seemed neither surprised nor concerned, merely resigned to the fact that this kind of foul-up happened routinely. Undaunted, Shrewin explained that my mother and I were foreigners and were thus entitled to the seats. The men were unimpressed; one even yawned loudly, showing blackened teeth. Losing patience, as the conductors were now banging on the doors, signaling the train's imminent departure, Shrewin exclaimed in a loud voice that it was a long ride to Suzhou and that my mother needed to sit, as she was old and ailing. Though my mother winced at this, she said nothing. Perhaps she sensed, as I did, that these exhausted men needed to sit down more than she or I. I looked around the car, searching for empty seats, but saw none. The aisles were filling up.

Shrewin threatened the men outright, saying he would have the conductor remove them to a second-class car, where they belonged. The men showed no signs of stirring. I found myself wishing I could speak Chinese so that I could tell them they could have the seats, because nothing mattered to me now but to leave them alone. I was ashamed to claim priority over them, embarrassed by Shrewin's bullying tone. Everyone in the car was staring. But now Shrewin must have viewed it as a matter of personal honor, because he thrust the tickets in the men's faces and demanded that they give up their seats. This caused them to shift uneasily in their places, but they did not get up. Several more tense moments passed, during which I wondered what Shrewin would do to follow up on his threat. Then my mother pulled out a carton of Marlboros from her bag.

The men eyed the carton as though it was a bar of gold. Wordlessly, they consulted with one another, then the man in the middle, apparently the leader, reached up and took the carton. Now I understood why my mother had insisted on bringing her blue bag along. We waited.

Slowly, wearily, the men rose to their feet, reached into the overhead rack for their few belongings, and shuffled through the car toward the rear of the train.

"Sit!" Shrewin commanded. We took the seats, which were warm with sweat and fatigue. My mother settled back in her seat with a sigh of relief. I was about to thank Shrewin for his efforts but saw he was already staring out the window, lost in his own thoughts. People were still crowding into the car, settling into the aisles, parking infants and belongings wherever they could. Moments later, the whistle blew, and the train began to move out of the station. We were finally on our way to Suzhou.

The train passed through the outskirts of the city, where laborers like the men we had displaced trudged along, balancing enormous debris-filled baskets hanging from either end of poles suspended across their shoulders. They worked in trenches along both sides of the track, digging with ordinary picks and shovels, slinging dirt and rock onto donkey-drawn carts. No bulldozers or other large machinery were in sight, only man after man digging and hauling and toiling as far as I could see. The train chuffed slowly beyond the edge of the city, a distance of several miles, and still there was no end to the laborers. Finally, only when we headed into the open countryside, did their numbers thin, workers giving way to peasants sloshing up to their knees in muddy rice paddies. Alongside were water buffalo which swung heavy, scimitar-like horns side to side as though scything grass. The pungent smell of rich black earth and animal manure poured in through the open windows of the train.

A few hours later, arriving in Suzhou, we were met by a cousin of Shrewin's, who had hired a driver to take us on a tour of the city. The driver, a young man who greeted us effusively and insisted on carrying our bags, proudly took us to his Toyota Crown car. When he proposed to take us to lunch at a certain restaurant, Shrewin protested, and the two of them launched into a violent argument, the words flying too fast for me to understand. My mother explained that Shrewin knew the restaurant was notorious for paying large commissions to drivers to bring foreigners, whom it charged exorbitant prices. Apparently this was a common scheme in China, where it was assumed all foreigners could afford to be shaken down a bit. Finally, the driver, who looked all of sixteen, took us to a people's restaurant, where we had a simple but tasty meal. He expressed his displeasure afterward by driving like a maniac, playing chicken with oncoming trucks, honking his horn, taunting them in a shrill, boyish voice as they passed. He dropped the four of us off at the Suzhou garden pavilion and pointedly ignored us, lighting a cigarette and turning on his transistor radio to loud disco music.

The temple grounds were serene and beautiful, though on a smaller scale than those in Shanghai. My mother, who had seemed unusually pensive, even low-spirited at lunch, suddenly spoke up.

"Yeh Yeh and Nai Nai's old house—I think it's near here," she said. "Did you know Aunt Lucy was born in Suzhou?"

I stopped dead, not believing my ears. "Is the house still standing? Can we go see it?"

My mother didn't answer but began walking in a purposeful way, taking the lead as we left the pavilion grounds. I recalled my neighbors' guidebook describing Suzhou as the "Venice of China," and as we continued walking, began to see validity in the claim. Graceful pedestrian bridges arched over a serpentine system of jade-colored canals which were abutted by stucco houses painted ochre and blue. Chinese boatsmen plied their watercraft through the canals using sturdy, bamboo poles. Made amazingly of concrete, the unwieldy, flat-bottomed boats looked difficult to navigate and clunked from one side of the canal to the other.

By now the afternoon was blazing hot, but this did not deter my mother, who seemed increasingly excited, hunkering down on her legs like a hound on the scent. She remarked that she had visited the house once before, on a prior trip to China, but that it had been a long time ago and she wasn't sure if her memory served her correctly. I tried not to get my hopes too high, but my heart pounded at the possibility that this other family house, *Aunt Lucy's birthplace,* still existed.

The streets turned narrow and dark. All around were signs of construction, large pits filled with rubble, half-erected walls covered with scaffolding. The entire area smelled like a cesspool. Shrewin and his cousin carefully picked their way through the debris. Though they wore neutral expressions, I sensed that they, too, were caught up in anticipation.

My mother came to an intersection and paused, looking left, then right.

Then, as if suddenly catching the scent again, she turned left, climbed up a steep hill, then abruptly disappeared from view. When we joined her, moments later, she stood before a crude brick wall, which, from the appearance of the roughly slathered cement, looked as though it had been erected only days before.

"It must be here," my mother said, more to herself than anyone.

She stared at the wall, as though not quite believing it was there. I put my hand against it, scraping crumbs of concrete with my fingers. It felt solid, immoveable.

"Are you sure this is the place?" I asked.

She nodded.

I tried to imagine what had stood there at one time—a house with a tiled roof surrounding a courtyard where my grandfather wrote his early poems, a home where my aunt, then a young girl, had grown up. But it was like trying to fathom an unknown tomb. In the way an unmarked grave gives off an unspeakably sad and lonely air, this wall evoked in me a haunting sense of loss for what I had never known, and now would never see.

A woman emerged from behind a flap of burlap from the *hutung* abutting the wall, which I had not noticed until now. She kicked along a bucket of human waste so stinking and full that even Shrewin grimaced and turned away. The woman stopped when my mother addressed her, replying hoarsely in a dialect I couldn't follow. Later, my mother relayed the woman's explanation that the government was razing the entire street, including the *hutungs,* for which the old woman rejoiced, as it meant all the residents could move into the modern high-rises on the outskirts of the city. The overpowering stench underscored her jubilation that her home was scheduled for demolition. Her *hutung,* a long wooden structure with a low, burlap-covered entrance that required occupants to enter crawling on their hands and knees, lacked plumbing and ventilation. It was freezing in the winter, sweltering in the summer, and was a breeding ground for disease. I had read in my *History of China* that every decade or so whole neighborhoods of *hutungs* burnt to the ground, incinerating entire families within. There was no question that removing them from the heart of every Chinese city was necessary and long overdue. Still, I could not help wondering what would take their place. Already, in Shanghai, I had seen cheap concrete structures utterly lacking in character or aesthetic quality spring up, looking not only boring and depressing, but unsafe. I hated to imagine entire Chinese cities turning out like so many American low-income developments which looked cloned from a single, cost-cutting plan. Though I knew I clung to naive, romantic notions of China, I couldn't help viewing the government's move toward modernization as an attempt to dress a centuries-old dowager in cheap, off-the-rack suits, giving her a shoddy, nondescript facade that stripped her of her inherent dignity and splendor. Who could deny that antiquity might well serve as another word for misery, and that the poor woman kicking her filthy bucket deserved a better place to live? It was just as well the argument was moot. Everywhere, the impact of hundreds of thousands of picks and shovels could already be seen and felt.

That Yeh Yeh's Suzhou house had been destroyed made me want more desperately than ever to go to Beijing. I wanted to walk up to my grandfather's house and place my hand on its wall to reassure myself that it, too, had not vanished in the way of the *hutungs*. How long would it be, I wondered, before the government laid claim to our family home? According to Da Bobo's letters, his neighbors were already selling out so that Yeh Yeh's house would be the only one left in their section of the city. As though this wasn't bad enough, I had read that morning in the *Herald Tribune* that Beijing was suffering a record-breaking heat wave. Air-conditioning was a rarity in China, and even electric fans strained the inadequate power supply. Large numbers of elderly people and young children suffered heatstroke and were being treated at hospitals throughout the city. I worried about Aunt Lucy, with her hypertension, wondered how she would hold up in the dangerous heat.

The next day, Shrewin showed up at the hotel where we had spent the night with a different car and driver. We headed for the countryside, driving down a narrow, unpaved road that appeared to be the main thoroughfare between Suzhou and Hangzhou. Swerving all over the road, as usual, were lorries, donkey carts, and bicycles loaded with families moving entire households. During the harrowing ride, I noticed that my mother seemed unmindful of the danger, only subdued and distracted by matters known only to her.

"You okay, Mom?" I asked.

She shook her head, looking away, clearly unwilling to say. I was puzzled, but not surprised. Whereas my American friends might have responded to my solicitous inquiry with an outpouring of their feelings, my mother's expression was her warning not to meddle. Whatever disturbed her was too painful or embarrassing to share. Preserving her pride and dignity was far more important.

When we arrived in Hangzhou, it was still too early for lunch, so we left our bags at the hotel and headed for the lake. According to my neighbors' guidebook, West Lake was one of the most beautiful lakes in all of China, and was the subject of much poetry as well as a popular destination for honeymooners. Why this was so became immediately clear when we drew up to the shore. The water was calm and veiled in a delicate soft mist, the color of midnight and smelling of green tea. In the middle of the lake, at some distance, were gently sloping atolls dotted with temples and pines. Standing on shore I felt an immediate sense of tranquility. Shrewin rented a boat and we began rowing out toward one of the atolls, leaving the driver to wait on shore. Shrewin took one oar, I the other, and after a few strokes, which sent the boat zigzagging erratically, we got ourselves headed in the same direction.

The sun met the water at the keel of the boat. I was struck by the contrast of temperatures, how the part of me inside the boat enjoyed the coolness of the lake while my shoulders and face felt the brunt of the heat of day. Other boaters rowed nearby in trance-like rhythms, and I wondered if they felt as I did. All my cares had fallen away and were replaced by a sense of well-being and peace.

Suddenly, my mother shifted in her seat and peered into the water.

"It jumped in the boat right here," she said.

She sounded agitated, so that instinctively I followed her gaze into the water.

"What, Mom?"

She did not reply, and the set of her face indicated she was not about to. I looked into the calm water, wondering what upset her, then remembered my sister's account of her family's visit to this lake, and how my parents had been in the same boat as she. She related that a fish had leapt clear out of the dead-calm water and landed in my mother's lap. According to Chinese superstition, a fish offering itself was a sign of extraordinary good fortune, but on West Lake, the lake of honeymooners, it had a special significance for marital happiness. My sister said she saw my mother's face light up in a way that only women with unexpressed hopes have, and that she thought the age-old tension between our parents vanished as they both grappled excitedly for the fish that had landed in their boat. They brought it to shore and asked the hotel cook to prepare it in the special West Lake style, and my sister related how my father offered the cheek of the fish, the most highly prized part, to my mother, adding that it was the most loving act she had ever witnessed of him. Sadly, the promise of the fish went unfulfilled. The next day, my father split off from the family, departing for Hong Kong, where he had business. A few years later, he and my mother separated.

So much for the power of superstition, I thought as I stole glances at my mother, who sat at the front of the boat. She seemed determined not to be read, keeping her face averted, staring fixedly toward shore. Though I respected her desire for privacy, I felt perplexed by her stubborn reticence, frustrated, as ever, that she kept herself and her extraordinarily rich personal history under lock and key. Was it because I was the daughter closest to the husband who had gone away? Was it pride? Or might it have been that English, already problematic as her adopted language, failed to convey the complex messages of her heart? Now, I began to understand her long-standing claim that only the Chinese language had the capacity to express the innummerable nuances and magnitude of loss. As we rowed toward shore, I saw a slope settle onto my mother's shoulders like a mantle of sadness, as though passing the spot where the fish had leapt reminded her of its betrayal. I wondered if her subdued mood earlier had been due to her dread of this place. I felt sorry for her, then felt profoundly sad that I had reached a point in life where I pitied my mother. I stared into the lake, searching for the ghost of the fish that had, in its unknowing way, revealed to me more than I was prepared to know.

Back at the hotel, the other guests, who were mostly Chinese, were having lunch. Waiters brought out a succession of famous Hangzhou dishes: tiny freshwater shrimp cooked in sweet-and-sour sauce, braised eels, crabs sauteed with ginger and scallions, snails in garlic and black bean sauce. Garlicky hollow-stemmed vegetables came next, then a fragrant eggplant dish with green peppers. All was accompanied by the ubiquitous salty orange drink and the local beer, which, though unchilled, was deliciously yeasty and full-bodied. I was hungry and thoroughly enjoyed the new tastes, but halfway through the meal I noticed waiters sneaking sideways glances at me. Perhaps it was because Shrewin announced, in what I thought were inappropriate, loud tones, that my mother and I were Americans, and that it was my first time in Hangzhou. And then I could have sworn that he winked at the headwaiter. I attributed his high spirits to the beer and tried to think nothing more of it. By that time, I had drunk half a large bottle myself and allowed that I might be imagining things.

At the end of the lunch hour, the crowded dining room took on an air of satiety and calm. People discreetly picked their teeth and commented lazily on the tranquility of the lake. I noticed waiters tittering and scurrying into the kitchen and began to sense the room shift subtly into a gear of anticipation. Simultaneously, as though responding to a secret signal, everyone in the room fell silent and turned to stare at our table. Feeling self-conscious, I saw my mother and Shrewin assume faces of exaggerated boredom and knew at that point that something was imminent. The tension in the room mounted so steadily that I imagined a drumroll starting up. Then the kitchen doors burst open, and a waiter, carrying a large platter overhead, sprinted to our table. With a dramatic flourish he placed the platter directly in front of me, turning it so that the fish lying on it faced me.

Since I had braced myself for something spectacular, what I saw before me was something of a disappointment. I had seen whole cooked fish before, and this one looked no different, though it was unusually large, and was artfully arranged atop chopped vegetables and sauce so that it looked propped up on its fins. I had no idea what kind of fish it was, probably a species indigenous to West Lake. It had a large, dissipated-looking face with an enormous lower lip, reminding me of the actor Charles Laughton, and was covered with a shiny brown sauce that was fragrant with garlic and fermented brown beans.

As the guest of honor, I knew what was expected of me, and picked up a large spoon to serve portions of the fish to my mother and Shrewin. To my horror, just as I was about to cut into it, the fish suddenly heaved itself up on its fins, pulled away from the sauce with an awful sucking sound, opened its mouth wide, and gave out a loud croak right in my face. I screamed and jumped out of my chair, backing away from the table, afraid of what the fish might do next. The next instant it flopped back into the sauce with a sickening splash, fanned its gills once, and was still. Gradually, I became aware of people applauding and saw that everyone in the restaurant was laughing and nodding with approval. The chef emerged from the kitchen and bowed proudly. Shrewin was laughing so hard tears were streaming down his face. Even my mother was smiling.

"What is this?" I demanded.

"West Lake fish," she replied. "This hotel famous for it. They catch fish, clean at last minute, then throw in hot oil so fast it fry alive. Then they put on secret sauce. You can tell cook is really good if fish still move when they bring it to table. Your fish still very frisky, so you see, chef here very good!"

"The best, the best!" Shrewin said, still crying.

I sneaked a look from behind my chair. "Is it dead now?"

Shrewin picked up a chopstick and poked at the fish. It lay in a glazed heap, motionless. By now the other guests in the room had turned back to their own affairs. I took the spoon I had dropped on the table and cut pieces of fish for my mother and Shrewin. I put a portion on my own plate, but when no one was looking, hid it under a pile of rice. My mother ate enthusiastically, and when all that was left of the fish was the head, took it and sucked it until all that remained were a few bones and the eyes, which rolled around on her plate like a couple of BBs.

Later, after *xiu shi,* our driver took us to the train station, where we boarded a train back to Shanghai. This time there was no problem with the tickets and we sat in a car marked first class, which proved to be exactly like the second-class car—packed with peasants, ducks, watermelon, and squash—hitched behind it.

By the time we arrived in Shanghai, I was tired and ready for bed, but my mother reminded me that we were expected at Auntie Aifong's to find out about our tickets to Beijing.

Biring had watermelon waiting for us, and we ate it in front of the ancient creaky fan. Auntie Aifong, looking more animated than I had ever seen her, asked whether I had eaten the famous West Lake fish. Apparently everyone had anticipated my experience and enjoyed a good laugh when I told them the fish had gasped its terrible death right in my face. I wondered if they plotted this encounter for everyone new to China. It gave them something to talk and laugh about for the rest of the evening, and probably for days after. Both Auntie Aifong and Biring begged for more details: what the fish looked like, what the sauce tasted like, how the other people reacted when I jumped out of my chair. At first I thought they were merely teasing me, but then realized they were eager for something new to talk about. Their enthusiasm inspired me so that I began embellishing my story, adding touches such as the fish flopped all the way across the table gnashing its teeth, the chef ran from the kitchen brandishing knives, and so forth. My mother raised her eyebrows, but she seemed amused by my tall tales. At least they made the hour pass more quickly.

Shrewin, already tired of the story, retreated to the balcony and began smoking one cigarette after another, glancing at his watch. By now it was ten fifteen. My fish story had long begun to pall, and we had fallen silent, all too aware of the minutes ticking by. Biring cleared the watermelon rinds, and we listened to the whirr of the fan and the other noises of the tenement as it settled down for the night. Ten thirty came and went. Shrewin tore open a fresh pack of cigarettes. Auntie Aifong dozed off. My mother sat quietly in her chair, but I could tell she was convinced our contact had stood us up. I had reached the same conclusion and pondered what it would be like to spend the rest of our time in China marooned in Shanghai, living on watermelon, and rehashing my sorry fish story.

Then we heard the faint *tap-tap* of someone ascending the stairs. Six flights later, Elvis appeared at the door. He was sweating profusely and looked as though he had not slept in days. Shrewin rushed to offer him a cigarette. Elvis claimed he had spent the last two days pursuing every possible avenue, then gave us the bad news: There were no tickets to Beijing. Shrewin slapped his forehead and moaned out loud. My mother and I stared at each other in disbelief. What were we to do? My mother asked Elvis if plane tickets were available. He shook his head dejectedly. If he was putting on an act, it was a convincing one, I thought. We looked to Shrewin, but he had gone back to the balcony to pace back and forth. No doubt he imagined the horror of having to look after us for another four weeks. My mother turned to Elvis.

"What other ticket you have?" she asked.

He hesitated, and a sly look flitted across his face. Pleased with himself, he reached into his jacket pocket and pulled out a folder.

"After searching whole city, I manage to get these. Plane tickets to Xi'an. Only ones left," he added proudly.

"Xi'an!" my mother exclaimed.

"Plane tickets!" I cried.

"Please excuse us," my mother said to Elvis, and pulled me into the tiny alcove off the balcony. "Well?" she whispered.

"I say we call the China Travel Agency tomorrow and get the real scoop," I said. "I think Elvis is trying to pull one over on us. How can there be no tickets to Beijing? Beijing's the capital of China, for heaven's sake."

"But what if what he say is true, that only tickets he can get are to Xi'an?"

I thought for a moment. "How long do we have to decide?"

We went back to the room, where my mother conferred with Elvis in Shanghai dialect. When she turned to me, her face was tight. "He say there are other people ready to buy tickets," she said. "He hold them until nine o'clock tomorrow morning, but no later. They cost one hundred seventy dollars apiece."

"One hundred seventy!" I sputtered. "I thought flying was cheap in China!"

I glanced at Elvis, who sucked on his cigarette, yanking it from his mouth in abrupt movements. No doubt he was offended by our distrust. I felt a pang of regret, but knew if it was between him or us, we had to look out for ourselves.

"Tell him we'll let him know by nine o'clock tomorrow morning," I said.

My mother relayed the message with a furrowed brow. Elvis made a sound of disgust, and stuffed the tickets back into his pocket. Shrewin, who had returned from the balcony to witness this latest phase in the negotiation, was clearly dismayed by our position. It was obvious he had invested much time and cigarettes cultivating his relationship with the contact, and now we had insulted both of them with our suspicion. He accompanied Elvis to the door, apologizing and thanking him for his troubles. Elvis muttered something, probably about the stinginess of pesky American women, and left.

The next morning, my mother and I called the China Travel Agency. To our astonishment, they confirmed Elvis's claim, explaining that, due to former-president Jimmy Carter's imminent arrival in China, every means of travel to Beijing was booked. Tickets would become available after Carter's departure, but the agency lacked the means to handle advance reservations. When we asked them about flights to Xi'an, they quoted a fare of three hundred twenty dollars, adding that they were sold out, as it was the most popular destination in China. Now we were down to Elvis, our last remaining hope, anxious that he had gotten fed up with our indecision and sold our tickets to someone else. We consoled each other with the fact that, up to now, he had honored his prior agreements. My mother reminded me that Xi'an had been in our original plan, following the visit to Beijing. Still, going directly to Xi'an, which was deep in the interior of the country, meant it would be several more days, possibly a week, before we could travel from there to Beijing, and that was only if we were able to get tickets. All this, added to the news that the heat wave in Beijing had worsened, killing several more elderly persons, drove me crazy. I was convinced that Aunt Lucy would die and that they would tear down Yeh Yeh's house while I remained trapped in Shanghai as helpless as a rat.

We waited in the hotel lobby until nine thirty, looking with hope at every person who came through the door. Nine forty-five. Finally, when I thought I couldn't stand it any longer, and when my mother was about to call the China Travel Agency to buy any tickets anywhere else in China, Elvis showed up. He looked as though he had slept and bathed and wore an expression of such satisfaction that I was sure he had sold our tickets. When my mother told him of our decision, he nodded calmly and said he had our tickets. My mother invited him up to our room, where she gave him a large bundle of foreign exchange certificates for the tickets. He slipped the money into his jacket pocket, thanked us politely, and left.

For several moments we stood there, disbelieving that the transaction had actually taken place. I examined the tickets carefully. They looked legitimate, though there was no way to be sure. My mother tucked them into her purse, and we went downstairs to send Da Bobo another wire, informing him of our latest change in plans. My mother also sent a wire to her friend in Xi'an, who had originally planned to meet us weeks later, to tell him of the new scheme. After that we went to meet Shrewin, who was accompanying us on our last day in Shanghai. I knew this meant more temples, more streets, and alleyways filled with people making widgets. Simply marking time. It wasn't that I was tired of Shanghai, but merely impatient to begin the next phase of our journey. I had read about Xi'an and was excited to see the excavation of the ten thousand terra-cotta warriors buried there, but more than that I was relieved that we were moving, however circuitously and with much uncertainty, toward Beijing, and Yeh Yeh's house, at last.

15

XI'AN

BIRING'S FAREWELL GIFT TO ME WAS A CONTAINER OF SHANGHAI PEARL FACE cream the size of a mayonnaise jar. It spoke volumes of what she thought of my American tan; still, I was touched that she considered me salvageable, and that, with the conscientious application of the cream, which contained strong bleaching agents, I could yet transform myself into a pale Shanghai woman. Biring, Auntie Aifong, and Shrewin had come to see us off and stood with us while we waited for our ride to the airport. I was surprised when a regular taxi drew up. Maybe, I thought, Shrewin had had second thoughts about pedicabs, or had relented and splurged on this, our last day.

An argument broke out when it became apparent all three intended to come with us to the airport. My mother tried to convince them it wasn't necessary, knowing that if they came they would insist on paying the driver, costing them the equivalent of an entire month's rent. I waited as they wrangled over this for several minutes, amazed as always by the time and energy Chinese spent to save face. Auntie Aifong was particularly fierce, as, befitting matriarchs, it was up to her to set the tone. Carrying on like Medea, she tried to push her way into the cab though my mother blocked her easily. They continued scuffling at the curb, pushing and shoving one another in histrionic but ineffective maneuvers. The taxi driver, used to such rituals, buried his face in a Chinese comic book.

Eventually my mother prevailed, but only after threatening never to return to China if they came. She pushed me into the cab, climbed in after me, and practically shut the door on Auntie Aifong's fingers. Throughout all of this, Shrewin showed no emotion but stood there with his usual heavy, toad-like expression. In spite of his brusque manner, he had proven himself to be a valuable guide, and I wondered how my mother and I would manage without him. It occurred to me that I would actually miss him. He demonstrated no such sentiments, but stared with that look of marginal tolerance, stoic in his task as our host as a dog is to a pack of fleas. In two years' time, he and Biring would move to California to live near their son, but at this moment it seemed as though seeing us off only convinced him he was fated to live and die in the stifling apartment in Shanghai.

The driver revved the engine. As we pulled away, we turned to see our Shanghai relatives waving at the curb until we were far away.

At the airport, everyone seemed to be in a state of high anxiety, breaking from one line to another forming at the entrance to the tarmac. As we waited to check our bags, I saw the reason for the panic. Beyond the terminal window, there was only one airplane parked on the runway, a medium-sized prop craft that looked as though it had barely scraped through World War II. Surrounded by ladders, fueling trucks, connected by hoses and encircled by scores of worried-looking men, it looked like a dying patient on life support. I thought of all the American newspaper accounts I had read of Chinese plane crashes, detailing how the Chinese fleet was made up of ancient Soviet hulks flown by pilots with little training and serviced by mechanics brought in from the countryside. The Chinese themselves seemed undaunted by their country's dismal aviation record, as evidenced by the scores of passengers waiting to board this lone, beleaguered plane.

I began to count the heads in our line, which by now had doubled and looped so that it stretched to the far end of the terminal. I doubted that my mother and I would make it. The plane carried thirty, maybe forty passengers, and already there were more than a hundred people in line, with more arriving every minute. The atmosphere grew tense, with everyone eyeing each new arrival as a deadly rival.

Anxious airline personnel tried to maintain order, exhorting passengers to stand back from the door to the tarmac, but everyone ignored them, pressing even closer on all sides. Suddenly the loudspeaker crackled to life, announcing that there would be a two-hour delay due to mechanical problems with the plane. The entire room groaned. We moved with several passengers to the adjoining waiting area, from which we observed a crew of four mechanics standing beneath the plane. Each grasped a corner of a large piece of paper, holding it aloft as though ready to fold it like a bedsheet. From the way they stared back and forth from the paper up at the belly of the plane, rotating slowly as they did so, it became apparent that the paper was a schematic of some kind and was key to the repair they were about to attempt. Every now and then one of the men would point upward while another would shake his head and peer more closely at the plan. At one point all four stopped and scratched their heads. This was not a good sign.

We waited for two hours. Three. Every so often I looked out to watch the four men climbing in and out of the plane. I tried to read my book, *Sense and Sensibility,* thinking it might be the last book I might ever read, while my mother knitted and napped. Other passengers harangued the helpless airline officials huddled by the door or paced back and forth before the glass window, muttering at the incompetence of the mechanics. Two children sprawled on the floor, playing a Chinese version of jacks. An elderly couple bickered over an orange. My mother woke up from her nap and stared at the people pacing back and forth.

"This remind me . . ." she began, but stopped to pick up the little rubber ball that had bounced from the two children.

"What?" I said.

The speakers emitted a garbled squawk, which caused everyone to look up. Glancing out the window, I saw that the four mechanics had disappeared.

"Hurry!" my mother said, grabbing her purse and her blue bag. Before I could stuff my book into my backpack, she grabbed my arm and pulled me through the confused crowd toward the tarmac door, where wide-eyed airline officials, backs to the wall, begged everyone to stay calm. Here I watched, amazed, as my mother thrust our tickets in the face of an official, demanding to board in a voice of such authority that the flustered agent stamped our tickets without even looking and waved us through.

Hurrying across the tarmac, I climbed the rickety ladder into the plane and saw how dilapidated it was. The engines and propellers were covered in sooty exhaust, and the nose was pockmarked, as though it had been battered by baseball-sized hail. When we boarded, the wings wavered up and down like weary arms. As my mother and I moved through the interior toward the rear, I concentrated on statistics supporting the case for sitting in back, the likeliest place for surviving a crash.

Hot air hissed from the vents in the ceiling of the plane. Having sat so long on the tarmac, the plane felt like an oven. Our row of seats was so tight that my elbow dug into the arm of the man sitting next to me, who stared straight ahead in a state of paralysis. The female attendants closed the door, and, while the engines revved, sprinted down the aisle, strewing things from trays hung from their necks. Hard candies, little plastic wind-up toys, and wooden blocks—which I surmised were the airline's version of cocktail peanuts—bounced between the seats and landed in our laps. This duty done, the two attendants strapped themselves into seats beside us. They looked twelve years old and wore thick pasty foundation that was melting. Pointy airline caps gave them the look of ice cream vendors. Their light blue uniforms were deeply stained under the arms and both looked bug-eyed, scared out of their wits.

The engines sputtered and howled. The propellers began to rotate spasmodically, then sped up until they were a blur. The plane lurched forward, balked, rolled slowly down the runway. I glanced at my mother, reminding myself that she had flown in China and survived. A woman of unshakeable faith and iron will, she attended church services and sang in the choir. She visited people older than herself, bringing them hot food. *God wouldn't let a person like that die in a plane crash,* I thought.

The whining engines propelled the plane faster and faster over the bumpy runway. We seemed to be on the ground forever, racing toward the outer rim of China. Outside the window, trees and buildings became a blur. I thought of all the people who had not made it onto the plane and wondered who was luckier. The plane kept going and going, shuddering and shimmying as if it was falling apart. Suddenly it hit a big bump. A bag fell from the ledge above and hit the attendant next to me on the head. She shrieked hysterically and kept on shrieking.

Finally, with the engines screaming as though they would explode, the plane rose heavily in the air and banked sharply to the left, piercing its own thick trail of smoke. I braced myself against the steep angle and looked out the window. Shanghai grew smaller and smaller below. The man next to me clutched my arm in a death grip. In his other hand, he held a wind-up toy that had landed in his lap. Mumbling an apology, he let go of my arm and looked out the window. On the other side of me, my mother knitted. I realized she had knitted like mad throughout the entire ascent of the plane, as though the whir of her needles would lift us into the sky. Now the cabin grew bright with the sun. The engines settled into a throbbing roar and the plane leveled off, heading west toward Xi'an.

Several uneventful hours later, the plane made its approach to Xi'an and managed a choppy landing. Waiting for us in the tiny terminal was Dr. Tsai, a friend and classmate of one of my mother's friends, and his young assistant, Dr. Liang. Both were opthamologists at the college in Xi'an. Dr. Tsai apologized, saying our sudden change of plans had prevented him from reserving a room in a hotel. Nevertheless, he had managed to secure a place for us at the hospital guest quarters nearby.

The air outside the terminal was even hotter and more humid than in Shanghai. Dr. Tsai drove a battered Russian sedan which he explained had been lent by the college, and after a brief ride we arrived at a spacious apartment with a window air-conditioning unit that hummed quietly, filling the room with heavenly cool air. A nurse brought us a tray of tasty cold dishes. As we ate, Dr. Tsai ticked off a list of sights he had arranged for us to see the following day as well as a special session with his students. He explained they had never before met a Chinese-American of their generation. His assistant, Dr. Liang, a slender young man with a gentle smile and rotten teeth, explained shyly in English that he was to be our guide. The nurse came to clear the tray, after which Dr. Tsai and Dr. Liang excused themselves.

Before leaving, the nurse unplugged the air conditioner, explaining it was the college's energy-saving policy. She opened the window, and warm, moist air seeped into the room, as well as the sounds of crickets, clicking beetles, and other flying bugs that banged against the screen. My mother carefully arranged the folds of her mosquito net around her as she got into bed.

"Leaving Shanghai today remind me of something," she said.

I looked up from Jane Austen, which I had been planning to read before going to bed.

"You know how people rush around, scared because not enough room on plane . . . ?"

I waited, hooking my thumb between the pages to mark my place.

My mother stared at her toes for a long time. "Did I ever tell you about when communists came to get us?"

I dropped my book on the floor and reached for pencil and paper. I could tell from the set of her face that she was about to relate an important moment in her life, and I didn't want to miss a thing. The story took a long time to tell because my mother's memory was like quicksilver released from a forgotten place, splitting like so many beads that skipped time and sequence and caused me to tumble after in confusion.

"Wait, Mom, can you back up? You mentioned secondary school. So you were around fourteen or fifteen when this happened?"

"No. I was ten or eleven when communists came. I couldn't be in secondary school."

That is not what I remembered her saying, but I crossed out what I had jotted down. "Okay. How many people did you say were in the house?"

"Eleven, including my parents."

"But didn't you have eleven brothers and sisters?"

"Yes, but two older brother and sister Anna live on own then, live in Shanghai."

"Okay. Where did this take place again?"

"In An Yuen, little town in Jianxi Province . . ."

I stopped, turned the pages of my notes. "Before, you said Hunan . . ."

"No, I never say Hunan. How you get that?" She was squeezing her thumbs, exasperated by my interruptions and sighs as I scratched out her words as fast as I put them to paper. She looked away as I erased the page. Already scrubbed twice, the paper ripped loudly, amplifying our mutual frustration.

"I'm sure you didn't say An Yuen in the beginning," I said. Hearing the accusation in my voice, I took a deep breath. "Do you think we could try to keep this in sequence, please?"

"I tell you things how I remember them!" my mother snapped. After a pause, she said, "Memory don't always come perfect order."

There was a husky catch in my mother's voice, something I rarely heard. I realized that our family had never heard her stories before, that our family lore was always about Yeh Yeh and his side of the family, not my mother's. I wondered if she had felt intimidated by Yeh Yeh's stature as a world-famous scholar, been further tamped down by my father, who demanded that she defer her personal ambitions to support his career and the needs of us children. Whatever the reason, somewhere along the way she had lost her voice, misplaced her own personal history.

"I have an idea," I said, pushing aside the protective netting around my bed, padding across the sticky linoleum floor. I searched my suitcase, took out my microcassette recorder and cassettes. *Why hadn't I thought of this before?* I had labeled each cassette AUNT LUCY, BEIJING, 1987, in anticipation of my talks with my aunt, but now I scratched through a label and wrote above it: VERA: AN YUEN, 1929.

"Let's try this," I said, inserting the batteries in the recorder and turning it on. Now I felt on a mission to right a wrong, to set the record straight. Seeing the tape machine, my mother cleared her throat, composed her face in the look of concentration a world-class soprano assumes when she is about to launch into her signature aria. She began her story again, from the beginning, and although she stopped several times to correct herself and jumped backward and forward in her chronology, I let the machine run. I kept notes as well, keeping an eye on the recorder timer in order to mark my own place in my mother's story. To this day, I still remember the process of editing my mother's rambling account, piecing together bits of her taped voice together with the copious notes I had written throughout the night. It took me more than a week, following our return from China. My imprint is everywhere, but what matters is that it is my mother's story and that it is on record at last:

VERA: AN YUEN 1929
THE DAY THE COMMUNISTS CAME

It all happened in one and a half days in 1929. I was living with my parents and nine of my brothers and sisters in the little town of An Yuen, in Jiangxi Province. My father was the foreman of a coal mine, which was the largest company in town. At this time the nationalist and communist armies were fighting for control of China. Every day it went back and forth—one day Chiang Kai Shek's nationalists were in charge, the next Mao Zedong's communists. For months we'd been hearing rumors that the communists were scourging the countryside, rounding up, torturing, and killing community leaders. They hunted down the rich and anyone else who had connections with the West, because they held them responsible for the corruption in China.

Hearing that the communists were getting close to our village made some people so jittery that they packed up and left. My father talked of leaving, but his company convinced him to stay, saying that, as foreman, he needed to set an example. He remained behind, even though he knew he was at the top of the communist death list.

Of course, being eleven years old at the time, I really didn't know what was going on. My older sister Anna was living in Shanghai, and my other sister Esther was sick with rheumatic fever, so I had only my brothers to play with. I was a tomboy and could outrun and out-jump most of the other children my age, even the boys. I had heard there was some kind of trouble brewing outside our town, but it seemed to involve grown-ups, so I was sure our town elders would take care of it. That was their job, after all.

Our town was divided into the people who worked for the coal mine, and those who didn't. These were mainly the shopkeepers, farmers, and people who ran other small businesses. My father's friends were company engineers and administrators, some of whom had come from Germany and Switzerland. My brothers and I played with their children and went to the same school. I don't know why we didn't play with the other town children. My mother never told me not to. They just seemed to avoid us, and we thought they were kind of odd, too.

Our house was always full of people. We had many servants, a cook, a gardener, people who delivered wood and coal, and of course the *amahs* who took care of us children. Our favorite *amah,* who lived with several other families in a building up the hill, would come every day to dress and feed us and make sure we did our homework. My mother oversaw everything but had a very comfortable life. She was tall and fat and had big feet! Her feet were so big that people in town gossiped about them. As the wife of the foreman she was a person of high rank, and so was expected to have bound feet, but my mother never had her feet done. Maybe it was because she came from Hawaii, from a family with modern ideas. Both my parents were second-generation Anglicans, raised in families converted by missionaries.

Along with her big feet, my mother also had a beautiful voice and loved to sing opera. She made all us children take up musical instruments. Every night we played chamber music—my brothers John, Henry, William, Paul, Richard, David, and Benjamin played violin, cello, piano, flute, and saxophone. I played piano. So you can imagine how the rest of the town saw us, living in our big house on the hill, running around with big feet, playing Mozart and Beethoven every night.

To me, it was a happy life. I had lots of friends, including the policemen who patrolled our street. They gave me money to buy them peanuts and would fill me in on the latest gossip. They said people liked my father because he gave gifts to the whole town at Christmas. Being a Chinese town, not everyone celebrated Christmas, but they liked my father's presents anyhow. The police seemed to know everything that was going on in An Yuen, and whenever I saw them I felt safe and that life was good.

In ordinary times, every town has something that lets people know that everything is all right. Like the sight of the postman delivering the mail, or the sound of bells chiming in the town tower. For us, it was the comings and goings of the company train between our town and Changsha, which was several hours to the west. Every day our train would meet the train leaving from Changsha at Ju Cho, the town that lay in the middle. In Ju Cho, the trains would exchange coal and money and then continue on their opposite ways. The nationalist army, which we thought of as our army, was then headquartered in Changsha. Since our train went there daily, we felt closely connected and therefore safe. We knew the bugle call of the nationalist army, which was different from the bugle call of the communist army. Our train carried the white nationalist army flag; the communist flag was red.

My older brother Henry had just returned home from his studies in the United States, where he had received a master's degree in aviation from the University of Southern California. I hadn't seen him in a long time, and he was so much older than me that I was scared of him. When he came home, he was wearing Western clothes and seemed like a total stranger. Gradually, I began to remember who he was, especially when we played music after dinner and sang all our favorite songs.

At dawn the next morning, my *amah* came running into our room shouting, "The mountains are red! The mountains are red!" We opened the window to look out, and sure enough, the mountains were not only red, but also moving strangely, as though they were alive. Then I heard a faint but clear bugle call. I didn't recognize it at first and then I realized it wasn't our bugle call at all, but the communist call! And then I saw that the mountains weren't moving but were covered with soldiers pouring down the mountainside toward our village, looking like a river of hot lava . . . hundreds, thousands of them carrying the red flags of the communist army.

Everybody panicked. We couldn't believe what was happening. My father ran around the kitchen shouting, "Where are my shoes? Where are my shoes?" until my mother pointed they were right by his feet. He put them on and left to go hide in the attic of the elementary school just up the road from our house. My mother and brother Henry ran to hide her jewelry, which was to be used as dowries for my sisters and me. They put some under loose boards in the floor, under flowerpots, wherever they could think of. My *amah* took my sick sister Esther up to her house on the neighboring hill. All the while I could hear the neighbors shouting that the army was getting closer and closer. I went outside to look, and this must have been when my mother took my four younger brothers to hide in our *amah's* house as well, leaving my brother Henry and me the only ones left in the house. When I saw the red soldiers coming up the street from the back door, which faced the road, I ran out the front door into the alley, bumping into my policemen friends just as they were running away. I begged them for help.

"Hide!" they said. "Disguise yourself! Smear dirt on your face, tear your clothes! Hurry!"

I grabbed handfuls of dirt from the alleyway and ran back inside the house. Henry was on the second floor, still trying to hide our family valuables. I smeared our faces with dirt, helped him tear his shirt and roll up his pant legs.

The red soldiers broke down the back door and began running through the rear of the house. I ran down the stairs in front. I could hear them moving from room to room, throwing our furniture around, shouting my father's name. I knew that any second they would reach the front of the house, where we were. I looked up through the upstairs bannister at Henry, who was frozen there.

"Jump!" I hissed. He looked at me as if he didn't understand, then slowly climbed over the bannister. "Jump!" I urged him again, nearly shouting. He jumped, landing heavily and stumbling against me. I pulled him toward the front door. The soldiers were right behind us now in the next room. Henry and I rushed out the front door, running into our neighbors who had come to see what was happening. They didn't recognize us. We pushed through them and ran up the hill to my *amah's* house.

Our *amah* took us up to the third-floor attic, where my mother and brothers and sister were hiding. From the window we could see the elementary school where my father was and our house. People were running in and out, stealing our furniture and linens. The looters were not company people but neighbors from down the street, the ones who whispered about my mother's big feet and complained about the music coming from our house in the evenings. I could see them at the windows of the upper floors of our house, throwing clothes and boxes and records out the window. I even saw them burst through the door from the inside, haul out my mother's grand piano, and roll it into the pond at the front of our house!

I was shocked, then angry. Why were they doing this? What had we done to them? When I saw them take my mother's records and skip them across the water, laughing as they landed, floating on the water like lily pads, something happened to me. I dashed from the attic, out of my *amah's* house, and down the hill back to our house. Since no one recognized me, I was able to mingle in the crowd and get inside our house. I had no idea what I was doing. All I knew was that they were robbing us and I had to do something. By now, the neighbors had taken nearly everything or broken all that the soldiers had left. I grabbed what I could, a couple of blankets, a pillow. One of our neighbors was clutching a shawl that belonged to my mother, and I grabbed that, too. She let go, as though she believed I was like her and entitled to a share of the plunder. Then I joined the others who were yelling and laughing as if they had gone crazy. It felt strange, how easy everything was. It was almost fun. Gradually, things quieted down. The neighbors, seeing that nothing was left, went back to their own homes. I took the blankets and my mother's shawl and went back to my *amah's*.

As soon as I got back, my mother burst out crying and scolded me for running away. Then we all calmed down and waited. The soldiers came three times to search the house, demanding that my *amah* tell them where we were, but she said nothing. Each time we crouched low and tried not to breathe. My youngest brother, Ben, had been diagnosed with tuberculosis, and was prone to coughing and crying, but he lay quiet under my mother's arm. When the coast was clear, our *amah* brought food, but no one could eat. We peeked out the window at the elementary school down the street, hoping to see my father, but it was too far. Even so, I knew he was watching us. We could all feel it.

Every hour throughout the rest of the afternoon, my *amah* brought news that so-and-so in my father's company had been caught, taken away, or gotten his head chopped off. She said the communists were swift and brutal. We shivered and waited, full of dread yet strangely eager to hear her reports.

Then, at four o'clock, our *amah* brought the miraculous news that our father's name had been removed from the death list. The communists had rounded up all the townspeople to determine who, of those remaining in hiding, was the most corrupt. Incredibly, someone had spoken up for my father, saying he was a good person. Maybe he remembered the gifts my father gave out at Christmas, or maybe he was one of the thieves stealing from our house who felt ashamed of what he and his neighbors had done. Even after hearing this good news, we didn't dare come out. What if it was a trick? The communists were known to trap people with such ruses. We talked about what we should do. Even if we dared come out of hiding, we couldn't run because Esther was sick and my mother was too fat. Besides, where would we go? Finally we decided to stay where we were. Nobody slept that night. My brothers sighed and whispered while Ben cried quietly under my mother's arm. I lay awake, thinking of our neighbors as they ran through our house, shouting like bandits. I saw visions of our sheets floating from the windows of our house, my mother's piano sinking into the water.

Many hours later, when it was still dark, we heard a cock crow. My brothers cautiously opened the shutters of the windows. The sun was just beginning to come up. In the distance, we heard a bugle sounding. We shushed one another to listen, and then my brother David shouted, "It's ours! It's our bugle!" Sure enough, it was the sound of the bugle signaling the advance of the nationalist army. We discovered later that, on the previous day, the communists had stopped our company train from going through Ju Cho to Changsha. Its failure to arrive alerted the nationalists that the Red Army had invaded our village. We crowded to the window to listen as our bugle calls grew shrill and clear, watching as the white flags came down the mountainside and the red banners retreated in confusion out of town.

I don't remember exactly what happened next. My father eventually left his hiding place at the school, gathered us all together, and took us to the train station. Nearly everyone in town followed us there, our friends as well as our bad neighbors. I remember the long walk to the station, past bodies in the street covered with blood, arms and heads chopped off. My mother put her scarf over my head, but I still saw everything. I'll never forget the smell.

At the train station, my father addressed the crowd. "Look at me and my family," he said. "We have nothing. We are refugees now." He looked into the faces of his colleagues and workers. Everybody was crying, even our neighbors. "I wanted to leave long ago, but you asked me to stay," he said. "Now, I ask you, where shall we go? What shall we do?"

There was a long silence, then somebody shouted, "Give them the train!" which was followed by a huge roar of approval. A railroad car was brought on the tracks and hitched to the engine bound for Changsha. We climbed aboard. People handed us food, clothes. Some even offered to go with us, but my father refused. Then the train began to roll, and we began our journey as refugees.

Several hours later, just as we were about to enter Changsha, my father told us he had watched our *amah's* house from his hiding place in the school to see if the red soldiers were going to capture Henry. "If they took him, I was going to offer myself up instead," he said. That made us very sad and frightened all over again. We talked about our future, what might happen next. Maybe because I was so young, I had no doubt that we would be all right. And sure enough, when we arrived in Changsha, officials from the Anglican church offered us a place to stay.

That is really the end of the story, though I remember pressing my mother for the epilogue. She told me that her family continued to retreat inland as the fighting between the two armies moved west. Her oldest brother George left Shanghai to join them, establishing an insurance business that kept the family going.

"And Ben?" I asked, thinking of the sickly little brother.

"He didn't have tuberculosis, after all. You'll see him in Changsha. He and Auntie Anna live there now."

"We're going to Changsha?"

"After the boat trip down the Yangtze River."

"Boat trip?"

"After we leave Xi'an."

"But I thought we were going to Beijing after Xi'an!"

"It doesn't make sense. Beijing's too far north. We may as well see as much as we can of central China while we're here."

I was about to argue the case for going to Beijing, but my mother's tone was final, and I remembered my vow to follow her lead. What choice did I have, really? Still, I was sick with disappointment and a sense of betrayal that my mother, who had apparently decided this after Elvis got our tickets to Xi'an, sprung this on me only now.

She didn't seem to notice my reaction, and sat there on the edge of her bed, swinging her feet. Brushing against the mosquito net, her legs made a carefree, swishing sound. A peculiar smile lit her face, as she savored that moment of triumph when she was eleven years old and had gone back to her house to save her family's belongings. I could picture very clearly the tomboy who knew about jumping down staircases and who had found her way across the terrifying fissures of war to land in America.

After my mother had gone to sleep, I unfolded my map of China and spread it across my bed. I located Xi'an, which was in the middle of the country, and Changsha, which was to the southeast. The Yangtze River traversed the huge area in between, twisting and turning like a gnarled vein. To the northeast, represented by a large dot at the extreme end of the map, was Beijing. Xi'an was on my pillow and Beijing lay on the floor, so I saw with heart-sinking clarity how far away we were from Yeh Yeh's house. Following my mother's new route, we were headed still farther afield. I stared at the map, feeling that I had lost grasp of all dimensions. In telling her story, my mother had taken us away not only in time, but in miles as well. I watched her as she lay sleeping on her bed, knowing that the deeper we probed China the closer we got to tapping her rich store of memories. First there was the story of her bomb, and now this. What other extraordinary events had occurred in her life? What other stories, prompted by our travels inland, were to be recalled? I wondered how she had gotten through the war and the difficult transition of those early years in America. Had she carried the episode of Henry leaping from the landing through every extreme moment of her life? *Sometimes you just jump.* I thought of how she had grabbed me and gotten us on the plane to Xi'an. That counted as a jump. And now, faced with more uncertainty, she was fast asleep, at peace in the currents of fate. We still had no tickets to Changsha, none for the boat down the Yangtze. I knew I wasn't a leaper like my mother, more of a creeper. For the first time I was seeing her as a source of limitless possibility, even audacity. Perhaps what I was searching for might not be in Beijing, among the ghosts or living relatives there, but much closer at hand. Lying right in front of me, in fact.

16

TERRA-COTTA

AT EIGHT O'CLOCK THE NEXT MORNING, THE ROOM WAS A SAUNA AND THE insects on the screen buzzed and snapped like a downed power line. Dr. Tsai arrived, bearing a telegram which he presented to my mother. She read it without expression and handed it to me.

SORRY ABOUT TICKETS. WE WILL WAIT. PLEASE DO ALL YOU CAN. LUCY IS FEELING POORLY. DA BOBO.

I looked at my mother, but she avoided my glance.

"I hope it's not bad news?" Dr. Tsai asked.

My mother explained Aunt Lucy's condition. I imagined my aunt's face before me, eyes bulging, foot kicking, kicking, as she lay on her deathbed in Beijing.

"I'm sorry," Dr. Tsai said. "It's unusually hot in Beijing this year."

"Mom," I could not refrain myself from saying, "can't Dr. Tsai help us get tickets to Beijing?"

She frowned, clearly displeased with my outburst, and turned to speak to Dr. Tsai in a dialect that sounded nothing like Mandarin, hardly like Chinese at all, but a series of glottal gulps and hisses. They pored over my map of China, running their fingers along the vividly colored terrain, tracing mountains, rivers, valleys, muttering all the while, two generals plotting war. After playing out many exhaustive but ultimately futile campaigns, Dr. Tsai began an extensive explanation that was a litany of hopelessness as far as I could tell. He finished with a regretful shrug.

"What did he say?" I asked.

My mother hesitated. "He say he try his best," she said.

"What does that mean?

"He say he get whatever tickets he can get. He say tour groups buy all tickets in and out of Xi'an for next month and a half."

"Oh, God!"

Dr. Tsai gave me a rueful look. "It's high season," he explained. "Everybody wants to see the terra-cotta warriors."

"What are we going to do?" I moaned.

"Dr. Tsai has contacts," my mother said, her voice polyphonic in its tone of warning.

Contacts. My guts heaved at the word. This could only mean more back doors leading us farther away from Beijing. I wanted to throw myself on the floor howling that I had had enough of this damned stupid bureaucracy— that I was going to Beijing even if I had to walk. My mother saw exactly what I was thinking and gave me a withering look. Dr. Tsai, grasping our situation, discreetly gazed at the windowsill, as if inspecting the dead insects heaped there. I began to hope a little, because however unassuming his demeanor, Dr. Tsai seemed a person who could get things done. My mother had informed me earlier that like so many of the faculty at the college, he also served as an administrator. From my experience in the Chinese community, I had learned how modest people who practiced scrupulous self-effacement often concealed the greatest ability.

There was a knock on the door, and Dr. Liang, Dr. Tsai's assistant, came in. Dr. Tsai excused himself, saying he would get on with the matter of the tickets right away. Left alone with us, Dr. Liang seemed to shrivel with shyness, looking down at the floor and clearing his throat with dainty stifled noises. He looked barely twenty years old, too young to be an assistant professor, with a smooth face and arms as thin as a girl's. Apologizing again for the heat, he said he had a car ready for us to tour the hills of Xi'an, where we would get an overview of the tombs.

Outside, the sun's rays were blinding and the buzz of cicadas deafening. The atmosphere was sodden, smothering, heavy as a wet quilt. My head ached and I wavered between excitement at seeing the terra-cotta warriors and despair from Da Bobo's telegram and the ever-receding prospect of reaching Beijing. The thought of riding around for hours in a hot car seemed overwhelming.

We climbed in a black sedan that reminded me of my family's first car, a 1949 Ford Roadster. As we rode, Dr. Liang spoke about the rule of Emperor Qin Shi, first emperor of the Qin Dynasty, who came to power in 221 B.C. "He was powerful, but monstrous, cruel," he said in a hushed voice, his eyes lowered, as though he still feared the eavesdropping of vengeful ancestral spirits. "Qin tortured poets and scholars, burned their writings. . . ."

The first Cultural Revolution, I thought. I looked out at the flat fields and gently rolling hills, the sun-scorched grass. Occasional plumes of dust spiraled across the unpaved road. A far cry from Shanghai and the other cities we had seen so far, there was not a man-made structure to be seen for miles. I thought of my friend Evan's account of the young American's arrest in a backwater area and wondered if he meant Xi'an. While everything looked innocent enough, there was something unsettling about the place. It was as if powerful evil forces still lingered, that the drifting sand, gusts of wind continued to whisper of the torment suffered. I wondered what kept everything under control in modern-day Xi'an with the ruling bureaucracy so far away in Beijing. I had seen few communist authorities other than the sleepy guard at the Xi'an airport, who barely glanced at my passport when I went through. Still, Dr. Liang's demeanor made it plain that this was no place to be inattentive. Xi'an was an area of inestimable archaeological wealth, a place where thousand-year-old mysteries and perhaps unimagineable powers were tapped daily, stirred from sleep. Reports were there had been plunderers and that the Chinese government acted swiftly to punish those caught defiling or stealing the precious artifacts. I was relieved my mother and I were under friendly escort, though I couldn't be sure if this meant we were immune from scrutiny.

In a guarded voice, Dr. Liang recited Emperor Qin's acts of madness: conscripting more than 700,000 workers to build his memorial, then slaughtering them in order to preserve the secrets of his tomb; murdering or forcing suicide upon his own relatives to provide himself with an entourage in the afterlife; filling his funeral grounds with gleaming bronze chariots, to which magnificent warhorses were harnessed, buried alive. I envisioned the terrified animals thrashing in their traces, screaming as dust poured down their throats.

The car bucked over large ruts in the road, climbed bare knolls of dirt.

The ruts reminded me of giant ribs, the gentle mound of a belly on the plain. All was covered in a layer of fine, yellow sand, soft and blowing, a coverlet of what had already been. Trees and grass, all that was alive or green, grew well beyond the area, as though still obeying the edicts of that first dynasty to keep clear.

We arrived at an area the size of a football field surrounded by a crude wooden barricade and protected by a plastic canopy stretched over a domed metal frame. Dr. Liang informed us this was only a small part of the burial site. No one knew what lay in the actual tomb of the emperor, which lay some distance away and on which excavation had not yet begun. Drawing closer, I saw that the site was a huge rectangular pit, bordered on all sides by towering mounds of dirt. Crude wooden signs marked a sloped path down to the entry. Dr. Liang spoke to one of the few guards, who seemed to recognize him. They chatted a while, then the guard waved us through.

"My friend is making an exception today," Dr. Liang explained, leading the way down the dirt-packed path. "The site is usually not open before nine o'clock, when the crowds arrive."

As my mother and I followed, I felt a growing appreciation for Dr. Liang, not only for arranging our preview, but for assuming that we were not like the other tourists. Perhaps he was merely acting in deference to my mother, but I was grateful for his sincere tone and for including me in his explanatory glance. As we followed him down the path to the inner sanctum of the site, I felt that I had a place, however small, in this land, and that what I had been feeling all my life in America were not mere romantic notions or wishful thinking, but ties as real as the earth I was walking on.

As we continued down the narrow switchbacks into the pit, I became aware of a peculiar smell of water commingled with pungent earth minerals. The smell evoked something immeasureably ancient and rare, signaling that we approached sacred ground. Then my mother stopped.

"Look," she pointed.

We stood against a barricade of rough planks at the rim of the pit. Several meters below, illuminated in a broad shaft of light streaming from a crack in the plastic canopy above, were row after row of trenches dug by the Chinese archaeological teams. Inside the trenches stood hundreds of human-like figures in various stages of restoration. The rounded domes of heads and shoulder caps jutted above the trench rims, poking up from the dirt like bleached bones. It was like looking down at the newly exposed skeleton of the earth itself. Shadows juxtaposed with flashes of sunlight reflecting from the dome's metal beams produced the illusion of movement, so that the figures seemed to advance along the excavated trenches in a stately and orderly fashion. In a reverent tone Dr. Liang estimated that the total number of figures in the site was six thousand. *But surely there were more,* I thought. The main column reached to the far end of the pit, then, like a spine, disappeared deep into the hips of the earth. I was certain there were at least several armies, if not entire city populations, down below.

Dr. Liang explained that the figures were made of terra-cotta, the clay of the region, assembled from pieces that were fired in huge ovens. It was clear, from their configuration, that the figures were part of a grand military scheme. Subtle differences in hair treatment and dress ornament signified varying ranks among the infantrymen, charioteers, officers, and generals. Also scattered about in the trenches were fragments of lances, armor, and war wagons. According to Dr. Liang, none of the figures was identical to another; each had been individually modeled after a living person. Squinting at the many distinctive details of the figures, I saw that it was true. All had faces of the same race, the same kingdom, yet each was undeniably unique. From the sheer number of the figures it seemed impossible that a single artisan could have made them, yet it was clear that those who had worked on them had labored under a single consciousness. In spite of their threatening numbers, the figures conveyed inextinguishable dignity and grace. How ironic that they had been created to reflect Emperor Qin's view of himself, I thought.

While I pondered this, my mother continued by herself down the slope to the farthest point jutting over the pit. There, she stood as though at the bow of a ship, directly above the first row of advancing warriors. By now the sun had climbed in the sky so that the shaft of light from the gap in the canopy shone directly on her. I was struck by how my mother blended with the elements of the tomb, yet remained somehow distinct. She seemed to straddle both time and being, standing half in antiquity and the present, half as clay figure and woman. Poised on this cusp, she embodied all the mystery and power of the site, her stillness reflecting a life as powerful and individualistic as those represented by the clay warriors below. It seemed natural for her to preside over everything, like an empress. I stared at her, transfixed in awe, until she abruptly turned and waved. This simple, ordinary gesture shattered the spell, turning the figure back into my mother. She climbed up the path toward Dr. Liang and me. It was only when she stood before us

again that I saw she was mere flesh and blood. Even then, she seemed transformed to me in some elemental way.

"What's the matter?" she asked, peering into my face. "You look like you
see a ghost."

At that moment we were interrupted by the first group of tourists de-
scending down the slope. There were about forty Americans and Canadi-
ans, yawning from being roused from their hotel beds, making jokes about
boogeymen and broken pottery. We met them just as they arrived at the rim
of the pit and were beginning to *ooh* and *ah* at the terra-cotta figures below.
Bringing up the rear was their guide from the China Travel Agency, a
frazzled-looking woman who kept up a barrage of warnings through her
megaphone: "Don't get too close! No smoking! Don't fall!"

I approached a middle-aged man, an American from the looks of his
Looney Tunes T-shirt.

"Where did you come from?" I asked.

He looked at me, startled. "Bal-ti-more," he pronounced carefully.

"Sorry," I said, realizing that he thought I was a native, taken aback that
I spoke English. "I mean, is this your first stop in China? Where did you just
come from?"

"Oh, Beijing," he said, pulling out a handkerchief to swab his face.
"Jesus it's hot."

"Beijing?" I felt like falling at his feet, as before a messenger from the
oasis.

"Yeah. Flew in two days ago on the plane from hell. Didn't think we'd
make it."

"How was Beijing?"

"Hot. Like this, maybe worse. Saw the Forbidden Palace, the Great
Wall. She kept us hopping, that's for sure." He looked around furtively,
spotting the guide who harangued members of the group on the other side
of the pit. "My wife got the trots the first day. That orange soda's the pits."

"Tell me more about Beijing," I begged.

"Oh, it was neat. Are you going there?"

"I hope so. We're having trouble getting tickets."

"Really? What tour are you on?"

"We're not on a tour. I came with my mother."

"Hey, that's the way to go. This is our first trip so we thought we'd go on
a tour, you know, where they take care of everything."

"So you've had no trouble with tickets?"

"Nope." He mopped his face again. "Sure could use a cold beer right now, though. Look out. Here she comes."

I turned away just as the CTA guide came up and bawled at the Baltimore man through her megaphone. Though he stumbled down the pit with her at his heels, I felt envious. He had been to Beijing.

For the rest of the morning, we followed Dr. Liang's itinerary to the Hot Springs, where Chiang Kai Shek was captured by the communists, then to the Banpo Museum, situated on a famous prehistorical site. The main attraction in the shabby building was the mummy of a woman in a glass case. The case was scratched and covered with greasy fingerprints, and the mummy within seemed to have fallen on hard times. Strained Chinese budgets hadn't allowed for proper care for her; her shroud was furred with lint, her bones covered with modern-day soot. Her leg bones poked through her burial wrapping, as though someone had carelessly bumped her, unraveling her shroud. Though tourists pressed close to the case, drawn by the mystery of death and at man's obsession with eternity, I turned away. Death was death, rotten and depressing.

After a simple lunch at a people's restaurant, Dr. Liang took us back to our quarters for *xiu shi,* saying he would return at four o'clock. I climbed between the sheets of my bed and fell immediately asleep.

Two hours later, Dr. Liang came by to introduce us to his class of a dozen opthamology students. There were two women among the men. All were bright-looking, shy, and fairly fluent in English. Dr. Liang began the session by asking me about the legislative process in American government. Though the students put on an interested face, I sensed a communal wilt at the topic. I talked about the House, the Senate, what little I knew of Reaganomics, all the while despairing at the light going out of their faces.

"Any questions?" Dr. Liang asked, looking around the room. The students went visibly rigid, clearly frightened that he would call on one of them.

Finally one young man shouted, "How much money do you make?" I looked helplessly at Dr. Liang, who cleared his throat in embarrassment. How was I to say that what I made annually, however modest an amount it was in America, was very likely more than what they would earn their entire lives in China? Hedging, I answered that I made enough to have a comfortable life, leaving out that I owned a house and car. Later, Dr. Liang told me

I needn't have worried, as his students were aware, from magazines and Chinese television, that all Americans lived like movie stars, rattling around in palatial homes with three or four televisions, eating beefsteak every night.

"Any more questions?" I asked.

"What about sports?" someone ventured.

"Sure, sports are big in America," I said. "Baseball, football, basketball, tennis."

Their faces registered polite interest at the mention of the first three, but at the mention of tennis, they lit up.

"Do you play tennis?" Dr. Liang asked.

"Yes," I said, realizing that I had really been missing hitting the ball.

"Our Mr. Liu here is rated number three on the college team," Dr. Liang said, indicating a tall, thin student.

"I didn't bring my racquet," I said, eyeing Liu's wiry build. His eyes had a wolfish gleam to them.

"Oh, we have plenty of racquets. How about a match?"

"Now?" I realized too late how alarmed I sounded. I looked at my mother for help, but she didn't blink. Her eyes had a peculiar shine to them, very much like Number Three Liu's.

"Why not?" Dr. Liang said, cheerfully. "It's the best time of day!"

A half hour later, after I had gone back to our room to change into a pair of walking shorts, Number Three Liu and I faced one another on Xi'an College's tennis court. The packed-dirt surface was hard as concrete, with tufts of weeds and grass growing in the intricate web of cracks, and the net was a tattered rope stretched between two rusted poles. Dr. Liang handed me an old wooden racquet that had somehow survived the war. Compared to my own racquet at home, an oversized, state-of-the art composite frame, the Chinese Spalding felt like a Stone Age club. Number Three Liu and I warmed up a bit, courteously lobbing the ball, which was worn smooth, having survived countless prior matches, back and forth.

By now, word of the match had spread all over the campus so that a large crowd had gathered courtside. Despite the sinking of the afternoon sun the air was so heavy and sultry that my shirt was soaked in a matter of minutes.

"Want to play game?" Number Three Liu called. He sounded friendly enough. The people gathered around clapped and made encouraging sounds. Though I still hadn't gotten used to the club I was using, I felt they deserved more than a casual practice session. "Sure!" I said.

The crowd fell into a hush. Some squatted along the lines and looked across the court with the intensity of spectators at Wimbledon. Number Three Liu insisted that I serve first. Rather than offend my hosts, I agreed. As I walked to the baseline I noticed that more people were trotting across campus to see what was going on. Soon we were completely surrounded.

I started with a three-quarter-speed serve that Number Three Liu smacked down the line for a clean winner. The crowd burst into cheers. *So much for a friendly game,* I thought. Number Three Liu skipped to the ad side of his court, crouched just inside the baseline, and intently awaited my next serve. I cranked up my best serve, aiming it hard and flat into his body. Off my own racquet it is usually an effective serve, at least against players in my women's league at home. Executed with the unwieldy Spalding, it pattered into the opposite court, setting up nicely for Number Three Liu to rifle it back. We rallied through several exchanges, both of us racing madly around the court, until I finally rimmed the ball into the net. I was out of breath, cursing the uneven court and my walking shoes, which offered minimal traction and no lateral support. The crowd cheered wildly for Number Three Liu, who jogged in place, awaiting my next serve looking very much like a Chinese Jimmy Connors. At 0–30 I served again, this time hard, with side spin, and again Number Three Liu whacked it so that I had to lunge just to get it back. A lengthy rally ensued, during which we both hit the ball as hard as we could. Number Three Liu, being stronger and taller, had the definite advantage. Finally I overhit the ball, sending it bouncing off a tree nearby. I lost my serve, and the next two games as well. At the changeover I glanced at my mother, who stood at the opposite end of the court, next to Dr. Liang. She was frowning, clearly disappointed with the way I was flailing ineffectually at Number Three Liu's laser-like shots. As I toweled off with a Chinese towel, which was like cheesecloth, only with larger holes, I glanced her way again. She seemed to be mouthing something, her lips forming what looked like the words "No way." *Thanks a lot, Mom,* I thought.

The match continued. Number Three Liu settled into an unstoppable rhythm, sending the bald black ball over the rope so that it skidded off the court and eluded my frantic lunges for seven consecutive points. At the next changeover, someone handed me a cup of water, which I gulped thirstily. Humiliated, exhausted, I buried my face in the cheesecloth and searched desperately for a way to finish the match with a modicum of self-respect. I sensed the tide overwhelmingly against me, with the crowd cheering with heightened intensity, conveying that what had begun as a friendly exchange had turned into a serious contest of honor between hometown boy and foreign visitor, man and woman, Chinese and American. Now it was a match of cosmic significance. I wiped my face with the cheesecloth one more time and trudged back on the court. Looking across the way I saw that Dr. Tsai had joined Dr. Liang and was talking to him quietly. Both looked worried, in contrast to the rest of the crowd, which was eager for the conclusion of the match. I guessed the doctor and his assistant were upset with Number Three Liu for trouncing me so thoroughly, for treating a guest with such utter disrespect. Perhaps, I thought, they were dismayed at the difference between the generations, between those born before the revolution and those after. Courtesy and political delicacy were the rules for those born before; rank ambition for those born later. I glanced at Number Three Liu to see if he had picked up on his professors' concerns, but he was grinning, bouncing up and down on the balls of his feet, poised to deliver the coup de grace. I wiped my face for the last time, preparing myself for ignominious defeat, then felt someone pinch me hard on the arm. It was my mother, who had made her way down to my end of the court.

"No pace," she whispered hoarsely. "Take pace off. Don't give him anything to hit."

No pace. That was what she had been trying to tell me before, not no way. My mother should know. At her club she was number one in her age group, sixty-fives and up. Whatever competitive drive I had, I had gotten from her. Nodding, I picked up my wooden club and trotted back to the service line.

The score stood at 0–5. Number Three Liu blasted a hard flat serve to my forehand. I blocked the ball, sending it in a high, lazy arc over the net. Number Three Liu rushed up, fixed wild eyes on the floater and smacked it into the next cluster of buildings. He slapped himself on the forehead, muttering, while someone ran to look for the ball. Several minutes later, after the ball was recovered, Number Three Liu served once more and again I blocked the ball back, sending it high into the air with underspin. Number Three Liu danced up to the ball, took his racquet back, and then, stymied by the lazy slow twirl of the ball, plopped it weakly into the net. Now I knew why he was number three, and not number one. He could only play with one pace, fast and hard. Anything else and he couldn't handle it. There were lots of club players like that back home. Opponents who moon-balled, dinked, and spun the ball drove them crazy. My mother had seen right away that I wouldn't be able to beat Number Three Liu at his own game, but that I might have a chance if I could take his game away from him. From then on, I kept the pace off the ball, lobbing softly, sending high-floating loopers into the air. It was not my preferred way of play, and it was not easy hitting the smooth black ball this way, but little by little, as I accumulated points from Number Three Liu's mistakes, we reached the score of 6–6. By this time, Number Three Liu stood heaving on the opposite side of the net, swiping his racquet at clumps of weeds in frustration. Thankfully, at this point Professor Tsai stepped in, and, congratulating us both in flowery terms, declared the match a draw. The crowd, who had witnessed the shift in the match with dismay, seemed relieved with the decision. No one had lost face. Number Three Liu and I shook hands over the net and bowed to appreciative applause.

As the crowd thinned, I saw my mother at the net, bending down for my soggy towel. She shook it several times, snapping the moisture from it, then folded it carefully.

"Here," she said. It was only cheesecloth, but taking it I felt as though I lofted the Wimbledon trophy over my head.

"Thanks, Coach," I said.

That evening, Dr. Tsai invited us to dinner at his house, where he lived with his wife. He entertained us with stories of his experiences during the Cultural Revolution, impressing me again with his command of English and straightforward, humorous manner.

When it grew dark, Xi'an's streetlamps came on, casting eery, greenish rays into the windows of the apartment. Exhausted from my tennis match, I could barely stifle my yawns. Ever the solicitous host, Dr. Tsai announced he would drive us back to our quarters.

"Oh, I almost forgot," he said. He disappeared into the adjoining room and returned with an envelope. "Here are your tickets to Chongqing. From there you will take the Yangtze boat to Wuhan."

My mother accepted the envelope and conferred with the doctor in the regional dialect. Mrs. Tsai joined in. The discussion sounded serious, complicated. I listened carefully but did not catch the word I was hoping to hear. At the end of the conference, Dr. Tsai turned to me. I saw in his eyes that he knew what I was thinking.

"I'm sorry," he said. "I wasn't able to get tickets to Beijing. Perhaps in Wuhan, after your boat trip, or Changsha. There are many helpful people there."

I was too exhausted to react much except to nod. *Whatever happened was fated to be,* I thought. *Best to bend with the wind.* Dr. Tsai took us back to the hospital guest quarters, driving along a road that wound past the outskirts of Xi'an. In the distance, looming and dim, lay the outlines of the Qin Dynasty burial mounds, reminding me again of the frightful human cost of fulfilling the emperor's journey into the afterlife. I tried to imagine the sheer amount of labor, materials, and planning required. In such a context, our situation seemed relatively trivial, however frustrating, and I realized I had actually enjoyed and learned much from the people and experiences along our detour. Still, Beijing seemed farther away than ever. *What else would it take to get there?* I wondered. All I could hope was that sufficient gains could be gotten from modest aims. As we drove beneath the shadows of the silent, towering mounds, I sensed that even this might be too much to hope for, in this land of irony and convoluted fate. I kept my hopes to myself, and watched the burial mounds as we passed in reverential silence.

17

CHONGQING

NEARLY TWO WEEKS HAD GONE BY WITHOUT MY HAVING SENT OR RECEIVED word from Fred. Communication was difficult enough inside China, but trying to get word outside proved virtually impossible except by mail. My mother and I had no telephones in our hotel rooms, there were no booths on the street, and the ones behind the hotel desks were guarded zealously by the clerks. As for other means, I could not see Chinese pigeons making it all the way to Minnesota. Perhaps it was just as well I was and am adverse to talking on the telephone, preferring by far to write letters and e-mail. Even so, the few aerograms I sent to Fred from Xi'an failed to assuage the feeling of being cut off from home and the outside world. The farther my mother and I were drawn inland in China, where cities and villages had fewer and less reliable means of communication, the more isolated and disconnected I became from the life I had known.

Back in America, the investigation of the Iran-Contra affair continued. The Minnesota Twins were on the way to beating the Detroit Tigers for the American League championship. As I wrote Fred's name, great waves of homesickness washed over me, how much I missed his loving and playful companionship, our dog, our friends, our yard with its masses of midsummer dahlias, and Twins games. Perhaps most of all I missed the simple pleasure of talking to Fred in English, of waking and retiring to the murmur of easy expression upon which our lives were based and which I had taken so much for granted. Though I was enjoying and learning so much from being in China, weeks of struggling to speak and understand Mandarin had a cramping, exhausting effect on my brain. Struggle with words led to struggle with thoughts, and that led to a wilting of the spirit. With each week, the gap in the life I had left behind and my ongoing Chinese experience grew so that it seemed insurmountable, especially when I tried to bridge it in the form of an aerogram weighing less than an ounce and which took its fluttery time getting from here to there.

Deprived of communication and contact, I found it difficult to comprehend how people, time, and events on the far side of the planet advanced concurrently in their own continuum. On blind faith, I wrote Fred telling him how my mother and I had strayed from our original itinerary and that I hoped to catch up with whatever letters he had sent me in Beijing, where he would have assumed me to be by now, leaving out the part that I believed I was marooned in China forever and that it would take a miracle before I thought I would ever see him again. After recovering from that melodramatic spasm, I wrote a telegram to Aunt Lucy telling her of our projected route, signing it, TAKE CARE. This seemed wholly inadequate when I really meant, *please stay alive,* as the latest news in the *Herald Tribune* was that the heat wave in Beijing had gotten worse and was not expected to abate for at least another week.

The morning after the tennis match, Dr. Tsai drove us to the Xi'an airport, where we climbed aboard a rickety-looking prop plane bound for Chongqing. The flight was smooth, made memorable only by the odd little toys and candies flung at us by the flight crew before takeoff. We landed a few hours later and boarded a bus which took us up the steep, winding road toward the city.

Chiseled directly into the side of a mountain, the road traversed a steep gorge. On the near vertical sides were small villages and fields looking as though they had been cut in the rock like facets on a diamond. The left shoulder of the road dropped abruptly into a deep chasm at the bottom of which the Yangtze River twisted like a dusky, twisted rope. Our bus climbed laboriously for an hour before it swerved around a forty-five-degree turn, crossed a narrow bridge over the gorge, then coursed down the hill into Chongqing itself.

The city's ancient, crumbling structures sprawled over iron-stained rock like a colony of barnacles clinging to a shipwreck. As we drew closer, I made out wooden huts covered with bits of canvas buttressed upon frail thickets of bamboo poles. Here the Yangtze River fanned into a broad sweeping

plain of silt-laden water, shallow enough so that the city's structural foundation, stained verdigris and reeking of rot and decay, took tenuous hold.

Enormous tourist boats, portholes weeping rust, plied up and down the
river, past factories at the river's edge which spewed smoke and flushed brilliant poisonous streams into the water. The dark, moss-green atmosphere
was acrid with the stench of primitive gases and coal smoke. If not for the
factories, I would have believed we had entered a giant, prehistoric fen.
There was an ominous feel to the place, as though things which ought to
have died out had somehow survived in grotesquely mutated form. I felt
strangely excited and afraid.

We got off the bus in the center of the city, near narrow, dirt-packed
alleyways crowded with pedestrians and vendors. Laborers trudged along
carrying baskets of bricks and stones, balancing them on shoulders streaming with sores. People dressed in drab blue shirts and trousers scurried
about with a no-nonsense, irascible demeanor, as though they knew they
were centuries behind and had little chance of catching up. The stench of
human waste was stupefying.

In the midst of the confusion, it was a miracle that my mother's contact,
Sun Ai E, managed to find us. My mother had written her months ago, informing her of our visit to China. Dr. Tsai had wired her from Xi'an, telling
her of our early arrival in Chongqing. We were lucky she was still able to receive us on such short notice.

Sun Ai E stood four feet ten, had lost all but one of her teeth, and was
growing out a disastrous Chinese perm so that her hair grew straight up
from the roots in a three-inch corona of ferociously fried hair. This fiery halo
gave her the look of a woman in a constant, blistering rage. Bluntly, without
ceremony, she told us to follow her, and walked away briskly without waiting for a reply.

We followed her up a steep maze of steps to a cluster of stucco buildings
that perched atop the city like a rookery. Although newer than the wooden
structures below, the place already had a decrepit look. The walls, with their
mosaic of cracks and fissures, looked like crushed eggshell. Children popped
from every corner, shrieking and tearing about. Entering her apartment, Sun
Ai E dragged wooden chairs across the bare concrete floor for my mother and
me to sit on. We made aimless small talk, in the way of people acquainted
solely through a third party, my mother's oldest brother, John.

Sun Ai E lit a cigarette and squinted through the smoke, speaking English in clipped tones. It became obvious that she disdained chitchat and assessed my mother and me as a nuisance she would have to tolerate for a long evening. As we talked, I heard voices from neighboring apartments as well as clinking pots and running water. Finally, during another lull in the conversation, I asked Sun Ai E about her life in Chongqing. Her expression brightened.

"I direct an actors' troupe," she declared. "Before the war, we put on classic plays, original material that I wrote. We were artists." She paused, stubbing out her cigarette before immediately lighting another. "Then the Cultural Revolution came. I was sent to work in a factory, inspecting bullets." She paused, then said with mirthless understatement, "It was not a good time." Sun Ai E inhaled her cigarette as though it were a lifeline, then continued, "After the revolution, I directed propaganda plays for the People's Liberation. In return, they gave me this apartment." She waved her cigarette to indicate the four walls around her in a gesture of mock gratitude. At this point a man, whose bony face and protruding ears reminded me of Kafka, came into the room.

"My son," Sun Ai E stated listlessly. "He doesn't speak English."

Her son shook hands with us politely. Calling out into the hallway, he coaxed a heavyset young woman to enter the room.

"His wife," Sun Ai E said, not bothering with her daughter-in-law's name.

A little boy, around three years old, rushed into the room, slapping the woman on the ankles with a stick.

"Their brat," Sun Ai E explained, narrowing her eyes at the boy, who, no dummy, kept his mother positioned between himself and his grandmother.

A folding table was produced, and we pulled up our chairs as the daughter-in-law brought dishes of *jiaoze,* deep-fried fish in brown sauce, steamed pork balls rolled in rice, stuffed eggplant, eggs and tomatoes, and soup with slippery mushrooms. Sun Ai E did not touch her plate but smoked throughout the meal, keeping baleful eyes on her grandson who lunged and grabbed fistfuls of food, howling when either parent made half-hearted attempts to control him.

"Do you have children?" Sun Ai E asked me abruptly.

"N . . . No," I stammered.

"Good!" she snapped. "If I had my life to live over again, I wouldn't have children, either."

I guessed that her son truly did not know English, as he showed no reaction to his mother's pronouncement.

Halfway through the meal, another woman came into the room. Seeing her, Sun Ai E's eyes grew almost tender.

"My daughter," she explained. Clamping her cigarette between her gums, she heaped food onto a plate for the younger woman, who made no attempt at conversation, but ate silently, with downcast eyes. She seemed worn out and depressed.

"All my children were sent down to the countryside during the Cultural Revolution," Sun Ai E said. "Nineteen-sixty-eight. Nearly twenty years ago." She exhaled a plume of smoke. "Only recently has my daughter been allowed to go to school to catch up on her education. She has to go at night, because of her job. It's been nearly three years now, eh?"

Intent on her soup, her daughter did not respond.

The daughter-in-law stood up, began noisily to pile the plates. Her face expressed nothing, but her raucous actions made her resentment clear.

"She has no education," Sun Ai E remarked, squinting at her daughter-in-law through the smoke. "But her family has money. Her little brat will have a better life than his father."

Sun Ai E's son shifted uneasily in his chair. Though he might not have understood his mother's words, I suspected that he was all too familiar with her tone.

"What does your son do?" I asked.

"Works in a factory," Sun Ai E said. "Makes bottles." She laughed, a bitter-sounding retort. "He serves his country well!"

The little boy climbed on his chair, placed a chubby knee on the table, and reached for the plate of pork balls. His grandmother snatched up a chopstick and rapped him sharply on the knuckles. He shrieked and began to roll around the table, sending the remaining dishes and chopsticks everywhere. His mother rushed over to pick him up. The boy kicked violently, thudding blows against her stomach. She tucked him under her arm and, glaring defiantly at her mother-in-law, grabbed a pork ball and fed it to her son, who gobbled it tearfully. Sun Ai E turned to me, her eyes glittering. "When you go back to America," she said, "tell them, in China, everybody is happy."

By now night had fallen so that we sat in the dark. The only light in the room was the glowing end of Sun Ai E's cigarette. She clenched it between her lips as she spoke, and I watched it go up and down, illuminating the deep terrain of hardship on her face. She never spoke of her husband. Later, my mother told me he had been killed in the war. Sun Ai E had raised her children alone, only to have them taken away to the countryside during the revolution. It was then I began to appreciate another meaning to her harsh statement about not wanting children.

"It will be another hour before the city lights come on," Sun Ai E said. She took a candle stub from the desk drawer, lit it with her cigarette, tipped it so that a blob of wax dripped on the desk, then stuck the candle there. She sat next to the desk so that the candle shone on half her face, giving it a mysterious, gloomy cast. She asked me if I liked drama, and when I nodded she talked about the Greek classics and the plays of Chekhov and Strindberg.

"I've always wanted to stage *The Cherry Orchard,*" she said. "Such nuance of character, such complexity! But then, what would be the point? It would never get past the censors here. They don't tolerate anything smelling of individual will, can't understand that people, even characters in a play, would dare think independent thoughts or entertain notions of romantic love. How subversive, they would think. How unpatriotic!"

"Haven't people protested?" I asked naively, ignoring my mother's warning look. "What about students?"

Sun Ai E looked at me closely, seeming to regard me in a different light. She looked as though about to say something, but changed her mind. She stubbed out her cigarette violently, pulled another from her pocket, and lit it. I was shocked that she spoke with such open disdain for the Chinese system. According to my research, government policies were more liberal now in that people were more free to express themselves, but Chinese history had always been one of tides that turned suddenly and viciously upon themselves. People were encouraged to speak then punished for openly expressing their thoughts. According to my friend Evan's report, Chinese students were growing bolder, but it was clear that Sun Ai E's view was that the tides had already carried her out to sea and that she was beyond caring. We sat in the candlelit gloom, feeling her mood burn as bitter and acrid as her cheap cigarette. Then, abruptly, she stood up. "I'll walk with you to your hotel. We'll go by the park. You can see the lights from there."

We descended the stairs into the hot, steamy streets, where people still hurried along the dirt-packed alleyways. Unlike Shanghai's active and bright nightlife filled with vendors and leisurely strolling citizens, Chongqing was stifled, muted, shifting about restlessly in search of relief. In the city park, we watched people dragging straw mats across the ground, arranging makeshift beds. Sun Ai E explained they came to escape their crowded apartments, the stench of the toilets, and the stultifying heat. People lay end to end talking quietly, smoking, the lighted ends of their cigarettes winking in the darkness like lightning bugs. We walked around the perimeter of the park, listening to the collective human murmur. All at once, the lights of the city came on, bathing everything in a watery, greenish glow. Drawn to the light like moths, children crowded beneath streetlamps to play jacks and twirl tops. Adults gathered there to gossip or finish chores begun during the day. One woman squatted over a plastic tub of live frogs. Using a pair of scissors, she snipped off their legs one by one for the next day's meal.

The hotel at which Sun Ai E had booked us a room turned out to be the former Russian Embassy, situated on a street where trolleys ran silently without lights to conserve electricity. I assumed they were empty because of their darkened interiors but as they passed, I glimpsed people silhouetted inside. Meanwhile, pedestrians continued to scurry through the streets, their shuffling shadows lending the city the air of a ghostly evacuation.

Sun Ai E promised she would send a telegram to alert our contact in Wuhan of our progress, then shook hands with my mother and me and disappeared. We entered the hotel to a shocking blast of air-conditioning, bright lights, and music, into a thickly carpeted lobby that was festooned with faux Baroque chandeliers. Caucasians wearing stylish linen and khaki outfits mingled about, speaking in French and German. My mother and I went to our room on the seventh floor, where I opened the window to look out at the city below.

I imagined Sun Ai E walking back to her apartment, alone, wondering how it was that she came by her love for Strindberg, Chekhov, and Eugene O'Neill. Probably in the same way Aunt Lucy came by her passion for the works of Nathaniel Hawthorne and Mark Twain, the music of Schubert. In both women, curiosity and passion had risen above politics, social convention, prejudice, and geographic distance. Neither accepted the notion of eminent domain or the narrow confines of intellectual origin or identity. For them, the Russians had no exclusive claim on Chekhov, nor Austrians on Mozart. I stared out at the green pall of Chongqing, feeling fortunate to have met Sun Ai E. Perhaps, rather than return to her bleak apartment, she had stopped to linger a while in the park. Undoubtedly there were more souls like her who wandered the city, their hearts bursting. I wished it were otherwise for people living in this city, where every hour seemed like twilight.

At five o'clock the next morning, when it was still dark, our alarm rang and my mother sprang out of bed. I stumbled after her down to the hotel lobby, where a taxi waited. Minutes later we stood at the top of the hill a hundred yards or so above the dock where our Yangtze River boat waited. All around us other passengers kicked boxes and bags down the slope. Rain had begun to fall, muddying the ground and making it slippery going on the steep grade. A man dressed in rags rushed up, grabbing our suitcases. I yelled at him and tried to push him away, thinking he was a bandit, but my mother, her face fixed in its forebearing look of experience, handed him a few *renmenbi*—old Chinese money, fifty cents at most—to carry our bags down to the dock. Here it was complete mayhem, with passengers rushing every which way, jostling crewmen who hoisted huge supply crates onto the boat decks. In one horrible moment one of the crates slipped from its ropes and crashed into the river, spewing water and drenching everyone on the dock. In spite of the chaos, my mother and I managed to find our boat among the three moored there. It took us several turns around the deck and up and down narrow stairways to locate our cabin, a closet-sized space with two bunks and a metal sink the size of a teacup. A stream of rusty water gushed from the faucet and wouldn't stop no matter which way I cranked the handle.

It turned out the boat was not due to leave for another two hours, so my mother suggested we try to sleep. I spread my jacket over the grimy sheet on the upper bunk and dozed fitfully, half listening to the noise of banging metal and shouting that continued to reverberate throughout the boat.

Sometime past eight o'clock, my mother and I sensed a different rhythm and went up on deck, where we discovered we had left port and were chugging down the river. The ship's engines emitted powerful, rhythmic vibrations that, for the next three days, were to become as much a part of me as my own heartbeat. We came to the viewing deck, an oval-shaped glass enclosure at the bow of the ship. The carpeted interior was furnished with upholstered chairs and dining tables laid with an elegant service for coffee and tea. My mother and I mingled with the other first-class passengers, tour groups from Israel and Belgium, Dutch schoolgirls on holiday, and three or four couples traveling independently. Sliding doors from this area led to an outer viewing deck, where, in spite of the rain, other passengers leaned against safety ropes to admire the view. Among them were three young Germans wearing mountaineering outfits who pointed excitedly at the sights along the riverbanks.

While my mother became acquainted with other passengers in the viewing area, I went out on deck, choosing a spot on the bow a respectful distance from the Germans. From here I watched the boat cleave through water which was dense, molten-looking, thick with silt and swirling in deep, treacherously shifting currents. Looking up at the mountainside, peering through the mist, I saw huts, crop fields, mile-long waterfalls and delicate-looking pagodas that poked up between gaps in the rock like tiny teeth. Tracing the verdant areas below were complex trails which I guessed were used by farmers and goatherds. Theirs was a harsh life, I imagined, but one that seemed strangely pure in its simplicity and remoteness. I wondered what it was like to live in perpetual struggle with the rock and gravity, which could easily pull one off the mountainside into the river. There were no telephone wires, roads, or a glimmer of electricity anywhere on the mountain that I could see, which left me to wonder whether people here knew of a world beyond the river.

Again, I felt that I had been transported back in time. Even the color of green, on the hills seemed brighter, more pure, and the smell of the earth itself, pungent from the dampness, primordially organic. Other tourists gathered on the deck to videotape the scenery, exclaim at the waterfalls. And then everyone fell quiet. I was stunned by the sense that the river took us to the precise spot where the past merged with the present. People lowered their cameras and stood in communal awe, the kind I have witnessed in concert halls by audiences inspired by music. We remained wide-eyed, wordless, as though filled with wonder at the possibility that the future, formerly so important and urgent to us modern people, suddenly seemed meaningless.

The chiming of a bell, announcing lunch, abruptly brought us back to reality. Eating with silverware, chatting in English, seemed wholly incongruous acts on this ancient river. Chinese waiters wearing the official white-and-gold uniform of the cruise line patiently answered questions about our boat, informing us that the ship was filled to capacity with more than three hundred passengers. It had three separate decks, multiple kitchens, and several lifeboats secured starboard and aft. Looking around the dining room, I counted the heads of first-class tourists: thirty-eight. If the boat was filled, then where were all the other passengers?

Later that afternoon, I went back on the outer deck, where it was still raining lightly. A thick fog swathed the mountains on either side of the boat, which pierced the river with a roaring, hissing sound so loud that the few passengers there gave up trying to shout over it. My thoughts turned to my *History of China* book and its description of the Yangtze River. Throughout the centuries it inexplicably jumped its banks to flood entire villages, killing thousands of people, giving rise to the belief that the Yangtze possessed a life of its own. In its dual role as source of life as well as ruthless killer, the river dominated the psyche of the Chinese people in the way of the most powerful despot. Recalling this, I backed away from the rope barrier. Looking directly into the face of the river seemed an act of reckless transgression. I grasped the rope tightly as I made my way back inside, trying to convince myself that there were scientific explanations for why the river abruptly shifted course. Surely, nature did not endow it with a demonic personality. I told myself that modern technology tempered the might of the Yangtze, that boats like the one I was on carved innumerable paths through the water, dividing the heavy yellow waves to render them harmless.

That night for dinner we enjoyed dishes of spicy chicken, red roast duck, fried pork with preserved vegetables, stir-fried green beans, tofu with red peppers, steamed fish with black bean sauce, eggplant with garlic, steamed bread, rice, beer, and, of course, orange soda. While the soy sauce used by the ship's cook was saltier than what I was used to, I hardly minded, since the preparation of the dishes was superb and the green tea at the end of the meal seemed to neutralize the salt. I ate and drank more than usual, including a large bottle of delicious Chinese beer.

Afterward, shyly at first, people began to sing songs. Some of the folk songs from Israel, Germany, Norway, and Russia were sad, expressing loneliness and loss. The looks people exchanged, even among those who had been initially cool toward one another, grew meaningful and intimate. Despite the unrelenting rain and gloom of the river outside, the mood inside grew expansive and warm.

My mother sang several Chinese folk tunes, which everyone found delightful, clamoring for more. Then my mother's new friends asked her to tell her life story. Touched by their interest, my mother complied, relating the story of her bomb and how she ran the hundred-meter hurdles while seven months' pregnant with my sister. This moved others to tell their stories. Within an hour, everyone was smitten by the kind of love affecting strangers filled with good food and drink and confined momentarily in close quarters. Glancing at my mother, I saw what an inspiration she was to everyone. I was struck by how getting to know her was to know a vital part of myself, and that she had been there for me all along, like eyeglasses I'd been searching for that had been right on my face the whole time.

We laughed and sang and told stories until the ship's bell chimed twelve o'clock when my mother and I bid our new friends good night, expressing the shared hope that the next morning would bring sunshine and a clear view of the famous Three Gorges.

I fell asleep quickly in my narrow, gritty bunk but woke up hours later with a raging thirst and the need to find a bathroom. Careful not to wake my mother, I put a jacket over my nightshirt and went out into the dimly lit corridor. No one else was in sight. Not even a crewman. *Strange way to run a ship,* I thought. I climbed down a staircase, went through another corridor, a series of twists and turns. At this point, I knew I should have been on the crew deck, but there were no doors, no sounds of life. The place was completely empty. Now I knew I was lost. Fighting panic, I decided to go back the way I came, but after a few more uncertain turns, stopped. Nothing looked familiar now.

I felt the bass-toned throb of the ship's engines travel up my legs, which only stimulated the need, already urgent, to find a bathroom. Reaching the end of the corridor, I turned left and miraculously found myself at a large communal bathroom. Moments later, sighing with relief, I re-entered the hallway to get my bearings. Before I could think of my return path, I saw a steep staircase immediately to my right which I had not noticed before. A faint light radiated from it, and though a warning went off in my head not to go there, curiosity led me to descend, following the sound of a dull throbbing that emanated from the very heart of the ship. The stairs seemed to go on forever, deeper and deeper into the depths of the hold.

Finally, reaching the bottom rung, I looked around and saw that I was in a huge space the size of a stadium that was completely filled with people. Rather than ringing with the clamor of excited fans, this place was eerily quiet. All along the walls people lay piled practically on top of one another in layered bunks. Most were small, sunburnt men with angular faces, wearing filthy rags, looking half-dead from exhaustion. At first I was afraid, since I had no idea how the men would react to me. I was relieved when the few who saw me registered only mild interest and went back to sleep or smoking their thick, hand-made cigarettes.

Elsewhere, illuminated by the flickering light of kerosene lamps hanging here and there in the hold, women and children lay dozing on filthy straw scattered about the floor. Bales of hay, cabbages, and melons were heaped everywhere as were piles of garbage. In the shadowy recesses, chickens clucked from wire cages. One had gotten loose and pecked at the feet of a tethered goat which stared with glassy eyes. I could hardly breathe from the reek of unwashed human bodies, excrement, and rotting vegetables.

Resounding throughout the metal hull was the relentless pounding of the ship's engines, which caused my head to ache. I wondered how it was possible that people were made to stay here, where it was like the inside of a colossal bell, the incredible concussion like that of a giant metal clapper pounding directly on one's skull.

I heard a shout above me. A ship's officer, climbing down the stairwell, grabbed me by my jacket collar. I felt his knuckle dig into my neck and the hot spray of spittle in my face as he shouted furious, incomprehensible threats while hauling me up the steps. I was petrified, but something in the tone of his voice conveyed, along with his fury, that he was as shocked and afraid to see me as I him, which helped me decide, at that instant, to try to escape.

I knew the rumors of how Chinese treated their prisoners, and I wasn't going to wait to see if he would have me thrown in jail, or tossed overboard. As soon as we reached the top of the stairs, I lunged, twisting away to break his hold. Before he recovered himself, I scrambled away into the maze of corridors. I was so astonished and relieved to be free that I ran through the corridors blindly, blundering through turns, up and down stairs, through doorways, not waiting to see if he followed, until incredibly I found myself inside the first-class viewing salon. Here in the semidarkness I made out the shapes of the dining tables, which were set for the next day's breakfast. I collapsed in an upholstered chair to catch my breath, waiting for my heart to stop pounding. I noticed that here the throb of the engines was barely noticeable, a mere gentle, lulling pulsation.

Though I felt safe for the time being, I couldn't help thinking of the people in the hold and the face of the enraged officer. I wondered how it was possible to feel ashamed and relieved at the same time, how I could sit here in the posh lounge while hundreds of peasants were crammed in abominable conditions in the hull. Hadn't the Chinese government abolished the class system? Hadn't the communist party boasted of its emancipation of the proletariat? Regardless of the official line, the faces of the people in the hold told otherwise. Now I understood the look of fury and alarm on the officer's face. I had witnessed firsthand the stupendous lie perpetrated by his government.

18

YANGTZE

SHUDDERING BLASTS SPLIT THE AIR ONCE, TWICE, STARTLING ME AWAKE. I SAT up and stared groggily about the cabin. The door opened and my mother appeared, fully dressed.

"Hurry up! We go in first gorge!"

As I dressed and clambered up the staircase behind her, the ship's horn sounded again, rocking the air with a percussive effect so violent I clapped my hands over my ears. All the other first-class passengers were already gathered on the viewing deck, rushing from one side to the other as they vied for the best vantage point. I joined the three German boys at the bow who trained their binoculars on the cliffs above. Shafts of morning sun pierced the thick condensation here and there, but were quickly smothered by gray banks of fog that rolled down the mountainsides.

"How much farther?" I asked the nearest German boy.

"The steward said fifteen minutes," he replied, lowering his binoculars. "Look! Down there!"

River craft, launched from the last village at the mouth of the gorge, sur-rounded our boat on all sides. The boats, like Chinese road vehicles, were makeshift structures of wood, metal, and canvas to which rudimentary diesel engines were lashed. No bigger than canoes, they bobbed in the waves like corks, their barefoot helmsmen, some dangling precariously over the water, hauling at the rudders. Buffeted by the clashing currents, a few boats veered so close they barely avoided slamming into the ship. I could think of no reason why they should come so near except out of curiosity, or to escort us like dolphins. Close to shore, barely visible in the fog, larger wooden boats looking like Dutch shoes cast from the village yawed in the waves.

More thunderous blasts sounded from the ship, alerting us to the fact that we headed into the first gorge, a ragged cleft between two sheer, dizzying, vertical walls of stone. A stubborn veil of mist hung here so that the rocky promontories, heavily streaked with mica, became visible only when sporadic wind gusts cleared the condensation. That the awesome face of the mountain was unmasked solely at the whim of the winds lent it greater power and mystery. I thought how easy it was to fall sway to the gorge's mystique as a place where Chinese sailors, lured by the mountain in the way Odysseus's men were seduced by the sirens, crashed to their deaths.

Suddenly, a huge rogue wave slammed the side of the boat, making it shudder. Knocked off balance, I barely managed to grab a guard rope as I fought to regain my footing on the slippery wet deck. I slid and flopped along the deck, hauling desperately at the rope to right myself against the powerful wind and the recoil of the boat as it was pounded by waves sweeping from one side of the gorge to the other. Blinded by icy particles lashing my face, soaked by cold water, I felt my hands grow stiff, numb. My throat filled with terror that I would lose my grip on the rope and be swept into the river. I imagined the impending crush of rock and water, the leap of my heart at the moment the wind and waves tore me from myself. I feared the heartless river had again turned fate on its head. It was not Aunt Lucy who would die, or the Beijing house that would fall, but I who would perish, here on the Yangtze, fulfilling the karmic edict of my family that I would never set foot in Yeh Yeh's house. In mindless defiance, I leaned straight into the wind, over the edge of the bow toward the magnetic core of the cliffs, my terror giving over to exhilarated surrender and utter detachment from the universe and everything that I had known. Another colossal wave struck the boat, drenching me totally. It was as though the river itself claimed me with such ferocity of will that I let go of the rope. For an instant, I was free-floating, completely at the mercy of the wind and the water. I saw the river loom up to claim me. Before I could give myself up altogether, one of the German boys grabbed my arm and hauled me back onto the deck. The look on his face was one of absolute horror, as though, against his better judgment, he had gotten ahold of a crazy person. "Thanks, I'm okay," I said. Looking around, dazed, I realized that he and I were the only passengers still on deck. The others had taken refuge in the viewing lounge, watching through the glass, their expressions mirroring the boy's. When I got to the door, my mother snatched me inside.

"What were you doing?" she demanded shrilly. From the look on her face, I saw she was badly frightened.

I shook my head, still in shock.

"You're soaked!" she scolded.

"I . . . I was looking at the gorge," I stammered, then stopped, unable to explain my near plunge into the river.

"Go change!" she commanded.

I went down to our cabin, put on dry clothes, and collapsed on my bunk to think about what had happened. A skeptic might claim that I had simply gotten light-headed or that I had tasted the mindless thrill that came of risk and danger. But I knew that something in the electric atmosphere of the gorge had in its ruthless, primordial way, stripped me clear to the bone. In the wild spray of wind and water, I heard the mountain call my name, one that I had never heard before, but one given to me by a source more ancient and true than that bestowed by my parents or grandparents. If asked today what that name is, I cannot say that it is even a word, but rather an instinctive sense of belonging. Hearing it, I felt an immediate sense of legitimacy as though I had finally stumbled on my true heritage.

The ship's horn sounded again, signaling our approach to the second gorge. Returning to the deck, I saw that heavy rain was falling now. The ship stewards had closed the outer viewing deck, and all passengers were looking at the gorge from within.

The second gorge was framed by several sheer peaks, taller and more narrow than those in the first gorge so that they looked like a line of jagged teeth set along the jaw of the river. Heavy mist swirled down from the peaks, revealing extreme summits that looked like those of the Himalayan range. Though impressed and awed, I felt a slight disappointment. Viewing the peaks from this safe place, behind glass, in the company of other people was not the same. I missed the naked, electrical charge of the air, the shock of the water, the feeling of exposure and danger. I longed for the physical proximity to the mountains, the icy wind of the peaks on my face.

Perhaps it is human nature to tire eventually even of miracles. As though in anticipation of this, the crew served lunch directly upon the boat's exit from the second gorge, setting out a sumptuous buffet of delectable Shanghai dishes. The passengers ate as though starved. Though conversation was of the gorges, their impact clearly had weakened. In the way people talk about art they view in museums, the passengers' own opinions and perspectives began to occupy them more than what they had seen. The German boys declared that as fantastic as the Yangtze peaks were they could not possibly compare with the Alps. The only other American aboard besides my mother and me, a cardiologist, claimed that the Grand Canyon was still the world's preeminent natural site.

Toward the end of the meal, when the stewards announced the ship's approach to the third and final gorge, people rose halfway from their chairs to look out the window. Seeing only the gentle sloping shoulders of hills dotted with farms and crops, a familiar vista, they turned their attention to dessert. I slipped out the doors onto the boat deck. The rain had stopped and was replaced by brilliant sunshine which streamed through gaps in the few remaining clouds, causing a fine vapor to rise up from the deck. Here the stretch of the river was calm, a serene postlude to the gorges as well as the approach to the city of Wuhan around the bend. The water looked translucent, green, its surface wrinkled with gentler eddies. Off to the port side, I spotted a large black-and-red flower floating. A peony, I thought, or poppy. Strange for the river to be so ornamented, I thought, moving along the rope in order to have a closer look. Then I saw that the flower had a head of black hair, the red was a pair of gym shorts, and that the flower was the body of a drowned man.

The sly river, as though to show off what it had snared, brought the body even closer to the ship. The splayed arms and legs of the man bobbed so that he looked as if he was sculling, taking a momentary pause from death to explore the river. Facedown, he might have been searching for something on the bottom. Who was he? A jogger who had accidentally fallen into the river? Strange that he wore no shoes. It occurred to me that people don't jog in China, that jogging was viewed as an activity of the leisure class, and, as such, wholly anti-proletariat. Possibly, he was a tourist from another tour boat who had fallen overboard. I stared at the mysterious body, which performed lazy, lateral cartwheels on the surface of the languid river current, until I became aware that someone approached me on deck.

I turned to face a man dressed in a green government uniform. During the trip I had glimpsed other such men, assuming they were assigned by the government to marshal river journeys. In a polite but firm manner, he asked to see my passport. I went down to our cabin and brought back my passport, certain that the ship's officer of the night before had reported me and that I was about to be punished. Several moments went by as the marshal paged through my passport. Reaching the final page he frowned, as though he had come upon incriminating evidence. Grasping for any distraction that might divert his attention, I said, as calmly as I could, "There's a body down there."

Pursing his lips, the official gazed at the horizon, which I took as an indication he didn't care, or was already well aware of the fact.

"There's a dead man in the river," I repeated.

The man glanced down in spite of himself. The hands of the body, caught in the waves lapping from the boat, moved up and down, as though waving hello.

I didn't dare say more. The uniformed man searched my face, feeling me out. He held my passport in his hand, casually, as though it were a deck of cards.

"What you doing here in China?" he demanded. His question could not have made its mark on me any more neatly than if it had been a knife at my throat. How could he have known this had been my own inquiry throughout my trip, that this question was as fixed before me as though it was the guiding hand on a compass? What, indeed, was I doing here but looking for myself, for clues, remnants of my ancestors that might inform me how to live? How was I to admit to him the self-centered nature of my quest?

"Why you come to China?" he barked.

"To see my family!" I said.

"Where?"

"Shanghai, Beijing."

"Then why you on Yangtze cruise?"

"I . . . we got delayed . . . we're sight-seeing."

"Who we?"

I hesitated, fearing to implicate my mother, but then I realized she was my only true representation, and besides, the official was bound to find out anyway. "My mother," I said. "She's Chinese, born here," I ended lamely.

The official's scowl indicated that his suspicions lingered.

"Unfortunate," he said, finally, looking out at the river.

What was unfortunate? I thought. That I had seen the body floating in the river? That I had stumbled down the hold of the ship? That I searched for myself in China? What?

Slowly, making a point, the official put my passport in his pocket. Then, before I could protest, he turned on his heel and left the deck. What now? What was I to do without my passport?

I looked over the side of the boat at the drowned man, as though he might have an answer, but he only floated there, waving, looking carefree, even lazy now that he had departed this life. It occurred to me that dead bodies in the Yangtze might not be uncommon, that, once they were taken by the river, all other claims, whether by government or family, were forfeited. All at once, I saw Chinese bureaucracy as a gigantic drift net, snaring the innocent as well as intended prey.

Not knowing what else to do, I went back to the salon, where my mother sat knitting. Though I had resolved to say nothing of what had happened, the first thing that came out of my mouth was, "I saw a dead man in the river."

My mother responded with her well-worn look. Naturally, she was not at all surprised.

"I think I'm in trouble!" I blurted, close to crying.

She put down her knitting. Her look of concern, so unpracticed, was nearly comical. "Why? What happened?"

I told her about the government official.

"It's probably nothing," my mother said, returning to her knitting. She was making a cap for one of my nieces, "Why would they bother with us small fish?"

I knew she was probably right, but doubts lingered. I had not told her Evan's story of his arrested acquaintance and could not shake the worry of having my passport confiscated.

After a sleepless night, I woke up to the third day of our boat trip. The sun shone bright and hot. The river was so calm the ship sliced through it as though it were molten glass. At breakfast, conversation among the passengers was understated and desultory. Most were looking forward to the end of the trip. A few, tired of boat life and scenery, talked of skipping the scheduled tour of Wuhan and taking a flight directly to Shanghai, where they could shop and enjoy lively nightlife. Since we had gone through the gorges and no other spectacular sights lay on the horizon, the day promised to be monotonous and long. After breakfast, I lingered on the deck, writing aimlessly in my journal while keeping an eye out for the official with my passport. I hadn't seen my mother since breakfast and assumed she was either visiting with her new friends or strolling about the ship.

While scribbling in my journal, my pen ran out of ink, and I went to our cabin to get another, pausing when I heard what sounded like laughter and strange music within. I opened the door to find my mother surrounded by several men who crouched on the floor of our tiny cabin. They were small and wiry and exuded a smell I remembered from the hold of the ship. Seeing me, they smiled and pointed to my mother, who sat on her bunk playing duets on her recorder with one of their companions, a man who played a crude-looking bamboo flute. My mother had packed her recorder in her blue bag but had not had a chance to play it until now. She raised her eyes to acknowledge me but was plainly absorbed in an elaborate improvisation with the peasant.

There is the expression, "The soul rides the breath," but I had never seen it exemplified until I heard this man play his primitive, handmade flute. He seemed to be in a kind of trance, his eyes opened but unseeing, fixed on some inner impulse. As he played, his eyelids fluttered in rapid, spasmodic movements, showing the whites of his eyes in the way of a mystic in a state of ecstasy. His lips were cracked and swollen from the sun, revealing, as he played, rotted stumps of teeth. Bobbing his head to the driving rhythms of the song, he moved his thick, calloused fingers over the keyholes with astounding delicacy and finesse. His right foot, which was entirely blackened with grime, pounded the floor in emphatic rhythms while his other foot hovered in the air, trembling from the exertions of his body and soul. The sounds he made were explosive, bursting from his gut, and were so harsh and shrill that I was tempted to cover my ears. His song expressed struggle and defiance and maddened joy, and as I listened I thought that nowhere, whether on concert stage or elsewhere, had I witnessed a more compelling performance. My mother made accompanying sounds on her recorder, but then the peasant took off from their duet, soaring away on his own. Lowering her instrument, my mother listened, her face radiant with awe.

To this day, I don't know how the flutist and his companions found my mother. Perhaps they had heard her practicing from their place in the hold of the ship, through the ducts or vents. Musicians have a way of finding one another. In any case, the flutist played, and we listened, nodding and weaving to his rhythms like a circle of cobras before a sorcerer. Eventually, at the end of his tune, he opened his eyes, looking amazed, as though he had no idea how he came to be in our cabin. He seemed content to listen as my mother played a Telemann sonata, joining the other men as they leaned close to music they had never heard before. At the end, they applauded enthusiastically, exclaiming in a tongue that my mother confessed afterward she did not understand at all. By this time, the flutist got a second wind and began to play another, more languid tune. My mother joined in, weaving in elements from her store of Western music. It made for a tangled and oddly colored braid, but the men listened with rapt attention, inspired occasionally to break into fragments of song. While their voices were hoarse and strained, their faces showed transcendent joy.

Sometime later, when the ship's horn sounded a deep blast, signaling our approach to Wuhan, the flutist and his companions bowed and bid us goodbye. Though my mother and I didn't grasp their exact words, we understood their sentiments and hoped they knew what we meant from our smiles and nods. When they left to go back to their place in the hold, I felt sadness and regret. I tried to write down the tunes the flutist had played, noting, by the way my mother worked out the tunes on her recorder, that she attempted the same. Between the two of us, we managed to put the bare bones of a few songs on paper, but we knew they were a poor substitute for what the flutist had spontaneously created. After a while, we gave up and packed our things, as the boat was entering its final approach to the port.

Before the ship sounded its three-note horn, signaling its arrival at the dock, I climbed the staircase to take one last look at the Yangtze. Making my way to the extreme end of the bow, I looked over the edge to see the ship slicing through the water so that waves unfurled on either side of the boat, falling back like heavy yellow curtains. I envisioned the waves joining seamlessly together again in the wake of the ship, making it seem as if the ship had never passed.

I realized then that the Yangtze was like a stream of time with no beginning and no end. I traveled through centuries on a river of years whose pulse and rhythm spoke to me in a way I could no more explain than I could describe the causal effect of music. All I knew is that even while I was on moving water I felt on solid ground, and that it was to this that Yeh Yeh had summoned me as much as to the threshold of his house. It was the entire experience of China he had wished for me, the sights and sounds of the cities and the river with all its myriad, poignant evocations. To his way of thinking we had always had this in common. All I had to do was to feel the river's pulse in order to realize how one generation flowed to the next, and that we were as conjoined as surely as currents in the water, no matter the passage of ships, events, or time itself. Nothing separated us.

I realized at this moment that my trip to China was fulfilled. Even if I never made it to Yeh Yeh's house, what I had discovered here swept doubt and self-recrimination from my heart, filling it with a sense of inheritance and newfound identity. The confluence of the water and the ship's rounding of the bend brought home the certainty that my experience of dual cultures needn't divide nor impede who I was but strengthen and serve. Realizing this set me free.

The ship sounded a final thunderous three-note blast. My mother and a few other passengers came to join me on deck to view the city of Wuhan. Built in the crook of the elbow of the Yangtze, it looked like a repository of all the flotsam and debris flushed from decades of floods. Even more so than Chongqing, Wuhan looked tattered, in rags, as though it had been washed ashore, patched together by bedraggled survivors using bits of canvas, sticks, and rope. The first-class passengers breathed sighs of relief that they had booked flights out the following day.

Getting off the boat was slow, as the ramp was blocked by thick crowds of people milling about on the dock. Just as we reached the railing, a rusty groan sounded behind us. I turned to see an opening appear in the hold of the ship. A long ramp descended, looking like a huge tongue uncurling, disgorging the hundreds of peasants from the hold. My mother leaned against me as she searched the stream of people blinking and stretching in the sun. Women and children emerged, followed by men toting belongings, herding animals. From the way my mother stood on her toes, searching the crowd, I knew she looked for the flutist. Though she squinted every few seconds and tensed the muscles in her neck, causing me to think she had sighted him, we never saw him again.

Meanwhile, I searched anxiously for the official who had my passport. As scores of uniformed men moved in to oversee those leaving the boat, I gave up hope, certain that I would be arrested in Wuhan and thrown in jail. Just as we got to the end of the ramp, my government official appeared out of nowhere and, surreptitiously, as though he were a gambler handing me the winning ace from his sleeve, slipped me my passport. I glanced down in disbelief, then looked up again to confirm what had happened, or at least acknowledge that he had made his point, but he was gone.

19

MOTHER HEN

WITHIN MINUTES ALL THE OTHER FIRST-CLASS PASSENGERS HAD DASHED from the dock, leaving my mother and me feeling deserted and lost. Not long after, emerging from the dust, came an elderly man wearing a stained undershirt and sagging pants, looking as though he'd just been roused from bed. He approached and peered into my mother's startled face, inquiring, "Wan Rui?"

"Zhao-Ji!" my mother exclaimed, delighted at the sight of her old classmate, who informed us he had received the wire informing him of our arrival just that morning. Apologizing profusely, he explained that he had expected us in a month's time as per my mother's letter, sent to him that previous spring. He had only just managed to reserve us a room in a hotel an hour ago, which explained his late appearance at the dock. Not only that, but he had planned months before to leave that very evening to visit his brother in Yunnan Province, meaning that he could not stay to entertain us. My mother assured him we had no expectations and were grateful for what he had already done.

Zhao-Ji gestured impatiently for a helper to carry our bags up the street. Though in his seventies, he hustled along with astonishing speed, muttering to himself and looking over his shoulder every so often with the harried look of the White Rabbit in *Alice in Wonderland*. At the hotel he waited while we registered, though it was plain he was anxious to be off.

Finally, he shook our hands and was about to leave when he suddenly remembered something. "Sorry, sorry," he repeated, his whiskers all but quivering. Digging in his pockets he came up with two train tickets printed CHANGSHA. That he had been able to get them at such short notice and that they looked untouched, pristine, told me that we were going someplace where few others, if any, wanted to go.

"It's only one night," my mother said, placatingly, later, as we sat on the sagging beds in our hotel room. The bare concrete walls smelled of mildew and the hard-bodied crickets made the sound of tiddly-winks as they bounced across the floor. I slept poorly, as the mattress was lumpy and the crickets clicked and clacked and scuttled around on metallic legs all night long. Even so I felt a strange calm, a growing sense that fate at last had changed for me.

Early the next morning we bought food at a market and arrived at the station to catch our train. Unlike every other terminal I had seen so far, this one was virtually empty, which confirmed my concern that few people were foolish enough to travel to Changsha. To make matters worse, as soon as the train left Wuhan proper, a man wearing the green uniform and red star insignia of the communist party entered our compartment. He was of medium build with a bureaucrat's potbelly and hands with manicured nails. The canny, point-blank look he gave me prompted me to slide across the cabin to sit next to my mother, leaving the entire opposite seat for him.

He brought no luggage with him, a sign that convinced me he was a spy. Though I pretended to study my map of China, I felt him staring at my mother and me. His blatant scrutiny made me feel self-conscious, more anxious to reach Beijing, as if there we might be safe. Out here in the nether regions I felt exposed, my foreignness an open invitation for trouble. I had hoped to ask my mother about what lay ahead of us in Changsha, but now, talking seemed unwise. My mother seemed unfazed by the official's presence, focusing her attention instead on the mulberry fields, rice paddies, and gentle hills flashing outside the window. As the train sped under leafy arbors, sunlight flickered in the compartment, dappling our faces. Despite the busy strobe effect, my mother looked content, peacefully engaged, as though she watched blissful dreams.

Resolving to ignore the official, I placed my finger on my map and traced the route from Wuhan to Changsha, seeing that we were traveling due south, directly away from Beijing. Once again the movement of my finger underscored the fact that the distance between us and our original destination was only widening. At least my mother looked forward to going to Changsha, where her sister and younger brother lived and where she had spent her early years. Again, I couldn't help think that it was here, deep in China's interior, where her true essence and happiness lay. I wanted to believe that the farther she traveled inland, the more the armoring layers she had taken up in America would be shed. Here she needed to convince no one of her rightful place. The simple fact of her birth justified her claim.

I was thrilled that I would witness my mother's return to the place of her childhood not only for her sake, but for mine. Her homecoming was, in an indirect way, my own as well. Even though I was beginning to adjust to being in China, I still felt enclosed in my separate little observational sac, a tourist struck dumb by the awesome and mercurial spectacles here. I continued to rely on my mother for practically everything. We were inextricably intertwined, she and I, as attached by my helplessness in this place as by that first rubbery cord at birth.

The train clattered on monotonously, as though it circled the earth. Beyond the window, the black soil looked plaited in neatly plowed rows stretching beyond the horizon. Everything indicated that life here was patterned on the infinite, yet I felt the keen sense that I was running out of time and that I would never discover the final piece of what I needed to know. Though I told myself Beijing and Yeh Yeh's house still waited for me, the fact remained that they were thousands of miles away, receding even farther with every mile we headed south.

Two hours into the trip, the conductor came to announce that food was being served in the adjoining car. Our official got up, stretched, and left the compartment.

My mother immediately opened our sack of food, taking out steamed bread, hard-boiled eggs, oranges, and Chinese candy that smelled like mothballs. As we munched the food, I asked my mother about Auntie Anna's family. She dug in her purse for the paper napkin, the same airline napkin from our first flight to China, and began to sketch the Changsha family tree, explaining, as she wrote, the various relationships. At the top of the tree was her sister Anna and her three daughters, Sho Mei, Sho An, and Sho Sung. Then my mother wrote down the names of the daughters' husbands and their children, explaining that Anna had been left a widow at a young age and had supported her family by teaching piano at the music school in Changsha. Now retired, she augmented her pension by teaching an occasional private student at home. All her daughters lived with her or nearby. Because she had remained with her brood in Changsha, far away from the rest of my mother's family, Anna had been given the name of *gi ma,* or mother hen.

"Why haven't you talked about them before?" I asked.

My mother put down the orange she was peeling. "When I first come to America and think of my parents and brothers and sisters back in China, I cry all the time. I cry so much I can't study or take care of you and your sister. Finally, I decide I have to stop thinking about my family or I go crazy. I was with Dad in America and I want to succeed in our new life. So I decide not to talk about my family in China." She picked up the orange, peeled it, and gave me half.

"What's it like for you, coming back?"

She looked out the window, thinking. "I don't know how to say in words," she said, after a while. "Maybe because we all getting older, but seeing your aunties and uncles help me remember what really matters. Things maybe change in China—the government, the economy, and so forth, but certain things stay the same. Like your Auntie Anna. She suffer a lot, but she haven't changed, not really. When you see her and her family, you know what I mean. That she stay the same remind me who I am. That, in spite of our difference, we still sisters. So, answer your question, it feel good to come back. It very important."

Talk of my mother's family made me think of my own home, and I began to reel with homesickness. I was sure Fred had not yet received the letter I had sent from Xi'an explaining our change in plans. Whatever letters he sent were undoubtedly waiting for me in Beijing, where he believed me to be. I realized now how much I needed those letters, how they served as lifelines that hummed with the comforting assurance that he held the other end. For the first time since my arrival in China, I began to think of my odyssey as possibly misguided. That in obeying my grandfather's summons I had given over to the belief that he drew me home, to the place of my ancestral origin, whereas now it dawned on me my real home was elsewhere, and that the longer I stayed in China the more I tarried from where I belonged.

Several hours later the train whistle blew, signaling our arrival in Changsha. Our mysterious official had not returned from the dining car. My mother and I had barely gotten off the train when seven pairs of hands reached out to pat us and take our bags. I recognized my Auntie Anna, who was a smaller, sadder version of my mother. Surrounding her in a protective circle were her three daughters and their husbands. Auntie introduced me to Sho Mei, Sho An, and Sho Sung, who were approximately my age and wore shiny dresses of silver, pink, and blue polyester. They looked as if they had just come from a wedding, but my mother told me later that they had dressed up solely in honor of our arrival. They giggled when their mother told me they spoke English, and we exchanged a few experimental phrases. My attempt at Mandarin embarrassed everyone and caused them to smile so hard their eyes disappeared. I wondered why we stayed on the platform, as all the other passengers had gone. My mother was deeply engaged in conversation with her older sister. They had their arms around each other and were chatting in Changsha dialect. It didn't sound that different from Mandarin except for certain words that had additional *shuh* sounds, the shuffling of soft slippers.

Presently a train pulled up to the adjacent platform. From the way my relatives anxiously scanned the disembarking crowd it became apparent we had been waiting for its arrival. They pointed to a lone, tired-looking woman who walked slowly down the platform. She wore the usual dark blue cotton jacket and pants and flat black Chinese shoes and was thin as a child.

"She your cousin," Auntie Anna explained, taking hold of my arm. "She ride five hours just to see you. You last one from America she not see."

The woman's face lit up when she saw my cousins and greeted them warmly. Then, seeing me, she approached, bowed deeply, and offered her hand. "Sung Lien," she said. My mother whispered her name in my ear and I spoke it aloud. It came out sounding wrong, but this cousin smiled anyway. "You come from far away," she said. "You come to China, it's good."

"Now we have tea," Auntie Anna declared, moving away. She walked unsteadily, veering a little, as if she had a balance problem. We headed en masse to the station tea room, a shabby corner with a few broken tables. A man set out a pot of tea and cracked cups. I asked my older cousin where she lived. She smiled vaguely and waved her arm, indicating far, far away. Her teeth were bad, like most everyone in China. Up close she looked at least sixty years old. Her wrists were bony and delicate but thick-veined, and her heavily calloused hands were covered with tiny, razor-like cuts. Auntie Anna explained that my cousin's husband and son lived in a town three hours to the west. They couldn't live together, because they had been assigned to work in different factories. My cousin saw her family once a month, when she received furlough to travel to the small town where her husband and son lived. In light of her hard life I was even more amazed and deeply moved that she had come so far in order to pay her respects to me, her distant American cousin.

An announcement sounded throughout the station, causing everyone to sigh. My cousin rose, told me again how glad she was to see me, then linked arms with her Changsha cousins and walked back to the train platform, where she boarded the train that would take her back to her village. She had been with us for half an hour.

"Why is she going?" I asked my mother, disbelieving.

"She only has twelve hour leave," she explained. "She has to get back to factory, or she lose whole day pay."

My cousin waved from her window. She was sitting in a second-class compartment so crowded she was pressed against the window.

"*Sheh sheh!* Thank you!" I shouted, waving.

The train began to pull away. My other cousins trotted along the platform, calling out her name. They were a strange sight, clattering along the concrete strip in their plastic high-heeled shoes, dressed in their shining best like fairy-tale stepsisters. "Look, look, she's waving!" my mother said.

I waved, straining to see my cousin's face, but it was a blur now that the train was at the far end of the platform. Tears welled up in my eyes from confusion and shame. She had come so far to see me, and already I had forgotten her name.

From the train station we rode in an assortment of borrowed cars and taxis to Auntie Anna's place. The air in Changsha was hot and sultry, but my aunt's apartment, situated on the fourth floor in a typical stucco building, was surprisingly well-ventilated and comfortable. As soon as we arrived, her daughters and sons-in-law disappeared, then quickly reappeared, changing from their shiny dresses to simple cotton blouses and trousers. I assumed everyone lived in the complex or very near, since they accomplished the change in a matter of minutes. The men went into the kitchen, where they began mixing dumpling dough. My mother and I observed the bustle while sitting in the living room of the apartment, which was bare except for a table, some chairs, and an old, scarred, upright piano.

We offered to help make dumplings, but Auntie Anna insisted there wasn't room in the four-by-six-foot kitchen. Her sons-in-law were tall and big-boned, unlike other Chinese men I had seen in the cities. Their faces were impassive as they kneaded the dough between calloused hands. Though they weren't quick, they were efficient and worked without exchanging a word. It was clear this was a task they could do in their sleep.

"They all teachers," Auntie Anna explained. "That one, he play trombone. That one teach electricity. That one teach physical education. All went down to the countryside, during Cultural Revolution."

I tried to read the faces of the men, wondering how they had come through their ordeal, when two of Auntie Anna's daughters approached us. Dressed identically in white blouses and blue trousers, they looked like younger twin versions of their mother. As long as they wore their silver, pink, and blue dresses, I could tell them apart, but now it was impossible. I remembered the song I made up about them: Sho *Mei,* Sho *An,* Sho *Sung.* Okay. But which was which? They must have seen the confusion on my face, because they laughed and pointed to themselves, pronouncing their names.

"They all pianists," Auntie Anna declared, at which they immediately bowed their heads and demurred shyly. "Look, their hands," my aunt persisted, taking up Sho An's hand to show me. "Strong palm, long fingers. Pianist hand." Sho An gently pulled her hand away, tucked it behind her back.

"I not pianist now," she said. "In Cultural Revolution, I go to countryside, take care of pigs. Make hands rough, stiff."

In a move that took my breath away, Auntie Anna suddenly wrapped her arms around her daughter and hugged her tight. "My daughter big talent," she said. "Sho Sung, Sho Mei, too. Before Cultural Revolution, they all play. I teach them myself."

My aunt's voice was thin but fierce. With her bony, triangular face, wiry arms clasping her daughter to her wide abdomen, she reminded me of a queen wasp.

Suddenly there was a loud bang, then the sound of many little feet.

"*Ai yah!*" Auntie Anna exclaimed.

Sho Sung, her third daughter, came in with the clan's children. Six tumbled into the room like tops that had been released all at once, careening into one another and against Auntie Anna so that they nearly knocked her off her pins. Screaming and giggling, they grabbed her skirt, rubbed their faces in the folds, then bounded off again, skittering across the floor. Auntie Anna snatched one child by the ear and steered her toward me, speaking sternly in Changsha dialect. The girl bowed and sang out her name, then hopped away. One by one, following Auntie Anna's strict command, they came forward, bowing to me and my mother, chanting out their names. The oldest was a nine-year-old boy named Gan Gan who impressed me not only with his happy bright face and high soprano voice, but little white ears that stuck straight out from his head. He was clearly regarded as the leader by the other children, as they kept their eyes glued to him and took his every cue, modulating their voices and movement to imitate whatever he did. Gan Gan seemed to revel in his special status, wearing it with a mixture of dignity and carefully gauged self-effacement. Mimicking Auntie Anna's stern voice, he ordered his underlings to line up in a row. As they did so, he looked up at the adults with a sheepish grin, conveying that, even as he shared their chain of command, it was all just a big joke to him.

There was another commotion at the door, and my mother got up to greet her younger brother, Ben. Though he was no longer the asthmatic little boy whose coughing threatened to reveal their family's attic hiding place during the war, he radiated a childlike innocence in the way he hung back in his humble, knock-kneed stance. His plain cotton shirt and shorts were limp on his soft, pear-shaped body, giving him an unprotected, vulnerable look. Standing behind him was his fourteen year-old son, a thin, morose-looking boy. Later, my mother told me that Ben, also a piano teacher, had recently been divorced by his wife, who had gone away to live in another city. This fact helped explain the father and son's look of helplessness.

The sons-in-law announced that the dumplings were done. They piled some on a platter and set it on top of the piano to cool, out of reach of the children. The rest were brought to the table. The men produced chairs and stools of assorted sizes, setting the larger ones aside for Auntie Anna, my mother, and me. They and their wives took little stools for themselves, so that they squatted far below the table, their heads barely reaching the edge.

The younger children, each gripping a bowl and a pair of chopsticks, huddled at the base of the piano, staring up at the platter of hot dumplings in reverential silence. At the proper moment, Gan Gan stood up, waved a spoon that was as big as his head, and announced that the dumplings were cool enough to eat. Shrieks erupted but were quickly subdued when Gan Gan ordered them to line up according to age. He carefully doled out the dumplings, beginning with the three-year-old, ending with Uncle Ben's son and himself. I saw Auntie Anna watching the scene with a judicious eye, catching the moment when Gan Gan glanced her way, at which point she allowed him a nearly imperceptible nod, which caused him to hide his reddening face deep in his bowl. It was a larger bowl than the others, as befitted his status, but not big enough to hide the sound of his happy slurps and the curl of his mouth grinning beyond the rim.

The dumplings were delicious and everyone ate hungrily. The steam from the circle of bowls formed a communal cloud of contentment. After a while, Auntie Anna addressed me.

"Did you know your mother play the ukelele? Our brother George brought it back from Hawaii. Your mother tune it to funny little song. What was song, Wan Rui?"

"My dog has fleas," my mother said.

"That's right! La da da *dee*!" Auntie Anna sang in her tinny voice. "My dog has fleas! Can you imagine?"

She looked around the table expectantly. Her daughters and sons-in-law nodded dutifully but without interest, evidently having heard the story many times before. Unfazed, even defiant, Auntie Anna fixed her narrow eyes on me and said, "I want you to know. Your mother have great talent."

I glanced around the table, wondering who she had meant to admonish. Then I saw that my aunt had resumed eating, done with the matter. Apparently her statement had nothing to do with me, but was rather a general proclamation defending her family's honor, which, in her mind, resided in their talent. I understood why she, as the mother hen, was driven to defend her daughters and sons-in-law, but why my mother? Did she know about my parents' separation? In the wake of her family's many tribulations, did she perceive her role as defending the essential worth of the wounded?

I became aware that the only other sounds at the table were of munching and the clicking of chopsticks. I was relieved not to have to converse in Chinese, though after a while, when everyone was on his second helping of dumplings, the silence began to feel oppressive. Back home I looked forward to meals as a form of entertainment, when people shared thoughts and observations of the day, or told jokes and stories. Though I felt the warmth of intermingled breath and the unquestioned peace of a unified consciousness at this table, I sensed that something was missing. What? Curiosity? Expectation?

I watched Sho Sung reach her chopsticks to spear a dumpling for her husband. Indicating that he had eaten enough, her husband pushed the dumpling back onto his wife's plate. She pushed it back onto his. This went on, back and forth, until the dumpling slid off the table and fell on the floor, where one of their children alertly pounced on it and ran off, stuffing it into her mouth. Auntie Anna, who had witnessed the entire scene, scolded the child for eating off the floor and sent her into the kitchen. The child's parents laughingly coaxed the girl back and caressed her under the table. Uncle Ben also observed what had happened, and stared at Sho Sung and her husband with a wistful, pained look.

After dinner, my mother reached into her blue bag and brought out presents for everyone. She gave Auntie Anna a bottle of Jergen's hand lotion and her three daughters different shades of lipstick. The sons-in-law each received blue cotton handkerchiefs. My mother pretended not to have anything for Uncle Ben, but then, with a flourish, brought out a shirt of a violent turquoise-and-aqua plaid, which caused him to blush and protest until everyone shouted for him to change. After retreating into the kitchen for what seemed an eternity, during which everyone clamored for his return, he finally slunk back, having put the loud shirt on over his own. To noisy, unanimous approval, Uncle Ben managed a wan smile, conveying good sportsmanship, though it was clear the shirt caused him untold embarrassment.

His fourteen-year-old son received a maroon polo shirt, which he put on, hanging his head like a pony waiting to be led to slaughter. The other children lined up for their customary gifts of red envelopes which my mother had stuffed with crisp new dollar bills. In exchange, Auntie Anna gave us the obligatory Chinese doodads, more figurines with mispainted faces, tins of tiger balm. This ritual over, it was time for watermelon, which the children served, then devised a contest of spitting the seeds across the room. This lasted until Sho Mei, scolding, made them sweep up the seeds with a broom. After the watermelon, Auntie Anna clapped her hands and announced that the children had prepared a recital in our honor. Again they lined up, twittering and scraping their shoes, joining forces to push the first victim toward the piano bench.

This was the three-year-old, who hung back, biting his lip and shaking his head until Gan Gan hoisted him up and slung him on the bench. The little boy stared at the keys, then burst into tears. Sho Sung, his mother, rushed over to carry him away, murmuring comforting words into his ear while offering apologies to us. Next, a little girl wearing a pink sundress climbed on the bench and began to plunk out "The Happy Farmer," her little arms pumping like pistons, making sure we knew her farmer tromped from measure to measure wearing big boots. After finishing she bowed to our enthusiastic applause, then, shrieking at the top of her lungs, vehemently whacked off watermelon seeds that had gotten stuck to her dress.

Next, an older girl played *"Für Elise,"* showing real musical talent in her phrasing and sensitive touch. Auntie Anna nodded to the rhythms of the piece, openly proud of her star pupil. The girl's mother, Sho An, watched from the doorway of the kitchen, her lips twitching with pride and vicarious nervousness. She stood with arms crossed, and, as her daughter played, moved her fingers along her arms in the rhythms of the piece, silently guiding her through it.

The last child to play was Gan Gan. Auntie Anna whispered in my ear that it had taken her all afternoon to persuade him to perform. He hated the piano and played only when forced. Apparently her eldest grandchild had decided to make the best of the situation. He went to the piano and began to bang out the Beethoven Sonatina in G with all his might. The piano, which was badly in need of tuning, jangled horribly. Though Auntie Anna called out, *"Mahn! Mahn!"* (slower, slower!) Gan Gan flashed her a smile and continued to pound louder and faster than ever, his elbows flying. It was clear he was determined to demonstrate, in front of everyone, how thoroughly unsuited he was to play the piano. While he played, he kicked his legs madly under the bench in a rhythm completely independent of the tune he pounded at the keyboard, revealing his considerable gift, since this required real coordination. When he finished, he jumped off the bench and sprinted from the room even before our applause ended.

The evening's entertainment over, Auntie Anna's daughters gathered their children and bid us good night. Their husbands swept the remaining watermelon seeds and stowed the chairs. Auntie Anna linked her arm through my mother's and led us to the dormitory of the music school, which was a few hundred yards away.

We went by way of a narrow lane behind her apartment building, through a grassy patch bordered by a thin stream. Few people in this residential area were out in the dark night; a lone man walked along, smoking, a group of women squatted in the lane fanning themselves, chewing sunflower seeds. Flitting about high and low were swallows, feasting on mosquitoes.

Vacant due to the summer break, the dormitory was built of cinder block and exuded the damp smell of mice and mold. Our quarters were lit by a single lightbulb and had the air of a bunker or bomb shelter. The bathroom was a cubicle with a cold-water sink and a hole in the floor. Next door the sleeping room contained two old-fashioned, wooden canopy beds on which flat bamboo mats were spread in place of mattresses. Heavy mosquito netting hung from the frames. I was relieved to see the netting but dubious about the mats. Our suitcases lay at the foot of our beds, where Auntie Anna's sons-in-law had left them.

My mother and her sister conversed in Changsha dialect while I swatted mosquitoes. The insects had been swirling around the lightbulb in the ceiling but had discovered us and were attacking from all sides. My mother and her sister hardly seemed bothered by the insects, only swatting at them from time to time when one landed on the other. It was a strange sight, the sisters talking earnestly within the swarm, gently slapping each other. Meanwhile, I hopped from foot to foot trying to dodge the pests. Then I heard the word *Beijing* in the conversation, at which point even the mosquitoes seemed to pause. Auntie Anna reached out, gently squished one on my mother's forehead.

"*Mayou banfa,*" she said. Even I understood this ubiquitous Chinese phrase. *Can't be helped.*

I was about to inquire further, but Auntie Anna took my arm and pronounced, in stilted English, a language she hardly ever spoke these days, "We try tomorrow."

I bid her good night and watched her move away in her erratic, lurching gait, as if even here she was buffeted by imaginary chicks.

20

CHANGSHA

THAT NIGHT I LOWERED MYSELF ONTO THE HARD WOODEN BED THAT creaked like a haunted stand of bamboo. As I twisted and turned, my bones grinding against each other on the flat bamboo mat, I saw myself flailing in the ashes of my dreams, the prospect of reaching Beijing retreating further away than ever. In contrast, my mother drew the mosquito net, curled up on the boards to which she was accustomed from her childhood, and was asleep in seconds. She had little to say when I asked her about our chances of getting tickets to Beijing, indicating only that Auntie Anna was aware of our dilemma. Neither of us spoke aloud what we both privately feared: It was unlikely a retired piano teacher like Auntie knew higher-ups in Changsha who could help us. We had gone to bed as we had on so many nights of our near two-week-long trip exchanging sighs of evaporating hope.

As I lay awake, listening to my mother's even breathing, I hardly dared think what we would do if we couldn't get tickets. I realized that I was getting used to not daring, not knowing. In spite of all my worry and frustration, I could feel my urgency for reaching Beijing wane, my sense of purpose wilt in the face of the never-ending obstacles and withering heat. It was far easier to let go and allow myself to be carried along by the prevailing currents of fate, like the poppy man drowned in the Yangtze. Perhaps I was experiencing the true meaning of time and nature; this was how life was really meant to be, the way animals experienced it, living hour after hour, day after day, until nature exacted death. Was this the real lesson of my trip to China? That only she obeyed the true rhythms of the planet, while the rest of the so-called civilized world whirled in a vortex of make-believe? Were my dreams and expectations wholly unrealistic and unattainable? These notions plagued me, combined with the hardness of the bed and the incessant whine of mosquitoes, so that I tossed and turned all night, attaining only a restless, shallow sleep, like a stone skipping water.

The next morning my mother and I went to Auntie Anna's apartment, where we ran into Sho Mei at the top of the stairs. Wearing an apron smeared with blood, waving a dripping cleaver in one hand, she grinned while babbling something in Changsha dialect. Auntie Anna appeared next to her, saying, "She say she make something very special for you for dinner tonight."

I stared at the bloody cleaver, not knowing what to think. Sho Mei gave a cackle and disappeared into the kitchen.

"What's she making?" I asked Auntie Anna.

"Cannot tell, big surprise!" Auntie said, holding her finger to her lips like a conspirator in a melodrama.

"What?" I turned to my mother.

She shook her head, frowning, a sure sign that she knew, but was not about to spoil her niece's surprise. At that moment, the trombone-playing son-in-law appeared, carrying a bucket of greens. He reacted strangely, seeming surprised and embarrassed, but recovered quickly, mumbling a greeting before hurrying to join his sister-in-law in the kitchen. Though the encounter was brief, I sensed my mother stiffening beside me.

"Now I show you Changsha!" Auntie Anna said.

We went down the stairs to the unshaded street, where the heat, in shocking contrast to the cool interior of the apartment, felt like a blast from a furnace. We walked through the residential district, past rows of barracks where women washed clothes and children played. In a few minutes, we arrived at the music school, at which Auntie Anna had taught piano for nearly thirty years. It was housed in a square cement building, deserted due to the summer break. The practice rooms were small and dank, housing the two pianos used by the entire school. Both were missing keys and in dire need of tuning. Crickets and slugs crept across the damp floor beneath the pedals.

We strolled into the commercial district, where the streets were crowded with shoppers, pensioners, idle youths dressed in communist uniform, and the usual meandering lanes of bicyclists. Elderly persons wearing pajamas and slippers aired their songbirds, clearly more concerned for the welfare of their canaries than the seemliness of their attire. Tanned, plain-faced women casually strolled down the street, arm in arm. Most wore their hair in old-fashioned, single long braids hanging down their backs. There wasn't a chic chignon or bicycle princess in sight.

Auntie Anna stopped at a Chinese medicine store for a special tonic. As the herbalist weighed out an assortment of dried leaves, twigs, powders, and fungi, I studied the jars and glass compartments in which there were dried turtles, lizards, toads, and snakes, looped like lariats, as well as pre-served animal organs that looked like nuts and beans. The place smelled like a stewpot of flora and fauna and a little like the monkey house at the Washington Zoo. Turning into a narrow aisle, I bumped into a wizened woman who muttered, *"Weiguoren!"*

"How did she know I was a foreigner?" I wondered aloud, to no one in particular.

Auntie Anna turned from the counter nearby. "You look like *weiguoren*," she said, pinching my upper arm, my cheek. "You got meat and fat on your bones. Not skinny, like Chinese. You walk with head first, eyes everywhere." She thrust her head forward, scooting through the shop in an imitation of me that was dead-on, devastating.

She paid for her medicine and led us back onto the street. As we walked, I glanced at my reflection in the occasional shop window and saw that what she said was true. I walked with my head jutting forward, as though I hurried after my thoughts, unlike the natives, who ambled directly beneath theirs. I also noticed that people on the street did not look directly at one another, but moved along in a shuffle that was self-contained, discreet.

"Come," Auntie Anna said, wiping her perspiring face with a handker-chief. "It's too hot. We go back."

Sho An had worked all morning to produce lunch, which included a tasty stewed chicken, stir-fried greens, pickled radishes, cabbage, and rice. Again the adults squeezed around the single table, clacking chopsticks, knocking el-bows, saying nothing. I looked warily at Sho Mei, who had changed into a clean shirt, but she gave no indication of following through with the threat she had made that morning. Afterward, my mother and I headed back to our bomb shelter for *xiu shi*. As we walked along, she shook her head, sighing repeatedly. After she lay in her bed, she exhaled heavily again, making the tell-tale sound of a troubled heart.

"What's the matter?" I said.

She hesitated, before confessing, "It's the trombone player. Two years ago he wrote and ask me to sponsor him. He want to come to States to study, to start new life." She paused, clearly struggling with her conscience, then sat up abruptly. "But I turn him down! I will have to pay for his tuition and all his expense. If he were young, maybe, not married, but he nearly forty! And trombone player! What a dreamer!"

She fell back again, sighing, and was asleep in a matter of seconds. Now it made sense, her discomfort at seeing him earlier that morning carrying the bucket of greens. In my mind, I replayed the scene at lunch, focusing on the trombone player's face, trying to remember whether he directed recriminating looks at my mother. I recalled only that he kept his face in his bowl, and whenever he lifted it, his expression was like that of his brothers and sisters-in-law: intelligent, patient, accepting. If he clung to thoughts of escaping his present life, I saw no trace of it. Not seeing did not prove that his longing might not persist. Who knew whether he still dreamed of teaching trombone in America, or of owning a house, a car? Or whether his desire was not specific at all but stemmed from the feeling that his present life, with its unending, day-to-day predictability, its confinement to his mother-in-law's apartment, was somehow not truly his.

I began to wonder if what I observed had any validity or meaning, if what I saw, as an American whose philosophic and cultural lens was centered on the individual, had any bearing or relevance here. People in Changsha seemed to live in a state of inversion, where life itself was a dream in which they were sleepwalking, and certain individuals, like the trombone player, strove to wake from it. An outsider like me could only skim the periphery of this life, ill-equipped to discern which was the real, which was the dream. To me, both states offered little promise, but who was I to judge? To the Chinese, whose perspective was developed over centuries of natural, social, and political disasters, achieving a life of tranquility and equilibrium was in itself a miracle. Better this than catastrophe and ruin. And better a pragmatic approach than disorder. Only anarchists dare lay claim that their lives are truly their own.

What I read in the trombone player's face was an expression that was perfectly in tune with his situation. Having the door closed in his face with my mother's refusal to sponsor him in America, he turned away from what he could not have and focused instead on what was before him. At dinner, he surveyed the bounty of food on the table, the faces of his children, and said, calmly, in a tone that was practical, fulfilled, though striking in its lack of nuance, "We have enough."

"That's right," Auntie Anna agreed. "Things are better."

"Is it because of the communists?" I asked.

"Whether or not we are party members, we all strive for the good of China," Auntie Anna replied, elusively. Then, assuming a pedagogical tone, she stated, "Our goals are, one: population control, two: adequate food supply, three: good economy, and four: good leadership. People join the party in order to serve the community, but not everyone joins."

"Do party members enjoy special privileges?" I asked.

"Yes, life can be better for party members," Auntie acknowledged. "But everyone may advance, *mahn mahn,* slowly, slowly."

"What about students?" I said, referring to the reports I had read in the *Herald Tribune.* "The increasing number of demonstrations must mean people are dissatisfied with government policies."

"Disorder and violence no good!" Auntie Anna countered, sharply.

"But doesn't that mean . . ." I persisted, warming up to an argument against statements that smacked of propaganda, but at that moment I felt a sharp elbow in my side. My mother was frowning and squeezing her thumbs furiously. The previous mood of open discussion had shifted abruptly. The faces at the table looked uncertain, shuttered, except for Auntie Anna, whose frown expressed her determination that no discord be permitted at her table. This made me wonder if my cousins agreed with their mother or were merely too afraid to say. What did they think of the student demonstrations? Suddenly Sho Mei jumped up, exclaiming that it was time for my surprise. All thoughts of politics and propaganda vanished as I recalled the scene of her bloody apron and cleaver earlier that morning. I realized I had been feeling a vague sense of dread all day. The sons-in-law cleared the table in front of me and everyone leaned forward expectantly.

Slowly, Sho Mei came in from the kitchen, carrying a large covered ceramic bowl. From her bearing and look of concentration, it was clear the bowl was extremely heavy and that it contained priceless treasure. She set it down before me and stood aside. I looked at my mother for cues on what to do next, but she only gave me a curt nod, indicating she could not help me now, and that what lay before me was something I had to go through on my own. Taking heart from the encouraging murmurs all around, I reached for the lid and lifted it, releasing clouds of steam that fogged my glasses and obscured the object within. Finally, the steam cleared, and I looked in the bowl. Floating there, its head and clawed feet bobbing in the bubbling broth as though it still swam in the wild, was a black, turtle-like creature. About the size of a football, it was shiny and soft-looking, as though it was made of patent leather.

"How . . . special," I stammered.

"It's *giao yu*!" Auntie Anna cried. "Very rare!"

"Very expensive," my mother whispered loudly. "You supposed to eat whole thing."

"No!" I said, laughing with disbelief. "This can't all be for me . . . here, let's all share!"

"No!" Sho Mei shook her head vehemently. "For you, guest of honor! Special surprise! Very hard to kill!"

Then she described, in gruesome, luxuriant detail, getting up from the table in order to pantomime the entire scene, how the creature had snapped viciously at her. She had baited it with a stick so that it stretched out its neck to grab it, at which point she was finally able to chop off its head with her cleaver.

"The shell is most healthy to eat," Auntie Anna offered helpfully.

"The . . . shell?" I said weakly.

"Whole thing!" My mother all but shouted, prodding me with her chopstick.

I poked at the thing with my soupspoon, gulping as it flopped over in its broth bath, revealing the scaly skin of its legs, its beaky, dead turtle face. One of my cousins helpfully reached over with his chopsticks and began to break the thing apart. The shell split open, the legs sank, and I peered into a gaping black hole that rapidly filled with soup. The cousin speared a fragment of meat and put it on my plate. "Eat!" he urged.

Cautiously I put the fragment in my mouth, chewed. It was fibrous, rubbery, like overcooked sea bass, but not unpleasant. Then Auntie Anna grasped a piece of shell, put it on my plate. "Eat!" she ordered.

Obediently I ate this, too, thinking I chewed a mixture of chicken cartilage and old Jell-O.

"What you think?" Sho Mei asked.

"Delicious!" I managed to say. "Thank you. I am truly honored. What a wonderful surprise!"

My mother smiled stiffly at my insincerity, but the others seemed pleased. I was thankful when they resumed eating the other dishes on the table, leaving me to hide the severed head of the turtle on my plate under a pile of cabbage. Eventually my mother took pity on me and accepted the pieces I secretly smuggled onto her plate. She ate all of it, even the head, with obvious pleasure.

Several days passed—how many, I lost count. One seemed to melt right into the next, made seamless by the heat and the monotony of the daily routine. I had given up asking about tickets to Beijing, because it put my auntie in the awkward and humiliating position of having to disappoint me. We spent the days wandering the streets, retreating into the cool interior of the apartment, eating, napping. I had all but given up attempts at conversation, my curiosity and sense of purpose gone dormant. Years later, looking back on that time in Changsha, I realized I should have asked my mother many things, but I was overcome by torpor. In any case, my mother seemed wholly engaged with her reunited family, especially her older sister. If not chatting with one another, she and Anna would simply sit quietly, side by side, hands in each other's pockets like Siamese twins.

One morning, Auntie Anna met us at the landing of her apartment, pulling my mother aside and whispering in feverish tones. My attention was diverted by noises coming from a black-and-white television that one of the sons-in-law had set atop the piano to entertain the children during summer break. They, as well as Sho Mei and Sho An watched, entranced, as Mickey Mouse, Chip 'n' Dale, Goofy, Pluto, and Donald Duck jabbered in Mandarin. I watched for a while, but quickly grew bored. I regretted that I had brought only *Sense and Sensibility,* which I had finished some time ago and longed for another book or means to pass the time, but there were no books, magazines, or newspapers in my auntie's place.

Auntie Anna announced that she and my mother were going out, giving orders to Sho Mei and Sho An, who turned away from the cartoons reluctantly.

"They take you sight-seeing," Auntie Anna said.

"Where's Sho Sung?" I said.

"At work."

"Where does she work?" I asked, recklessly.

My cousins' eyes went blank. They immediately excused themselves, saying they would return. I looked at my mother, confused. She beckoned for me to come close, whispered in my ear, "Sho Sung is janitor at music school. She sweep the floor. Sho Mei and Sho An are laborers, too, but to-day their day off."

"Never mind," Auntie Anna said, seeing my embarrassment. "You go with Sho Mei and Sho An. They take you sight-seeing."

"Where're you going?" I asked.

Auntie Anna waved her hand dismissively. "We see you later."

Slipping her arm through my mother's, the two left the apartment. Shortly after, Sho Mei and Sho An reappeared, dressed in smart dresses of rayon georgette. They both wore sheer nylon anklets and plastic heels, and had carefully applied the lipstick my mother had given them. I felt totally drab in comparison, wearing what had become my tourist uniform, a plain white cot-ton shirt and blue skirt. Even though I had stopped wearing makeup the day after I arrived in China, I already felt greasy due to the early morning heat. It was a strange turn of events that I should feel like a refugee, I thought, and was grateful my cousins did not react one way or another. Leaving the chil-dren in the care of one of the husbands, we left the apartment.

It was another sweltering day, with the sun beating down so hard I imag-ined myself popping and sizzling. We picked our way slowly, keeping to what-ever shade was available. There appeared to be a tacit understanding between us that, since we shared little language in common, it was perfectly all right to say nothing. We felt relaxed in each other's company. Soon we reached the business district.

Sho Mei stopped at a dress shop, pausing before a row of dresses identi-cal to the one she was wearing. She ran her fingers along the hems, inspecting them closely, nodding, as though satisfied she had picked the best of the lot.

"You like?" she asked, pointing to her dress, then the ones hanging.

"I like," I said.

"You want?"

I hesitated, running through the possibilities in my head. If I said no, which was the truth, she might be offended, taking it to mean that I did not like her dress. If I said yes, it would almost certainly mean that she would in-sist on buying it for me. I knew Auntie Anna's mandate reached that far.

"I like, but you look better in it," I said.

Sho Mei laughed, shaking her finger at me, then removed a dress from the rack, held it up to me. Of the three sisters she looked most like Auntie Anna, and her voice pulsed with the tones of the next-in-command. "You want? We buy for you."

"I like," I insisted. "But I want to look more. Okay?"

Sho Mei seemed satisfied. We left the shop, continued down the street, a sister walking on either side of me. It was then that Sho Mei slipped her arm through mine. It was a simple, natural gesture, one I had seen undertaken by many women in China. Still, I was so surprised by the act that I stopped in my tracks, then pretended to stumble in order to cover my shock. Sho Mei laughed, pulled me up. I looked in her face, seeing in her warm brown eyes only simple attention, uncomplicated by judgment or expectation. In the firm support of her arm I felt a closeness I had not felt anywhere else, a simple unspoken intimacy and connection for which I realized I had been searching in China but not experienced until now. That I was so moved seemed to embarrass Sho Mei, causing her to look away. Her arm stayed linked in mine, and we walked on, though we both felt awkward and pressed for something to say. With each step, we gradually relaxed, realizing that, even if we knew the other's language perfectly, there were no words to tell one another how we felt, and that it was enough to move along like this, in tandem, if only for a while. I was happy, because with this one simple act my cousin linked me not only to herself, but to China.

We walked on and on in the near-empty streets of Changsha. It was still morning, but the air was already sodden with the turpitude of late afternoon. Few bicyclists were about. Through a shuttered doorway, I heard a man cry out as from a dream. For the most part, the city was silent, as though baked to a standstill. Here and there were a few figures dressed in the communist uniform but they leaned against shaded walls, hats pulled over their eyes, as overcome by the heat as everyone else. I plodded along, feeling utterly depleted of energy and will, submitting to the city's state of total suspension.

Finally we headed back to the apartment, where Sho Sung, on her break from work, and the brothers-in-law were preparing the midday meal. Auntie Anna and my mother were back from their mysterious sojourn, sitting together with legs stretched out, sipping glasses of soda. Browned from walking in the sun, my mother now looked like her sister's twin, perfectly aligned not only in appearance, but intention. There was something calculated in their ladylike sprawl. When I searched their faces for news of their morning outing, I gathered nothing.

Sho Sung and the sons-in-law set out an impressive display of food, but even this failed to stimulate our faded appetites. Everyone nibbled at the dishes but mostly drank bottles of water and soda. The electric fan in the corner whirred, making noise but little headway in the thick, moist air. The children fell asleep even as they chewed. *Xiu shi* descended like a great crushing wave. For once, when we left the table and returned to the coolness of our bomb shelter, my creaking wooden bed looked almost inviting. The room seemed to spin as I closed my eyes. My final thought, before falling asleep, came as a revelation: To live in China was merely to bide the long hours before and after *xiu shi*. It was that simple.

When I awoke again, it was late in the afternoon. My mother's bed was empty. I assumed she had gone back to her sister's place. I got up, sponged myself with cold water, and rinsed out my clothes. After putting on a fresh shirt, I felt better. As soon as I left the relative coolness of the dorm, I broke out in a sweat, for the day was at its hottest, the ground heated through so that the heat came at me from below as well as above. As soon as I arrived at Auntie Anna's apartment, I felt a sudden change in the atmosphere. Though it was no cooler and there were no clouds in the sky, there was a charge in the air, the kind one feels before a gathering storm. Auntie Anna and my mother were standing together, barely able to suppress excited cackling, looking like the Doublemint twins from hell.

"Gan Gan!" Auntie Anna called, summoning the little boy from the kitchen. Gan Gan appeared, chewing on a watermelon rind. Refreshed from his nap, his face smeared with pink juice, he gave me a brilliant smile, beckoning for me to follow.

"Go!" my aunt said, pushing me toward him.

The last thing I wanted was to go traipsing out again in the heat, but I sensed I had little choice. I was about to ask my aunt the reason for going out, but Gan Gan grabbed me by the sleeve and pulled me down the stairs after him.

I followed him into the yard, toward a back street I had not noticed before. Gan Gan skipped ahead, singing aimlessly. Occasionally he would point to something and call out a word in Changsha dialect. His high-pitched warble, sung in the tones of his provincial dialect, gave him the sound of a young turkey. I guessed he was trying to teach me the names of things along the way: the wall, the stream, the fence. Somehow it didn't matter that I couldn't understand a word of it. It was enough simply to follow him in his trail of exuberant good will.

Gan Gan's spindly legs carried him swiftly over the concrete rubble and loose stones so that I had to scramble to keep up. We went through several back lots and came upon a newer neighborhood where barracks were surrounded by corrugated metal fences and a stagnant canal. Plastic bottles, wire, and sooty rags clogged the viaduct at the end. We arrived at another row of houses, where, with an authoritative chop of his hand, Gan Gan signaled me to stop. I stood panting while he disappeared into the alleyway. Several minutes went by. I listened to the whine of insects, the cluck of chickens scratching in the dirt nearby. A man pushing a clumsy dung-filled cart passed. I began to review the route we had taken, in case I had to find my way back alone. Finally, tired of waiting in the brutal sun, I went into the alleyway to look for Gan Gan.

The neighborhood here looked fairly typical, with clotheslines strung in yards cluttered with bicycles and other rubble. As I walked along, I saw women moving about in the dark interiors of the houses, beginning preparations for the evening meal. Halfway down the street, I saw Gan Gan talking with a man. They stood in a recess in the alley wall, beneath a tree, so that they were partially hidden. Whether they purposely chose this spot I couldn't tell, but the nervous way the man kept looking around him conveyed the meeting was clandestine. I ducked behind a small shed in the alley where I could observe what was going on unseen.

The man was perhaps in his thirties, wearing a uniform. From my hiding spot, I couldn't tell for sure if it was a communist uniform, but it looked enough like one with its greenish cast. What was taking them so long? Shading my eyes, squinting into the alleyway, I saw that the uniform was not a communist uniform after all, but that of a city official, perhaps a trolley conductor or street inspector. His jacket was unbuttoned, hanging loose, so I assumed he was off duty. He and Gan Gan continued to talk in a casual manner, heedless of the time or the heat. Gan Gan kicked at pebbles with his shoe, sneezed in the dust. In an unhurried motion, he took something from his pocket and handed it to the man. The man slipped it under his jacket, then gave Gan Gan something in return. Gan Gan stuck it under his shirt. He bowed and, waving cheerfully, watched the man retreat to his house behind the wall.

By this time, I was hurrying back to the spot where Gan Gan had instructed me to wait. There he rejoined me, singing again. We headed home. Along the way he pointed out more things, teaching me the names in Changsha dialect. I dutifully repeated the words after him. The noises of my efforts made him laugh so hard he could barely stagger on. I was glad to humor him, although the whole time all I could think of was what he had hidden under his shirt.

When we got back to the apartment, everyone was busy making dinner, even though it was obvious they had been waiting for us. The three daughters and sons-in-law, covered with sticky flour and bits of pork filling, rushed at us. Auntie Anna dropped her pan of string beans. Even my mother, who had been chopping scallions, got up to greet us.

Auntie Anna grabbed Gan Gan and hugged him as though he had returned from a dangerous reconnaissance mission. Then she whispered in his ear. Slowly, he came toward me. All the others, including the children, pressed close. Gan Gan took an envelope from his shirt. After pausing dramatically, he handed it to me with mischief in his eyes. The envelope was creased, worn, as though it had survived many previous transactions. I looked at my mother. She gestured impatiently for me to open it. I lifted the flap. Inside were two strips of paper covered with Chinese characters. At first I had no idea what they were. Then, taking them out, I saw the images of airplanes stamped on the tops of both strips.

"*Fay gi, fay gi!*" Gan Gan shouted.

I realized I knew that Chinese word. Even in Changsha dialect, it was clear what it meant. *Airplane.*

"Tickets?" I said, barely able to speak.

"Look!" Auntie Anna poked me violently, unable to stand my stupidity.

I looked again at the script, and this time saw the words printed faintly, in English, beneath the airplanes. BEIJING.

"Tickets to Beijing?" I croaked.

"Tickets to Beijing!" my mother shouted, exploding in a kind of glee which I had never thought her capable.

"Shit!" I yelled, clamping my hand over my mouth before I realized I was in China where no one could possibly know what I meant. *Glory Hallelujah.* I grabbed Gan Gan with both hands and whirled him around, then grabbed my auntie and whirled her before she slapped me smartly on the wrist and told me to calm down. Even then I couldn't stop hopping up and down and twirling, inciting all the children to start jumping and shouting at the top of their lungs. And as I spun giddily past my mother I glimpsed her face which, for once, did not look disapproving, but soft, lit in a strange way that I hadn't remembered seeing in what seemed like forever.

That last night in Changsha, I reviewed the scene at dinner when Auntie Anna revealed how she and my mother had gone on their secret mission to get our tickets. Having successfully diverted my attention that morning by sending me off with my cousins, she had brought my mother to meet her contact, an engineer who was married to one of her former piano students. This engineer, who worked at the Changsha airport, had a friend who worked in the ticketing department. For the right price this friend had managed to wrangle tickets for flights leaving the city in the past. It was a delicate matter, and he was not always successful, as it depended on who else was working in the ticket office, and whether this colleague was "flexible." The contact promised he would look into the matter and notify my aunt later in the day.

The news came, via messenger, around three o'clock, an hour before I woke up from *xiu shi*. My mother, who had been too keyed up to nap, had stolen back to her sister's in time to receive word, sent by the engineer, that he had gotten tickets issued for the flight leaving for Beijing the following day. My mother suggested the brilliant final stroke of having Gan Gan take me to go fetch the tickets from the engineer.

"But why the secrecy?" I asked Auntie Anna.

"Your mother want to surprise you. She know how much it mean to you."

I glanced at my mother, who sat quietly with a strange smile on her face. I would never have suspected her of pulling off a caper like that. I sensed her smile was not only from the success of her dramatic plot, but also from the pleasure of my unexpected discovery of her.

I could hardly believe that our dinner that evening was to be our last in Changsha. In spite of the many long days we had spent there, it seemed I had only just gained entry to the family, through Sho Mei. I felt sad now that it was time to leave. As I looked at my relatives, trying to imprint their images in my mind, my eyes kept returning to Sho Mei, whose face was as smooth as a river-swept stone and whose grace throughout a life of upheaval and deprivation shone as clearly as the bitterness borne by our playwright acquaintance, Sun Ai E, in Chongqing. I realized now that it was Sho Mei who had granted me my passport to China. It had not occurred to her, as it had me, that my deficiency of language, limited American perspectives, or habit of speed-walking prohibited my acceptance. For her, that we were of the same family sufficed. In return I longed to give her something more significant, more tangible than my gratitude. She seemed to sense this, shaking her head whenever she caught my eye. There was nothing she wanted, at least that I could provide, and I finally understood this to be her essential wisdom. She accepted life simply as it was.

My mother and Auntie Anna spent the rest of the evening holding hands and talking in intimate tones, separate from the rest of the family. Throughout, Auntie Anna nodded and patted my mother's hand, as though renewing a pact they had made long ago. When we finally bid everyone good night, preparing to return to our bunker, Auntie Anna grabbed me by the arm.

"Remember!" she said, intently. "Your mother very smart, she think of sending Gan Gan with you to get tickets. Remember, your talent, you got from her."

An hour later, I looked over at my mother lying next to me. Viewing her through layers of gauzy mosquito netting as she lay in her shallow wooden bed, I saw her as a mummy resting in a crude sarcophagus. I was unnerved again by the awful truth that time was unrelenting, and my perception of its standing still was merely an illusion brought on by the soporific air of Changsha. I thought of the many times on this journey I had gazed at my sleeping mother, filled with sadness that we were running out of time together, both in terms of our stay in China and in our lives.

I saw by the pale light of the moon that her arm was raised above her head, a sign that she was awake.

"It'll be hard to leave tomorrow," I said.

She sighed. "No harder than when I left thirty years ago."

The next day the entire clan came with us to the airport and waited on the tarmac while we boarded the plane. As usual there was confusion and delay as the airline officials attempted to sort out the passengers and tickets. When my mother and I were finally permitted to climb the gangway onto the plane, I turned to wave a final good-bye. Our thirteen family members were gathered beneath the hot sun, the adults using their hands and an assortment of improvised fans to shade their children's faces. My cousins looked exhausted from all the shopping and cooking and cleaning of our visit. Even Gan Gan drooped a little. I pictured them returning, after our departure, to the coolness of Auntie Anna's apartment to drink orange soda and eat watermelon. I missed them already. Seeing me wave, my cousins called to us one last time, their voices wafting faintly on the shimmering wind. I wondered if I would see them again. Just before I ducked into the plane, everyone waved once more, all except Auntie Anna, who stood perfectly still, not moving at all, like time itself.

21

BEIJING

OUR FLIGHT TO BEIJING BEGAN SMOOTHLY ENOUGH. THE OLD SOVIET CRATE bumped along the runway, then, groaning, hoisted itself into the air. A half hour later, we ran into a storm that caused the plane to buck and sink and make loud snapping noises, as though it was breaking up around us. My main thought was that the cosmos couldn't strike us down when we were so close to Beijing, simply to prove, in a final grand gesture, that the forces of irony were greater here in China than anywhere else.

My mother's wide eyes revealed that she spoke her own silent prayers. Turbulence spanked the plane repeatedly from side to side, then up and down, causing people to shriek and moan. Everything in the overhead bins fell out, passengers threw up and fainted. Having run out of prayers, I surrendered myself to whatever end fate had in mind for us. Then, abruptly, the plane ironed out, settling into the monotonous drone of higher altitude.

Two hours later, the pilot informed us over the intercom that we were approaching Beijing, and that if we looked out the left side of the plane, we would see the Great Wall. I turned my head, and sure enough, there it was. From our vantage, the wall looked less like a man-made structure than a giant, twisting snake. As we drew closer, I could make out the huge stones, mortar, and ramparts and the tiny dots that were people crawling up and down it. I was amazed that we were actually passing over the wall, though it had been built to keep me and all other intruders out.

Until the moment we got off the plane, I had not actually dared to imagine seeing Da Bobo and Da Mama again, but there they were, looking as they had when they had come to see me in St. Paul. Da Bobo spoke my Chinese name as he embraced me. In his forthright eyes, I saw that he, too, had suffered impatience and frustration for the circuitous route my mother and I had been forced to take. But Da Mama, as usual, was steps ahead of him, squeezing me and shouting, "*Wah!* You here at last!"

The rush of seeing them made me forget myself. "Where's Aunt Lucy?" I exclaimed, disappointed at not seeing her.

Da Mama's face darkened as though someone had pulled the shades.

"She's only just been feeling better, since the heat wave lifted," Da Bobo said carefully, avoiding Da Mama's eyes. There was placation in his voice, the echo of arduous argument. "She was afraid the trip to the airport would be too much for her."

"That's okay," I said, but couldn't help noticing Da Mama shaking her head furiously.

While Da Bobo and Da Mama argued whether we should take a pedicab or bus, my mother hired a taxi. It took us on the perimeter route into Beijing, swerving recklessly between cars and donkey carts and bicycles. I noticed an unusual number of black sedans occupied by self-important-looking bureaucrats. Arriving in the center of Beijing, amid the vast Soviet-style squares I had read about and seen in the photos my brother had brought back, I recognized the Great Assembly Hall of the People, Tiananmen Square. The entire area was striking in its lack of trees or greenery, curved lines or ornamentation. It was as welcoming as a barren desert or cubist landscape. I supposed this was exactly the intent of the ruling party's architectural committee: to project, in its capital design, its incontrovertible, uncompromising will. The sprawling scale and vast acreage of concrete only confirmed that the country's consciousness had turned to stone. After being in the more remote, backward areas of China for nearly three weeks, arriving in Beijing was like being catapulted back into modern times. I was struck by the intense, preoccupied expressions on the faces of the people, the overall feeling of being at the nerve center of the country.

The taxi turned off the main boulevard onto a street which had a residential air with its trees, small shops, and strolling pedestrians. It hit me then how close I was, that I was finally on the last leg of my journey to my grandfather's house. Yeh Yeh's words came to mind:

> Ours is one of the very last private houses remaining in Beijing. From the street you would never know it is there, as a high stucco wall surrounds it. In the middle of the wall there is a door, which is painted red. When you come, walk through this door, for it is the gate to my house.

Then it came to me. The description was from Yeh Yeh's last letter that I now carried in my viola case. I fixed upon the final line of that letter as a beacon guiding me through those early years of fog: *Sung Lien, come soon, for I am failing.* Everything described by my grandfather seemed familiar now, in the way of the long elusive tune suddenly remembered.

The taxi slowed to a stop, and we got out on a street that was bordered by a ten-foot-high wall. Retrieving our bags, we followed Da Bobo along the wall until he stopped before a door, digging in his pocket for his keys. At first I thought the door was made of rusted metal, but then, looking closely, saw that it was wooden, its paint faded to the color of dried blood. My heart began to pound. Da Bobo turned the key and pushed the door open. He passed through, then beckoned for me to follow.

Even now, so many years later, I remember the sensation that came over me the moment I crossed the threshold. I felt light-headed, dazzled in a way, though I continued to see everything clearly.

"What's the matter?" Da Bobo said.

Da Mama looked at me closely. "She have long trip. Better we go in." She took hold of my sleeve, pulled me along.

"I'm fine," I insisted, staring at the path of cracked bricks beneath my feet.

"Sung Lien!" called Aunt Lucy, who appeared from another wing of the courtyard. She peered into my face. "Are you sick?"

"Bring her inside!" Da Bobo ordered.

I followed my aunts, but not before looking over my shoulder into the courtyard. There was Yeh Yeh's plum tree, his plot of chrysanthemums, the snagged clothesline belonging to the peasant neighbors of whom he had complained so bitterly. Scattered on the ground were stray clods of dirt, weed stalks, feathers. I had not imagined the yard to be so small and unkempt. Then my foot struck something, and I found myself at the first step of the house, before a sagging wooden portico supported by uneven beams. With my uncle at my side, I entered the cool tiled foyer before the central chamber of the house. At the exact point of my entry, the house seemed to exhale, breathing into my face the odors of ancient oils, expired pungency, and pain. While my relatives bustled about throwing open doors, hauling suitcases across the floor, I stood rooted in the middle of the maelstrom trying to track the source of my confusion.

The room had a dim, cave-like aspect. The windows were covered with dust, blocking sunlight. After my eyes adjusted to the darkness, I saw massive, Western-style furniture, shelves stuffed with books and papers. A huge television set presided in the corner. Then I saw it: Yeh Yeh's portrait, hanging on the east wall of the room, and on either side, his scrolls of calligraphy. It was here that the trail abruptly ended. Rather than experiencing revelation and relief, I felt painful upheaval as expectation, memory, the sedimentary layers of my imagination separated and collapsed. I had assumed that my nostalgia, that compelling, complex thing that evolved from Yeh Yeh's letters, my family photographs, my wishes, would interface neatly with the experience of my arrival. But now that I had finally arrived and confronted the real, I was unable to make sense of my cherished memories, all that I had lovingly imagined.

I stared at Yeh Yeh's photograph, as if I would find the answer there. It was a black-and-white portrait, the kind displayed at memorials and funerals, in which he struck a formal, stiff pose. He looked dignified, yet rueful and resigned, as though he hadn't been able to deny the conventional wishes of his family and knew he would be hanging on the wall. I examined the calligraphy scrolls on either side of his face. Executed in classic Chinese, they remained inscrutable, fulfilling their function as beautiful artifacts rather than prescriptions for my emotional ease. Each seven-foot-long scroll was executed in a different style, the first in the expressionistic "grass" style, in which the characters were flowing and curved, the other in more academic, block style.

"Which one do you like?" Da Bobo said, startling me.

"I don't know. They're both beautiful."

"Yeh Yeh left one for you. Pick one."

I felt him studying me and grew increasingly uneasy under his angular gaze. I sensed he knew what was going on with me.

"No hurry," he said. "Plenty of time to decide later. Come on, I'll show you the house."

He guided me into the dining room and from there to the newly finished bathroom, which was twice the size of the central chamber. Da Bobo's feet clapped across the tiles as he proudly pointed out the bathtub, toilet, and cold-water sink, each affixed at opposing walls. The cavernous space smelled of damp grout, reminding me of the communal shower of my junior high gym class and its memories of excruciating embarrassment.

From here, Da Bobo led me out to a path that encircled the house, leading us back to the courtyard. He held my elbow gently, as though I were fragile cargo. I was grateful he avoided going back through the central chamber, skirting the spirit center of the house.

We came to a makeshift kitchen, built onto an exterior wall of the house, where my mother and Aunt Lucy watched Da Mama and the maid preparing dinner. Da Bobo explained they had improvised the primitive cooking area after the government had taken over the section of the house containing the original kitchen. The maid, a young woman who was already stooped and toothless, fried garlic over a grimy propane stove. Da Mama chopped cabbage on a tree stump, rinsed it in a cement trough set on the ground. The packed dirt floor beneath her was strewn with wood chips, vegetable scraps, more feathers. The entire place reeked of stale grease and smoke. Aunt Lucy tugged my sleeve. "I live over there," she said, pointing in the direction of the courtyard.

"She can go there tomorrow," Da Bobo said.

"The BBC is coming on soon," Aunt Lucy persisted. "Handel's *Julius Caesar*. Something you would appreciate. Authentic instruments, I believe."

"She hears Handel all the time," Da Bobo said, taking a step that placed him between me and my aunt.

I stared helplessly at my relatives with their flared pinions. Finally Aunt Lucy said, in her high, imperious tone, "Very well. Do what you want," and turned away. I noticed that she walked heel-first, not on her toes as before, and that her air of nervous agitation had disappeared.

"She does seem much better," I said.

"Yes," Da Bobo agreed, somewhat ruefully.

Later, over dinner, Da Bobo told us about the construction of the bathroom, how it ended up costing so much money that he had had to dip into his pension.

"But it was worth it, because now you and your mother don't have to use the *ma tung*."

I sucked in my breath at the mention of the filthy wooden waste receptacle used in the old days, recalling the old woman in Chongqing with her foul bucket. My uncle seemed not only gratified by my response, but took it as encouragement for him to elaborate further about his ordeal.

"It turned out the workers were not bathroom workers at all, but road laborers who were moonlighting for extra money," he complained. "Not only were they lazy and incompetent, but they demanded cigarettes, and beer, and snacks!" He went on and on, describing his tale of frustration and extortion in a narrative that was clearly well-worn. Da Mama and Aunt Lucy listened with an air of heavy resignation, in the way they endure a family member's snoring. Finally Aunt Lucy lost her patience.

"What did you expect?" she cried. "We live in China!"

Making a bid for peace, my mother took out photographs of her grandchildren and passed them around. While my mother and aunts clucked over the photos, I looked around the room more closely. It was hemmed in with bookcases bulging with books and old papers like the rest of the house. Next to the door, there was a small refrigerator, atop of which there was a Mr. Coffee machine still wrapped in plastic. Scattered in other corners of the room were a toaster, microwave, bamboo steamer, box of preserved duck eggs, and several jars of herbs and ointments. The room exuded an air of antiquity teetering inexorably toward modern life. Despite its clutter and incongruity, it exuded a strange harmony and comfort. Sitting there, listening to the sound of my relatives' voices, I felt completely at home.

Turning slightly, so that I looked through the arched entryway of the room into the adjoining central chamber, I glimpsed again the shrine-like arrangement of Yeh Yeh's portrait and his scrolls of calligraphy. Once again I grew uneasy, unable to come to terms with all my feelings. This time I could not even name them all. I felt like a tiny country at war with itself, its many factions shifting allegiance so that their identities became blurred, the main impetus of their struggle lost.

I may have stayed in this state had not Da Bobo announced that it was time for our baths. This involved him carrying bucket after bucket of hot water, heated on the primitive kitchen stove, through the outer passageway around the house into the new bathroom. After my mother's bath, he insisted that I have one, too. Rather than having us reuse the precious hot water, he insisted on emptying and refilling the tub. Despite our protests, he toiled on, sloshing the buckets, panting, his neck muscles straining. As dismayed as I was by my uncle's stubbornness, I saw how it was consistent with his character. Even as he embraced the conveniences of modernity, he still held fast to the old rules of Chinese propriety.

It was nearly midnight when we retired for the night. Despite our protests, Da Bobo and Da Mama insisted that my mother and I sleep in their bedroom, on the west side of the central chamber. Amid more shelves stuffed with books, clothes, and a table covered with vials of Chinese medicine, there was a large bed that smelled of moldy silk and sandalwood.

"Where are Da Bobo and Da Mama sleeping?" I asked.

"In the room off the other side of the dining room," my mother replied. "Yeh Yeh slept there, before he died."

She had already slipped beneath the sheets. Though I had taken off my tourist's uniform and put on my sleep shirt, I sat on the other side of the bed, on top of the heavy coarse coverlet. Another daughter might not have hesitated to share a bed with her mother, but I felt strangely reluctant, or, more accurately, prevented, as though the points of our heads and feet, like magnetic poles placed positive to positive, negative to negative, repelled one another. After a while, I slid under the sheets.

"Was this Yeh Yeh and Nai Nai's bed, too?"

"Hmmm," my mother said. She was already drifting off.

Carefully maintaining a space between us, I tried to settle into the uneven hollows of the bed, shifting my back and shoulders until I sank into what felt like the contours of another body that had already made its permanent impression in the mattress. The impression felt deep, made over a long period of time, its edges soft and rounded, like a surface planed by wind or sand. My head lay in what felt like a skull-scooped indentation, my hips and shoulders settling into broader shallows. I lay still for a long time, hardly daring to breathe, my mind churning with theories and imagined narratives: that I lay where Yeh Yeh had slept; that this bed supported a succession of Chao family members, from Yeh Yeh to Da Bobo to me, and that this moment, when all their spirits conjoined with mine, was my rightful inheritance. I felt overwhelmed by the enormity of the moment, the possibility that all might be wishful thinking and fantasy.

I listened to my mother's breathing and the sifting of the night wind as it sought passage through the old house. The breeze was cool, the first of its kind since our arrival in China, and stirred the damp curtains of air like branches of palm. As if in relief and celebration, the house sighed and lifted itself. It was then that I knew. It was not a matter of consciousness or effort, but of allowing myself to surrender to what had already been there waiting to embrace me. All I had to do was to meet it, not by straining or struggling, but by being still. Every Chinese knows this. You wait, and the answer will come. And so the night passed. I lay quietly, feeling my body slowly filling the depressions in the bed, like water seeping into footprints left in sand.

22

DOGHOUSE

DA BOBO MADE AMERICAN-STYLE COFFEE BY POURING BOILING WATER INTO powdered Nescafé and condensed milk. "You know," he said, "our new bathroom, it wasn't cheap. I asked Lucy if she would pitch in, because she's rich now, after the government returned all her back pay. But you know what?" He dropped his spoon, whether from sheer outrage or dramatic effect, I couldn't tell. "She refused!"

"She do nothing!" Da Mama added, rocking back and forth, her lips pressed tight. "She not shop, not cook, not clean. She stay in her room, read read read, listen to music. We do everything!"

In the background, the television, which Da Bobo explained a big shot had given him after they had won a tennis tournament, roared from its place in the center room. From the corner of my eye, I glimpsed a program on hydraulic dams. The volume, which Da Bobo had turned on high, as he had still not put in his hearing aid, made it sound like Niagara Falls.

"We feel sorry for Lucy," Da Bobo said, handing me the coffee. "She must be lonely. Sometimes her old students come to visit her, but nobody else. We invite her to eat with us. . . ."

"But she no like us, no like nothing," Da Mama said.

"Where is she now?" I asked.

"Where else? In her *go ooze*."

"*Go ooze?* You mean doghouse?" I had heard of the Chinese term before, meaning a wretched place of exile.

Da Mama nodded. "That what she say."

"Why doghouse?"

"You go see yourself!"

After breakfast, I excused myself and went into the courtyard, where the
day felt pleasantly warm. Beyond the wall came the myriad sounds of
Beijing's white noise: jackhammers, bicycle bells, buses rumbling by. I walked
the twenty or so steps across the courtyard and knocked on Aunt Lucy's
door, which swung open to reveal her seated before a tray of food on a small
table.

"I'm sorry. I'll come back later," I said.

"No! Come in! I was just finishing."

I stood beside the table, feeling awkward. There was only one other chair
besides my aunt's, and it was covered with papers and several books. On either side of the chair, on the floor, were two stereo speakers. More books lay
in stacks and in disorderly piles all over the floor. I noticed Aunt Lucy chewing on something, a yellow sphere that looked like a tennis ball.

"*Mao tow,*" she explained, swallowing. "Millet ball. Mao Zedong ate
them on the long march. It's peasant food, but nutritious, low-fat. I eat one
every morning. Would you like to try?"

The *mao tow* smelled like birdseed, the kind I used to feed my parakeets.
It looked dry and crumbly, with the consistency of mulch. "Thanks, I already ate," I said.

"Bao Ai E!" Aunt Lucy screeched.

The maid, who had been sitting outside, scrambled to the doorway.

"Take the tray away. And don't forget, I want my bath at four o'clock."

The servant picked up the tray and left.

Aunt Lucy turned to me. "Would you like to look around?"

I glanced about the room, which was lit by a single small window set
high in the wall. Beneath this was a narrow cot, made up with coarse-
looking sheets and a wool blanket. Next to it was the small table, where my
aunt sat watching me expectantly. I approached the larger end of the L-
shaped room to her right which was divided by rows of freestanding book-
shelves so tall they nearly reached the ceiling exuding the smell of crumbling
paper, musty binding, old glue, and dust. As I walked down the rows I noticed volumes of history, philosophy, poetry, and fiction written in English

and Chinese. At the end of each stack, standing like elegant bookends, were beautiful pieces of furniture: a chest of drawers, a carved stand of rosewood, a table with legs as slender as a fawn's. Beyond the far end, behind the last row, I came upon a small tiled space with a hole in the floor. A sour smell rose from it, and I realized, with embarrassment, that I had stumbled upon Aunt Lucy's toilet. I doubled back through the rows, nearly colliding with my aunt, who stood before a wall-sized unit of shelving and drawers which appeared to be carved from a single piece of wood. Exquisitely made, the piece glowed with a rich patina like that of my old Italian viola.

"All these pieces are from the Ming Dynasty," Aunt Lucy said, waving in the direction of the furniture behind the book stacks. "When the Red Guards came to arrest me, they took everything. Decadent spoils, they called them. They took these, too."

She opened a drawer, drew out an ivory medallion. It was the size of a scallop shell, so minutely and intricately carved that it looked to have been rendered by artisan ants. From another drawer, Aunt Lucy removed pieces of jade ranging in color from that of skim milk to moss and deep emerald. Each stone gleamed softly from having been polished by loving and expert hands. My aunt held up a translucent, tear-shaped pendant.

"The best jade is cold to the touch," she said, placing it in my palm. I closed my fingers around it, amazed at how cool and heavy it was, like a fragment of frozen sea wave.

One by one, Aunt Lucy pulled out the remaining drawers, showing me antique combs, mirrors, hairpins, ornamental knives, and other artifacts that she had collected before the Cultural Revolution. A few pieces, she explained, she had inherited from Yeh Yeh. Most were from the Ming Dynasty, an illustrious period between 1368–1644 regarded as having produced the finest of China's ornamental arts as well as significant advances in literature and culture. I viewed the priceless artifacts with awe and an indefinable sense of privilege. In a tone of pride that had less to do with ownership than with recognition of the intrinsic value of the pieces and their place in Chinese history, Aunt Lucy described each piece, explaining in detail how and when she had come by it. Holding up a hairpin made of bone, she regarded it as a splinter of history.

"I never thought I would see my pieces again," she said. "But when the communists released me, at the end of the Cultural Revolution, they told me to go claim my things. At first I didn't know what they meant. I thought they had destroyed everything, as they had threatened. But they had kept them all, you see. Catalogued in a warehouse. Here, look."

She took a curl of paper from the last drawer and handed it to me. The look in her eye conveyed that here was the crowning piece of the whole lot. Not the jade pendant, not the Ming tables and chairs, but this strip of faded yellow paper. I unrolled it. It looked like a laundry list, vertical columns of Chinese characters followed by five-digit numbers.

"This says jade," Aunt Lucy said, pointing to the paper. "The first item is a pendant, a carved eggplant, tagged 54367. The next item is a ring, tagged 54368. And so on."

She rocked back and forth on her heels, nodding. I stared at the paper. The handwritten list was meticulous. Obviously not the work of a peasant, more likely a clerk or accountant assigned by the communists to perform bureaucratic latrine duty.

"So there is something to be said for Chinese bureaucracy," I said, handing the paper back.

"Hoo hoo hoo!"

"But why? If the communists wanted to wipe out China's so-called decadent society, why didn't they destroy these as well?"

My aunt shrugged. "Peasants may be ignorant, but that doesn't mean they don't know beauty when they see it. Also I think they were superstitious, afraid to risk incurring the wrath of the spirits of the emperors who had commissioned the pieces." She paused, reflecting. "But now that I think of it, maybe the communists had never meant to destroy them. Maybe it was more important to them that I not have them. I was the so-called traitor, after all, not the things themselves. Even so, the Red Guards had no idea what they had gotten into. They couldn't risk having the artifacts stolen and sold in foreign markets, so they had to put them in warehouses, catalogue and guard them. Just imagine, my things were only a small number among the hoard that was taken from the thousands of people they arrested. Think of the labor involved, keeping track of everything! Hah! Served them right!"

Now I noticed a photograph, framed in ebony, that lay in one of the cases. The subject's face was handsome, severe. Following my gaze, Aunt Lucy picked up the portrait. "My husband," she said.

"Aunt Lucy," I began, but hesitated, remembering our conversation in St. Paul, how we had stalled at this very juncture. I thought of how everyone throughout my journey in China had suffered as a result of the Cultural

Revolution, from Auntie Aifong, Sun Ai E, and my cousins in Changsha. How odd that I was brought full circle back to Aunt Lucy where again I peered into the chasm of her personal history, afraid of stumbling over my curiosity into the realm of trespass.

"It's all right," Aunt Lucy said, looking directly at me. There, for the first time, in her eyes, I saw her permission, her view that here, in her doghouse, there was no transgression.

"My husband and I were totally opposite," she said, replacing the photograph, locking the case. She moved back through the stacks to her alcove, where she sat down. She gestured for me to clear off and pull up the other chair.

"I preferred to spend my time reading and writing, whereas my husband loved parties, dancing. His professors predicted a brilliant career for him in archaeology, but he was not ambitious. We married quite young."

She paused. I felt her eyes searching my face, anticipating my reluctant questions.

"My husband and I were in Chicago, in 1949, when Mao Zedong summoned all Chinese to come home. We came back as soon as we could, thinking it a tremendous honor to be asked to help our country. Before, we never had a leader who envisioned a unified China, or who demonstrated the power and the will to succeed. Because of Mao Zedong, there was great hope in our country, a patriotic fever. My husband and I believed we could contribute by teaching what we had learned in America, helping our country overcome the ignorance and backwardness that had crippled it for so long. Because of Mao we felt proud to be Chinese, no longer ashamed in the face of the world.

"But when we got home, it was not as we hoped. The infrastructure was destroyed. People were homeless, starving. The communists branded intellectuals and artists as elitists and traitors who corrupted their proletarian society. They went house to house in the middle of the night, rousing us out of bed to interrogate and harass us."

Aunt Lucy took off her spectacles, rubbed her eyes. "When I told Yeh Yeh we had made a mistake, that we should not have come back, do you know what he said? He said we were not true patriots, that true patriots do not think of themselves first, but rather of their country, their countrymen. 'Keep sight of the long view,' he said. 'Be patient.' This, even as the communists beat him, burned his entire life's work in front of everyone in the town square.

"Terrible years of suffering passed. Crops failed. Thousands of people died of starvation and disease. Mao Zedong's Great Leap Forward, a plan designed to organize the country's labor force into communes, was a complete disaster. Then came the Cultural Revolution in 1966. The Red Guards hunted down teachers, purging the universities. One by one, we heard of our friends and colleagues being arrested, sent down to the countryside for hard labor and 're-education.' As teachers, my husband and I knew we were on the list, but we had nowhere to go. There was nothing to do but wait."

Aunt Lucy paused. After a long time, she said, "My husband had a favorite white shirt. A button had come off. There was only a bit of black thread in the house, so I used it to sew on the button. It did not look right, of course, but it had to do. This was the shirt my husband managed to put on the night the Red Guards broke into our home. Everything happened so fast there wasn't even time to say good-bye. They locked me up in an old abandoned school, shaved off half my hair. Only half, you see, only the right side of my head, so I was doubly humiliated."

My aunt's leg began to kick; her left hand picked at imaginary threads in her blouse.

"Aunt Lucy," I began, backing away from the chasm, but she shook her head.

"They kept me locked up for six months. Whenever my hair grew back a little, they shaved it off. There was little to eat, some hot water with a bit of rotten turnip. My hair began to fall out. I was actually pleased at this, you see, because then the shaving meant nothing. I thought, *the less there was of me, the less they could humiliate.* Sure enough, they found a way. I had been allowed to have paper and pen, but one day they took these away, too. My thoughts became homeless, having nowhere to go but around and around in my head. I couldn't sleep. Night after night, I lay on the floor, feeling myself melt away. To keep busy, I began counting my bones. Have you ever done this?"

She raised her hands, placed them on the top of her head, indicating for me to do the same.

"When you have not eaten in a long time, your skull begins to feel bigger. It isn't, really, but because there is less flesh, the bone feels more prominent. Here, tap yourself, right on top."

She tapped her crown. I did the same.

"When you are starving, your head sounds hollow, like a melon. An overripe melon, past eating."

She kept her hands on top of her head for several moments, then slowly lowered them.

"One day, the guards came in and gave me a pile of clothes. At first I was confused. *Whose clothes were these?* I wondered. *Why have they brought them to me?* But then I saw the white shirt, the one with the button sewn with black thread, and I knew that my husband was dead. Later, they told me he had hanged himself. Some say he had been weak, that only weak people kill themselves, but I think they are wrong. It may have been true that my husband had lost hope, that he believed he would never be free again, but this didn't make him weak. I had thought as many times to kill myself, only I did not have the courage." Aunt Lucy paused, as though still pondering this. "Years later," she continued, "I found out they had locked him up in a building right next to mine. Who knows? If there had been a window, I might have looked out and seen him."

We sat for a while, not speaking. From across the courtyard I heard the television blaring, Da Bobo arguing with a neighbor. I knew I stood deep in the chasm, amid the reverberations of my aunt's story, and tried to muster the nerve to ask my final questions. Then I realized it was too late not to, as I was already there, at the bottom.

"Aunt Lucy. At the end . . . do you think Yeh Yeh still believed?"

She thought for a long time. "I don't know. He was so tired and lonely. But I think he had come to accept that a person cannot hope to see all things pass in his lifetime, and that, finally, even though he could not be there to see the changes in our country, he still thought they might happen. I think, at the end, he accepted everything, your father too, for not having come home. This, among everything else, was what allowed him to die."

She stopped, rubbed her eyes again.

"Aunt Lucy . . . what they did to you . . . are you . . . bitter?"

She blinked, fixing her small eyes on me with a look indicating I should have known better. "The Chinese have a saying," she said. "*Che ku*. Eat bitter. That says a lot about the Chinese character. You eat bitter, it becomes a part of you. To be otherwise means to separate yourself, to indulge in conceit. Why should you think you are special, that you suffer more than anyone else? Am I bitter? Who am I to be bitter? I have my books, my music, my work, my little *go ooze*. It is enough."

It is enough. Who said that before? I recalled my cousin-in-law, the trombone player, who had given up his dream of coming to America. I thought of my cousins Sho Sung, Sho Mei, Sho An, with their pearly faces of acceptance, and tried once more to understand their way of yielding to a single greater consciousness. Yet how could I, an American whose beliefs were founded on the rights of the individual?

My aunt grew suddenly restless, as though she was tired of the subject, and pointed to the pile of books stacked on the floor.

"Those are my translations of Walt Whitman," she said. "I would give you one, but you don't read Chinese."

I felt my face turn hot with shame, and I saw the chasm open up again, yawning deep and wide, but something in the tone of Aunt Lucy's voice made me pause. Looking up, I saw in her face her simple abhorrence of waste, her acceptance of the practical nature of things, and that her remark had nothing to do with whether I was Chinese or how I was Chinese. She was not remotely interested in these matters. As soon as I realized this, I was suddenly liberated. The moment was pivotal and transformative, as though I were a fish emerging from the sea to walk on land, a lizard sprouting wings to take to the air. And yet neither of us felt compelled to mark it in any way. It was simply the nature of things.

I heard Da Bobo call my name from the courtyard.

"I guess I have to go now," I said. "They have sight-seeing planned."

Aunt Lucy tilted her face in the direction of Da Bobo and Da Mama's wing of the house. Light glinted from the lenses of her spectacles.

"Yeh Yeh's not there anymore."

"What do you mean?"

She rose stiffly from her chair. "All they do is watch television, gossip, listen to popular songs. That was never his way."

Da Bobo called me again, louder.

"Come back at five o'clock," Aunt Lucy said. "The BBC is playing Monteverdi."

"Thank you. I love Monteverdi," I said, before turning to leave.

"Yes. Yeh Yeh did, too."

That evening, my mother and I were the guests of honor at a small party that Da Bobo and Da Mama organized. They introduced us to two older couples, card-playing friends they had known for more than twenty years. They sat with us in the center room, listening to tales of our trip, adding sympathetic commentary. They spoke missionary English and sounded like different versions of my uncle, only not as loud. Da Bobo served cherry-flavored Kool-Aid, given to him by a big shot back from a business trip to San Francisco. Later we all sang my uncle's favorite songs, including "Blue Skies," and then some old Broadway favorites: "Surrey with the Fringe on Top," and "GiGi." The voices of the old folks quavered, but their memory was unerring, nodding encouragement and prompting me when I forgot the words. Between songs they joked and teased one another in affectionate and familiar tones. I got the sense they met regularly to sing the same songs and tell the same jokes over and over. Across the courtyard, drifting in on the mild night air, I heard Aunt Lucy's stereo playing Schubert's *Death and the Maiden* quartet. It is a work I love and admire, but on this evening, juxtaposed with "Oh What a Beautiful Morning!" the piece sounded grim and histrionic.

Out of the blue, Da Bobo asked me to demonstrate disco dancing.

"I don't know how to dance disco, Da Bobo," I said, mortified.

"Oh sure you do, a young person like you?" He put on a Henry Mancini cassette. The sounds of "The Baby Elephant Walk" burbled in the room.

"I don't think that's disco," I ventured.

"It has a nice beat," Da Bobo mused. He swung his hips back and forth experimentally. "How about the twist?"

"I don't think that's disco, either."

"Disco! Disco!" Da Mama and her friends clamored.

"Here, you pick," Da Bobo said, handing me his box of cassettes.

Reluctantly, I went through the tapes. Toward the end, astonishingly, I came across the Bee Gee's "Stayin' Alive."

"Where'd you get this, Da Bobo?"

"I think your brother sent it."

"All right. Put it on."

The silly beat sounded throughout the chamber. Feeling idiotic and self-conscious, I began to screw my feet around on the slippery tiled floor and throw my hips and shoulders in opposite directions.

"Teach me!" Da Mama shouted, jumping up, joining me on the floor. She began to heave herself around enthusiastically. *"Ai yah!"* she whooped. "This hurt my back!"

The other seventy-year-olds joined us and, carefully at first, then, with more abandon, began to hop and bend to the beat, looking like dried cornstalks creaking in the wind. The song ended, but the tape went on relentlessly to the next tune without skipping a beat. Da Bobo seemed to have gotten the hang of it, managing to hoist himself around like a slightly rheumatic John Travolta. He pulled my mother out of her chair, cajoled her to dip her knees a little and shrug her shoulders to the music. Watching them move across the room I glimpsed Yeh Yeh's portrait on the wall looking on with his rueful expression of accosted dignity. That he was ignored, eclipsed in his own house, made me feel vaguely ashamed, so I ducked out onto the portico, where the disco beat was transmuted into a din of clicking insects. Across the courtyard, I heard the last strains of *Death and the Maiden,* sounding louder now, signifying not only the climax of the piece, but that Aunt Lucy had cranked it up in order to drown out "Stayin' Alive." A faint light shone in her window, a stubborn square star in the night. Now I knew that the meaning of *go ooze,* doghouse, according to Aunt Lucy, meant self-imposed exile, because she had refused Da Bobo's invitation to mingle with his friends.

The disco music faded. In its place came the sounds of clinking and laughter as Da Bobo refilled the Kool-Aid glasses. Across the yard, Death finally claimed the Maiden. An eery peace filled the courtyard. I stared at the light in Aunt Lucy's window, which remained pale but steadfast, until it abruptly went out.

23

PILGRIM

"I FORGOT, THESE CAME FOR YOU," DA BOBO SAID, HANDING ME A PACKET OF airmail letters.

They were five aerograms from Fred, the first dated a few days after my departure from St. Paul, the last written a week before our arrival in Beijing. He reported that our lilacs were blooming, as well as the Queen of the Night and Apricot Delight tulips I had planted the previous fall. Also, Maya had escaped through a gap in the hedge and gotten into the Dumpster behind Applebaum's grocery store on Grand Avenue. *I took her to the emergency animal clinic,* he wrote. *The vet took an X-ray of her stomach showing a whole fish floating along with other abstract-looking debris, like a Paul Klee painting. He had to pump her stomach—Jesus, the bill came to $233.00!*

In another letter he described the Grand Old Days parade, which began at Fairview Avenue, near our house. *The horses crapped all over the front yard,* he wrote. *But the Twins are in the playoffs against the Tigers. I hope you and your mother are having a great trip. I miss you!*

In the final letter he wrote: *Yay! It's good to hear from you! I was beginning to think you and your mom had been arrested by the Reds. Sorry to hear about the hassles, but it sounds like the detours have led to adventures you might not have had otherwise. Still holding down the fort—Maya's fine. I miss you.*

I read the aerograms quickly, then again. Even after the second time I was still hungry for word from home, feeling like I had gobbled pills instead of a meal. It hardly felt like three weeks had gone by since I had left home, more like several months. A tsunami of homesickness, carrying the essences of life at home and the awesome Minnesota Twins swept over me. I ached for Fred's arms around me, pizza, the luxuriant shade of oak trees, and, almost more than anything, the English language. Yet I knew there were still two weeks left before I was to go home.

When I joined my mother, uncle, and aunt at breakfast, the conversation sounded serious. Da Bobo stroked his temples thoughtfully, as though counting with his fingertips the exact number of his last remaining strands of hair.

"...if the government claimed eminent domain, we'd have no choice... we'd have to sell," he was saying.

"What are you talking about?" I said.

"We might lose the house."

I stared at Da Bobo, feeling as though he had just socked me in the stomach. I had known of the possibility of their losing the house, but to hear it expressed aloud in such clear terms, and by my uncle, the longtime guardian, made it sound as though everything had already been decided.

"It's getting to be too much," he said, his words coming in a rush, as though they had been building up in his head and only now found an escape. "The repairs, the bills, the government officials bothering us all the time. What choice do we have? Because we don't have children, your brother is the rightful heir, but he said he doubted he could establish residency in Beijing in order to inherit the house."

"How long does it take to establish residency?" I asked.

"Six months."

I'll do it, I thought.

"Look what we went through with the bathroom," Da Bobo said. "Next there's the roof, the windows, the kitchen. Your brother says it doesn't make sense for him to move to Beijing. He's too busy, and, besides, he wants to raise his children in America."

So he had already talked to my brother about it. I searched my uncle's face, seeing not even a hint that I had come up in the discussion. My feelings stuck in my throat even as they rose. I was a woman, after all, and women didn't inherit property in China as long as there were male heirs. Glancing at my mother I saw confirmed in her sad expression how well she knew to what Chinese women were entitled. It made no sense for me to make a claim. What would I do with a house in China, this great, sagging place that cried out for a complete overhaul? Not only was it beyond me financially, but I couldn't even begin to imagine establishing residency. Nothing was clearer than the impossibility of it all, yet the thought of abandoning Yeh Yeh's house was unbearable.

"Did you know this is one of the last private houses left in Beijing?" Da Bobo went on. "It's worth hundreds of thousands of dollars. If the government makes a good offer, we could buy two new apartments, one for Da Mama and me, one for Aunt Lucy, and still have enough money to live on for the rest of our lives."

He was massaging the area above his right temple where a network of blue veins throbbed faintly. It wasn't clear if he had a headache, or whether he was probing the path he might take: whether he was to honor family obligation by finding a way to stay in the house, or sell, and liberate himself from financial worry and endless hassles. My uncle's eyes looked troubled and doubtful, yet there was a flinty spark there, too, reflecting a sensibility that overlooked nothing, especially opportunity. It became clear to me that, above all, Da Bobo was a pragmatic man who set his sights firmly on the future. He had had his fill of the decrepit house and the burden of obligation, which he had borne for so long alone. I saw that he was capable of relinquishing even the most deeply held sentiment in the face of the right offer. In spite of my own sorrow and regret, my vague sense of guilt, I knew that I had experienced none of what he had sacrificed. It was up to me to nurse my phantom pains as best I could.

"Oh, by the way," he said, "my contact got train tickets for you and your mother to Shanghai."

The reminder that my mother and I were scheduled to fly home from Shanghai came as a thunderbolt. Though I was eager to go home, this latest news of the probable loss of Yeh Yeh's house now made me feel like a deserter, leaving my uncle alone once again to defend the family fortress. There was something else in my reluctance to leave which I couldn't even explain to myself. Something still felt unfinished, unfulfilled, as if my having finally arrived had not yet sunk in, or that I had not comprehended what Yeh Yeh's house truly meant to me. With the prospect of demolition, I realized I might never know.

I went out to the portico to stare at the tall wall, where it became all too clear that my grandfather's house was under siege. Convoys of buses rumbled past the courtyard, shaking the very ground, while bicycles circled in a swarm.

Looming nearby, encroaching the periphery, were concrete high-rises, man-made peaks that spiked the dirty horizon. A far cry from the dingy hovels of the *hutungs,* they signaled that the day of the *ma tung* was drawing to a close. Soon, I thought, there would be nothing left of the old China except for a solitary wooden bucket preserved in a museum. And who would mourn but tourists, and wayward pilgrims like me?

A trip to the Great Wall had been planned. I slathered on sunscreen and put on my sturdy walking shoes. While Da Bobo locked the house, I waited with my mother and Da Mama in the courtyard, listening to strains of Schubert lieder coming from Aunt Lucy's window. Her door was closed, looking pursed, like a mouth that has decided it is pointless to speak since no one pays heed. I wondered what her feelings were regarding the sale of the house. In spite of her powerful role in the family, she left all practical matters to Da Bobo, not only because she felt it was incumbent on him as the eldest son, but also because such matters were beneath her. Perhaps there was more to it. Perhaps she deferred to her brother because he had rescued her when she had lost her mind during the Cultural Revolution, and she felt she owed him for that. In any case, I couldn't imagine Aunt Lucy ever leaving her doghouse. Beijing could turn into a hideous concrete desert, but she would remain forever in her little den of books and Ming furniture, drowning out the sound of modernity with Monteverdi and Schubert. This gave me some comfort, because in my mind Aunt Lucy stood for Yeh Yeh. As long as she stuck to her guns, he lived on.

We arrived at the Great Wall after an hour's drive in a hired car. Though it was still early in the day, tourists were swarming all over. Most were Chinese from Hong Kong and Taiwan, but there were quite a number of Chinese Americans, too, from the looks of their husky limbs, baseball caps, and neon-bright butt packs.

We climbed the long staircase of stone and stood breathless atop a fortress cresting the uneven hillside. The wall coursed in an angular undulation up a natural spiny ridge, looking like petrified movement, a quiver deep from the earth that had become, through some natural phenomenon, suddenly stilled as molten lava is shocked by its headlong spill into the sea. At this junction, where the wall split in two directions, my mother stopped and waved me to go ahead. She had climbed both paths over the years, and now her knees were as spent as her awe. She joined Da Bobo and Da Mama, who were browsing the concession booths abloom with Mickey Mouse I WAS AT THE GREAT WALL T-shirts and balloons and other paraphernalia.

I began to climb the steeper path, the one that looked as if it led to Mongolia. The stones beneath my feet were more than two feet long and a foot and a half wide. I tried to remember the statistics given by my old *History of China* book, but could only think of the thousands of workers whose backs were broken and who lay buried within the wall.

Under clouds that were mere wisps falling away from the sun, the wall kept going on. After an hour, I was still climbing. Every now and then I stopped to peer over the sides, viewing a sheer drop of fifty feet and more. Few other tourists had come this far. At an elevated thickening, a joint in the wall, which had once been a lookout post, I stopped to scan the horizon. From this spot, more solitary than a lighthouse promontory, the air seemed thin. What did a lookout see beyond the vast stretches of gray-green plain? More miles of sky? Enemies? Tiny dots far away below, or, more likely, distant pinpoints in the paranoid imaginations of the rulers building the wall? Who would dare to challenge this looming edifice, this man-made Himalaya?

I listened to the wind, watching it chase clouds so that their shadows flitted over the ground like schools of fish. There was little other sound. For a moment, I imagined that here was a spot that modernity could never disturb. Had the thousands of souls conscripted to build the wall known what it would come to stand for? Could they have grasped the nature of the real foe to China—not the dreaded barbarian hordes of their own century, but the far greater evils of a time they could not have imagined? Possibly, they had. Why else the gargantuan dimensions, the terrible cost? They must have known what havoc men could make. Perhaps it was not so extreme after all, this single, fearful consciousness.

Imagining myself a lookout, I turned to face Beijing. Above the horizon lay a dark amorphous mass, a gathering of burnt waste that was the collective exhaust of the city. Though it was suspended, stationary, its edges expanded and contracted with a peculiar ominousness, signaling imminent invasion, like a swarm of locusts.

I hurried back down the wall, which was more difficult than the strenuous steep climb. Pounding the rock, my knees ached, my teeth rattled in my head. After what seemed like endless miles, I arrived at the junction, where a great horde of tourists had gathered amidst a sea of red, white, and black,

Mickey Mouse all over, where the wall had been transformed into another backdrop for Fantasy Land. I spotted Da Bobo leaning against the stones, licking an ice candy. Da Mama and my mother sat nearby in the shade, fanning themselves.

"What do you think?" Da Mama asked.

I opened my mouth, but no words came. For the first time, I understood what mountain climbers must feel when they descend from heavenly peaks. In my case it wasn't fatigue or lack of oxygen that prevented me from speaking, but the fact that I was still there, far away, and not likely to be at sea level for some time. Something kept me there, something unmarked and pure, beyond human experience and all that was common and mundane. Even though by reaching that place I might have sullied it somehow, I felt graced by it nonetheless, filled with gratitude that there was something yet untouchable in the world.

Later, back at the house, during dinner, tumultuous rain fell, splattering through leaks in the roof. Aunt Lucy watched indifferently as Da Bobo and Da Mama scurried about, setting out pots and pans to catch the deluge. Turning from them, she inquired about my next day's itinerary of sightseeing.

"Forbidden City!" she huffed. "So touristy! If you want to see the real China, I'll take you to Liulichang Street."

"The Forbidden City is real China," Da Mama said, looking up from her hands and knees. Her face had flushed dark. The Forbidden City was her idea. She had offered to take me there, just the two of us.

"Everybody goes there," Aunt Lucy retorted. "You'll suffocate. Besides, all the best things have been stolen or stored away." She raised her chin, fixed her eyes on me. "You really don't want to waste your time there."

"Actually, I've heard a lot about the Forbidden City," I said, carefully. "I'd like to see it."

Aunt Lucy seemed momentarily taken aback. Then, recovering quickly, she rapped her chopsticks against her plate. "This chicken," she declared, knowing full well that Da Mama had cooked it, "is much too salty!"

The next day, Da Mama and I set off for the Forbidden City. We took two buses and walked several long blocks toward an edifice with tiled rooftops that swept upward like albatross wings. As usual, the streets were choked with pedestrians and bicyclists. Everyone was coughing and squinting in the hot, sooty air. Da Mama trotted along at a fast clip, snatching quick backward glances to make sure I was still with her. Though I tried to keep my arm in hers, onrushing people repeatedly broke our link. I was tired of being bumped and jostled, of tripping headlong in a rhythm set by the mindless frenzy of the street. Again, I noticed several black sedans conveying important-looking bureaucrats moving through the lanes of bicycles. More officials dressed in the green-and-red communist uniform strolled the streets of Beijing than anywhere else in China, giving the city an authoritarian if not military aspect. Finally, we arrived at the gates of the Forbidden City and entered the first of the great halls.

The large foyer was dark, already steamy from panting tourists. Guides chanted through megaphones in Mandarin, Japanese, and English, addressing three separate groups. The sound of their scripts, ricocheting from the walls, sounded like underwater babble. I focused on the English group, led by a young woman who reeled out, in a singsong voice:

"In the year 1406, Ming emperor Yong Le began the construction of the Forbidden City to house the Imperial Family and its attendants. Today you will be seeing the Hall of Supreme Harmony, the Gate of Divine Military Genius, the Hall of Mental Cultivation, the Hall of Manifest Harmony . . ."

She paused for breath. It was obvious she gave this speech several times a day, day after day, and that it bored her to death. She inhaled deeply, closed her eyes, and continued:

"In its heyday, the Forbidden City was residence to, in addition to the emperor and empress, more than two hundred cooks, over a thousand eunuchs, one hundred and fifty concubines plus their ladies-in-waiting, more than two hundred children, nine hundred ministers, advisors, administrators, secretaries, two dozen scribes, over one hundred and fifty *amahs* and their helpers . . ."

Her voice droned on in the cold dispassionate tone of an IRS clerk. Even so, I found the numbers, all that remained of the occupants in this awesome place, strangely compelling. As we walked through the labyrinth of rooms, winding hallways, and stairwells, our guide intoned: ". . . and here you see the chambers of the palace concubines, who vied for the emperor's favor. Those who bore him sons rose in the ranks, assuring themselves rich pensions in old age." She indicated a long divided hallway along which doors opened on both sides. The rooms within looked like cells in a beehive. As we passed, wooden beams creaked beneath our feet, and I imagined the nightly shuffle as concubines vied to carry out their imperial trysts.

We entered a display room of the empress's jewelry, housing gem-studded headpieces, necklaces, rings, opium jars, mirrors, combs. Although the pieces were replicas, they were still impressive, ornate and intricate in design. There were also court gowns, made of exquisite silk covered with rich embroidery, cut so that the armholes were tight, the aprons stiff-looking. They looked shiny and rigid, more like armor than cloth. At the rear of the display was a life-sized painting of a court lady. She was depicted seated on a cushion in an attitude of utter stillness, her face, with its exquisite, tiny mouth and minutely plucked brows, expressing nothing. Perhaps she awaited a summons from the emperor. She looked suspended, as though frozen in a state of waiting, her blood turned to stone.

Then we came upon a bewildering maze of staircases that crisscrossed the walls of the palace. The wooden steps were scooped out from the feet of the thousands of palace occupants who had trod their daily routine of boredom and intrigue. As we went up one staircase and down another, Da Mama stepped on my heels. Turning around, I saw that she looked bored and restless, leading me to believe she had seen this place countless times and had come only for my benefit.

At the far side of the palace our guide paused, took a deep breath, and launched into another recitation of statistics. Looking around, I spied a large gap in the palace wall and peeped through it. Beyond was the street, where vendors were setting up shops in the alleyway.

"Come on," I whispered, pulling Da Mama's arm.

We went out into the street, where there were endless bins of cassettes, key chains, toys, clothes, and scarves fluttering from metal stands. Though it was clear she had no intention of buying, Da Mama examined everything that struck her fancy.

"Look!" she exclaimed, hoisting a packet of cosmetics costing four dollars, then tossing it back indignantly. "For four dollar, I buy two chicken!"

Linking arms, we strolled down the length of the alley. Midway, we paused to watch a young boy wheedle his mother into buying him a pair of Reebok knockoffs. She resisted at first, then, after persistent begging from her son, finally relented. The boy's noisy crowing made the entire alleyway pause. Curious onlookers gathered as the boy sat on a crate to lace up his precious sneakers. As he rose, flushed, his feet encased in dazzling white leather and the all-empowering, though fake logo, they burst into applause. Then a strange thing happened.

Little by little, then in a rush, as though an airborne virus had swept through them, people began to buy. Sneakers flew out of the bins. The tower of scarves toppled as women snatched at it from all sides, its bright swatches of color swirling like flames. It was as though the purchase of that one pair of sneakers had expunged the age-old taboo of fulfilling material want. Reebok, or rather a Reebok wannabe, had prevailed.

Why shouldn't Chinese live as others in the modern world? I thought. *Why shouldn't they be free to choose?* Da Mama and I sensed, with a mix of fearful excitement and uncertainty, that life in China changed before our very eyes. As people grabbed things, spilling coins all over, I saw that it was not merely greed that was at the heart of the matter, but frustration and anger. All the centuries of pent-up want and denial were straining at the gates, rushing through each tiny crack that was forced open. By breaking the taboo, people broached the underlying philosophy of their government, challenged the hypocritical edicts and corruption of their leaders. Soon, I thought, chaos would erupt; all order would be at risk.

Two years later, in fact, in 1989, Chinese students demonstrated at Tiananmen Square and were put down in a display of brutal force that all the world denounced. When I stared at the television, seeing with horror and disbelief the tanks and gunfire and smoke, the students screaming and running in all directions, I relived the day Da Mama and I had strolled down the alleyway and experienced the reaction of the boy to his new sneakers and the tumbling tower of scarves.

Still, there were those who did not see or ignored the signs. Among these was Aunt Lucy, who moved along the sidewalk unperturbed by the noise and crowds. She was taking me to Liulichang Street, the lane of the last remaining artisans, the day after Da Mama and I came back from the Forbidden City. As we walked, Aunt Lucy's air of self-containment was such that I was reluctant to take her arm. She moved slowly through the crowds with a lofty air so that everyone made way. We took one bus, then another, winding through the back streets of Beijing in a serpentine route. The weather had turned hot again, like a furnace. I wiped my face, felt sweat dripping down my back. Aunt Lucy, on the other hand, looked cool as a piece of jade.

We got off in a section of town that was carved with narrow winding lanes and alleyways, along which were low wooden buildings that emitted from their doorways the dank smell of antiquity. Not many people were about: a few octogenarian men squatting on stools, feeble old women hobbling on bound feet looking like crippled birds. In this rare neighborhood, even the breezes fell still, becoming as fixed as the years. Though there were no vendors, there were signs in Chinese and English pointing the way to shops promising good prices. I sensed, with a sinking feeling, that this area was as doomed as my grandfather's house, that soon there would be nothing authentic left in China, nothing left to venerate but profit.

Aunt Lucy paused to get her bearings, looking left and right, breathing deeply, as if only here she trusted the air. Then she pointed down a street that was laid out like a horizontal wave, and said, in a low voice meant to cast spells, "Liulichang."

The street was narrow, bordered on either side by shops. Hanging from the door frames were scrolls of calligraphy. The scrolls were highly individualistic, signifying the distinctive styles of the artists within. I stood there in a paralysis of wonder and indecision until Aunt Lucy prodded me gently.

"That one," she said, indicating a doorway to our left. "He specializes in the grass style. Very distinguished."

We entered via the narrow doorway into a small room that was dark except for a shaft of light from the window. Within its faint beam, an old man sat with ink brush in hand, poised over a curl of rice paper. He wore a black silk skullcap.

What little I know about the art of brushwork comes from my mother, who took up Chinese painting when she was nearly sixty years old. She says brushwork is like playing music. First, you have to imagine the stroke in your mind, practice it, try to feel the rhythm, before you put your brush to the paper. Then you must play it. Because ink soaks into the paper, there's no erasing it, so you only have one chance to make the stroke. You must prepare your mind and body totally beforehand. Brushwork is meditation, a matter of spirit.

I held my breath as the old man silently considered the paper before him. His eyes looked open but unseeing behind the thick lenses of his spectacles. His brush hand was arthritic-looking, a puzzle of blue veins, but unwavering. In a swift, sure motion, he lay his brush to the paper, and in a continuous, swirling stroke, created a character that looked like the aftermath of dance. He contemplated his work quietly. The ink dried. Throughout, he seemed unaware of our presence. My aunt leaned over the paper to examine the character, nodding approvingly. I accepted her critique, even though I couldn't tell whether the character was well wrought or not. I only knew that at the moment of its creation I felt I had witnessed a kind of small miracle.

Again, I wondered why my mother had not come with us. Despite our invitation, she said she had been to Liulichang many times before and preferred to stay at home with Da Mama. She seemed anxious, preoccupied. Though initially puzzled, I didn't think more of it, accepting again that she and I were bound to experience our China stay in different ways.

Finally, the old man looked up at us with his deep-set philosopher eyes and nodded to my aunt, indicating a stack of scrolls leaning against the wall. I went over and carefully unrolled the scrolls, one by one. A musty smell rose from the delicate, porous paper, and bits of fiber drifted to the floor. The scrolls were clearly old, precious, and revealed lines of calligraphy brushed in the flowing style that evoked fields of grass tousled by wind. Though I couldn't read the characters, I was struck by their elegance, how they embodied movement and music.

At the bottom of one scroll dangled a price tag of several hundred dollars. I was shocked at the expense, then reasoned that the scrolls were all that remained of the calligrapher's early works, and that the artist himself, though seemingly in good health, was nearing the end of his productive life. Surely work from his hand would only appreciate in value. I replaced the scrolls, hoping that neither he nor my aunt read my calculating thoughts. I wanted one of the scrolls badly. But which one?

"They're all so beautiful," I said to the calligrapher in Mandarin, or at least that is what I hoped I said. He inclined his head, accepting my compliment. I tugged on Aunt Lucy's sleeve.

"Can you help me? I can't decide."

She stared at me in disbelief. "What? You want to buy?"

I felt myself waver before her piercing look. "I know. . . . But they're so beautiful."

I wanted one so badly my throat ached. Aunt Lucy murmured something to the calligrapher, who nodded and calmly went back to his work. Then my aunt took my arm and steered me to the door. When we were safely outside, she said, "All his original work, done in his prime, was destroyed during the Cultural Revolution. What you saw were reproductions. Mass-produced. Worth a few dollars at most."

"But the paper seemed old!"

"Faked. Easy to do."

I felt my face turn hot. We walked on, passing several door fronts through which we saw other old craftsmen bent over their tables.

"So he makes his living selling fakes?"

"Occasionally he'll sell to a tourist who claims to know Chinese art, or who obviously has money to throw away. But mostly he supports himself by copying poems, inscribing memorials."

"He seemed perfectly willing to sell one of those fakes to me."

My aunt shook her head. "He only invited you to see. But there was no question of you buying. We know one another, he and I."

We walked along for several moments, each absorbed in our own thoughts. Then my aunt pointed to another doorway. "Let's look here," she said. "Another interesting style, though more contemporary. This one has real flair."

The calligrapher here was a younger, solidly built man who crouched over his table, rising on his legs as he painted characters in bold, swift strokes. His thick brush splashed across the paper, leaving broad trails of ink pooling on the surface. He turned to greet my aunt and me. My aunt spoke a few words, after which he set out another, smaller piece of paper. He considered it for a brief moment, then swept his brush over it, leaving characters that seemed to twitch even after he finished. When the paper had dried a little, he picked it up and held it out to me. I looked at my aunt, astonished.

"What does it say?"

"Your name, Chao Sung Lien. Take it. It's a gift."

I took the still-damp paper and thanked the calligrapher profusely. When we were outside the shop, I held the paper up to the sun so that it dried completely. Even then the characters seemed to roll and tumble in the light. I rolled it loosely.

"Take good care of it," my aunt cautioned. "He is one of the most important calligraphers today. His father was a colleague of mine. A Longfellow scholar."

I looked at my aunt, familiar questions on my face.

She anticipated them quickly. "Sent down to the countryside in sixtyseven. Disappeared. His son searched for him for many years. We think his father died soon after he went down, but no one knows for sure."

"What do you mean no one knows? How could they just lose someone?"

My aunt shrugged.

I thought of her Ming furniture and pieces of jade that had been so meticulously catalogued and stored, how these antiques had been so carefully saved, while her colleague had vanished.

A commotion erupted at the end of the street. White men dressed in dark suits ran down Liulichang, waving for people to clear the way. Old men knocked over their stools as they stumbled from the curb while the old women hobbled into the safety of their doorways. My aunt and I watched as a procession of black Mercedes sedans swept by. In the middle was a long black limousine, escorted by plainclothesmen trotting alongside, eyes probing the street. The progress of the cars was slow but inexorable, as though they were taking part in a scrupulously planned invasion. Then the procession stopped. A silver-haired white man got out of the limousine. Straightening, he turned to view both ends of Liulichang Street. His attitude, from what I could see, from a few hundred yards away, was that of admiration and wonder. Recalling an article in the *Herald Tribune* that had announced his arrival in Beijing, I recognized his face.

"Jimmy Carter!" I said, more to myself than anyone. I turned to my aunt. Obviously she was not particularly impressed by foreign dignitaries. Nor, I noticed, were the other residents of the neighborhood, who stood in their doorways looking on with an air of mild curiosity, nothing more.

I stood on my toes, straining for another look at the former president, who had now disappeared into one of the shops along the street. His anticipated visit had caused all the tickets to Beijing to vanish, given over to dignitaries from all over China who vied to meet him. I had voted for him, felt sad at the lapse of his presidency, and still admired him greatly as a man. But what I felt at that moment was the sheer excitement of seeing another American.

In a rush, I understood what it had meant to be a foreigner, a person in a state of perpetual alienation throughout my entire trip. My feeling of otherness had been based not only on how people reacted to me, but on my own response to how people saw me, and ultimately how I saw myself. Seeing Jimmy Carter, I realized that at my core I was American, that I had a country to go back to. Even though I was an "other" there, too, a non-white, it was where I was born and where I had made my home. I knew it was time to go back.

When Aunt Lucy and I returned to Yeh Yeh's house, we heard the sound of people talking and laughing, my mother's voice ringing high and clear above the others. Her laughter was rare, like the sound of an exotic bird that calls but once a year. Inside the house we found Da Bobo, Da Mama, and my mother sitting with an older couple, whom I knew at once from their photographs. The man with the round face and the Lin family jowls was Uncle John, my mother's oldest surviving brother and with him his wife, Elsie. They had traveled all the way from the western provinces to see us. My mother's face was radiant as she made the formal introductions. Now I understood why she had stayed home from our excursion to Liulichang and why, indeed, she had come to China.

24

STORM

UNCLE JOHN, A LARGE MAN WITH A THICK, STURDY TRUNK, WAS EIGHTY years old and appeared to be in fairly good health, though my mother confided afterward that he had heart trouble and arthritis in his knees and hip. The only sign of his frailty was a metal cane he used to steady himself. When he offered me his hand, he suddenly lost his balance and keeled against me, toppling like a tree. Though I tried to support him, his weight brought me to my knees. Shocked by the feel of my uncle's body and what it had transmitted in that brief moment of contact—his age, his dignity, and his great physical presence in spite of his disability—I could only watch as my mother cried out and impulsively threw herself beneath him.

Her gesture was startling, strangely deferential, conveying not only her adoring regard for her oldest surviving brother, the reigning patriarch and linchpin of her family, but her view of him as the central male figure absent from her life for so long. Her concern, while natural, surprised me with its peal of panic. Suddenly my mother seemed fragile, vulnerable, lapsing into the traditional ways of the submissive Chinese female, unlike the proud woman who had fought loneliness and hardship for so many years in America. Was being back in China causing her to revert? Was seeing her brother in decline stirring her fears that her last remaining ties here weakened?

Uncle John seemed embarrassed by my mother's outcry, waving her off weakly while murmuring thanks. Auntie Elsie's face had tightened momentarily at her husband's near fall, but she quickly resumed her calm, pleasant expression, her wide-set eyes radiating a wry view of the world and a generous spirit. She smiled sweetly while my mother and I helped her husband back to his chair, indulging the fact that brother and sister had not seen one another in more than two years. Looking at her more closely, I noted the stiff, sallow skin of her face, and realized she had her own, possibly more threatening health problems.

Both Uncle John and Auntie Elsie spoke English fluently but carefully, as though it was a precious artifact they displayed only on special occasions. They apologized for not meeting my mother and me in Chongqing, where they lived, explaining that Uncle John had been called suddenly to speak in the place of an ailing colleague at a medical conference in Yunan Province. They had learned only recently from a wire sent by Da Bobo that we had finally made our way to Beijing.

"But none of our troubles matter anymore, do they?" Elsie said, smiling. "We are all together now."

Da Mama served orange soda while my mother recounted our trip: our visit to Anna's home in Changsha, our encounter with Sun Ai E (at this Uncle John and Aunt Elsie shook their heads, murmuring, *"ku, ku,"* bitter, bitter), and our trip down the Yangtze River. Both were eager and appreciative listeners, exclaiming aloud at each episode. At one point Auntie Elsie reached over and grasped my mother's hand, stroking it affectionately. My mother beamed with happiness, clearly looking like a woman in the loving lap of her family.

At Da Bobo's urging, they began to sing their favorite songs. Even Aunt Lucy joined in, warbling, "I Could Have Danced All Night," in her tremulous soprano. "Seventy-six Trombones" followed, then songs from *Carousel.* I sang along as best I could, humming when I forgot the words, which was more often than not, as I didn't know the popular medleys of their generation. Da Bobo acted as the indefatigable group prompter, shouting the upcoming chorus whenever the others faltered. In a short time they were singing full throat, except for Auntie Elsie, who moved her lips delicately, as though she were sipping tea, and Da Mama, who chanted along in her tone-deaf monotone like a Tibetan monk. It immediately became clear that it was Uncle John who possessed the true gift, a sweet, effortless voice that soared above the others like that of an Irish tenor. The only drawback of its thrilling power was that it incited Da Bobo to raise his own voice to a fevered pitch.

The afternoon would have slipped unnoticed into evening except for the fact that Uncle John's voice faded and Auntie Elsie confided they had left his heart medicine where they were staying, in the apartment of friends across town. Though Da Bobo urged them to take a taxi, Uncle John insisted on taking a bus back. A former chief surgeon and university president, he emanated a firm conservatism as well as an unimpeachable authority in his view of taxicabs as emblems of decadence. We filed out to the street to wait for the bus with him and Auntie Elsie.

Though it had been decided that her brother and sister-in-law were to return in a few days to join in the celebration of our final night in Beijing, my mother seemed anxious about their leaving. She hovered close to Uncle John, making a place for him in the bus line. I had never seen her make such a fuss before, not even with my father. Thankfully, the bus, on arriving, was nearly empty. People made way for my uncle and aunt, waiting patiently while he laboriously climbed the steps. When the bus pulled away, my mother waved until it turned the corner and disappeared. When she dropped her hand at last, I saw her face assume its furrowed medical technician's brow indicating a bad prognosis.

A cool wind, whistling in a thin, piercing tone, rose as we headed back toward the courtyard. As we entered the house, a summer storm had begun to blow, the skies turning purple, green, and black, like a horrific bruise. Bolts of lightning snagged through the sky and the wind howled, pitching debris through the yard and rattling the windows. By the time everyone went to bed, gusts rocked the house and bits of tile broke off from the roof and rattled into the courtyard. The bursts were erratic and violent, causing the walls to thump and moan. The noises sounded more like the work of *guei,* Chinese demon ghosts, than of nature. I lay in bed listening to Yeh Yeh's house shudder and quake, thinking it would collapse right on top of us.

Sometime later, I woke to a loud noise. At first I thought I dreamt it, but then it sounded again and this time there was no mistake: *Bang! Bang! Bang!* My immediate thought, struggling from sleep, was of the three strident chords in Shostakovich's Eighth String Quartet, thought by many to signify the KGB pounding on doors to roust suspected dissidents in the dead of night. *Memory stains a house,* I thought, remembering how, twenty-one years before, the Red Guards of the Cultural Revolution had come for my grandfather as he slept.

Bang! Bang! Bang!

I sat up, staring wildly through the darkness, bracing myself for a cadre of Red Guards to burst in. I scrambled into my clothes.

The wind shrilled through the cracks in the windows, causing the entire house to creak wildly, like a frigate tossed on a stormy sea. It came again: *Bang! Bang! Bang!* My mother murmured fitfully in her sleep, but stayed immersed in her dream. Heart pounding, chills of fear running down my back, I crept toward the double doors of our bedroom. Placing my hands on each portal, I took a deep breath and pushed them open, stepping into the central chamber of the house. Here it was dim except for flickering light cast through the front glass doors by the moon, whose face was obscured now and then by clouds racing by on the wind. The first thing I saw, after my eyes adjusted to the semidarkness, was my grandfather's portrait on the opposite wall, his scrolls of calligraphy hanging on either side. His pale face stood out in the darkness and drew me toward it. The wind sang beneath the doors, chilling my ankles and feet as I crossed the cool tiled floor. Gusts swirled throughout the room, causing the lampshades to tremble and the white cloths Da Mama had draped over the arms of the furniture to quiver and flap like ghostly hands.

Surely this was the work of *guei,* I thought, trapped in the house to remind those of what had happened here so many years ago. There were as many different kinds of *guei* in the world as bad memories and I wondered if among them were ones sent from my ancestors to punish me for not coming to China, for having answered my grandfather's summons too late.

The pounding sounded again, and I turned in the direction of its source. Now I saw the wooden batons weighting the lower ends of the calligraphy scrolls being hefted by the bursts of wind and then released to fall back against the wall. The gusts, made quirksome by having snaked through the many cracks and fissures of the house, caused the scroll on the right to bang twice on rebound, resulting in the three-stroke pattern. I watched as the wind lifted the batons from the wall, furling the scrolls like slender sails, then dropped them back again to drum the wooden panels on either side of my grandfather's portrait. After a time the wind slackened, so that the banging became a soft, irregular tapping.

Thoroughly chilled by now, I stared at Yeh Yeh's portrait, waiting for him to speak. It seemed the proper moment, now that all was quiet. I longed for him to give voice to his house and all the offenses committed against it and his life there—his public humiliation at the hands of the Red Guards, the burning of his life's work. And for what? So that China could be handed over to Mickey Mouse? That his home, our family seat, could be torn down to make way for a high-rise?

I stared at his face, waiting, but he said nothing, only looked down at me, his face fixed in that serious, solitary gaze. He had given his life to reflection and expression of the classic Chinese ways, fulfilled his patriotic duty, and now the country he had known and loved was gone forever. The look in his eyes seemed lonely, yet clear, free of illusion, and slowly I began to understand the gift that he offered to me. All my previous expectations and romantic notions of him and China, all that had stood between us, fell away.

By answering his summons, I had seen China's face and felt its pulse, and by doing so joined my memory with his. My journey on the Yangtze had taught me this. Revolutions had changed the course of our family in the past and might yet again in the future. *Only look and remember,* Yeh Yeh seemed to say. *Learn.*

A final gust of wind stirred the scrolls so that the batons lightly brushed the wall. The sound came as a signal that my appointment was over. I had come to stand before my grandfather like a novitiate before a master, and now I had received his blessing. I could not simply turn away. Something called for me to celebrate the moment. In the one gesture I knew, one I had practiced all my life as a musician and which I now embraced as a granddaughter, I faced Yeh Yeh, and hoping to convey all that was in my heart—honor, communion, and gratitude—I bowed.

25

GOOD-BYE

ON OUR LAST DAY, DA MAMA TOOK ME TO THE LARGEST OUTDOOR MARKET in Beijing, saying it was only here she could be sure of finding the foods she wanted to prepare for our last, celebratory feast. We arrived early in the morning, when the day was still pleasantly cool, the food stalls not yet crowded.

The market was a huge open field divided by lanes of long wooden tables. The tables on the right were virtually empty of wares, tended by listless men and women who stared vacantly or dozed in scattered piles of hay, whereas the tables on the left were piled with fresh produce, tended by vendors who energetically sang their praises.

"What's the matter over there?" I said, pointing to the right-hand tables.

"They communist farms," Da Mama replied. "Guarantee money. They get pay no matter what, so why work?" She clucked her tongue in disapproval, marched to the tables on the left to inspect a handful of peppers before putting them in the string bag slung over her arm. The vendor, already focused on his next customer, flipped her coins into his metal box. Like those of the other independent vendors, his face was agleam with entrepreneurial zeal. Wearing a T-shirt and jeans, he bobbed to the beat of disco music sounding on a cassette player nearby.

Next, Da Mama picked out fresh mushrooms, hollow vegetables, thin long green beans, garlic, and green onions. Then she headed to the poultry section, where she eyed a brace of pullets held high in the air by a farmer, peering into their bright red eyes and poking them in the breast. Making a face, she informed the farmer that the birds looked sickly. He squawked indignantly, bouncing the chicks in the air so that they clucked and flapped their wings. Finally, after additional close scrutiny, when it seemed she had counted all the feathers on the birds, Da Mama held out several pieces of script. Pocketing them, swiftly, the farmer handed her the pullets.

"Here," she said, handing them to me. I was surprised at how heavy they were and how hot their feet felt in my hand. At six weeks old, their beaks were still soft, nearly transparent. I held them high, careful not to let their heads bang the ground as I followed Da Mama through the lanes. Part of me felt sorry that I was an accomplice to their demise, while another wondered if, when cooked, they would be as tender as Da Mama promised. I resolved to try to make their final hours as comfortable as possible.

Next, we approached a large metal drum that appeared to be dancing and swaying with a life of its own. Drawing near, I saw that it was filled to the rim with fish swimming frantically round and round so that they roiled the water, rocking the drum. Now and then the fishmonger reached in and hauled a fish out by the tail. It flailed mightily and was so heavy that it caused the fishmonger's arm to warp back and forth like a strip of rubber, splashing water everywhere. The carp was dark green with huge yellow scales on its underbelly, and had fleshy black whiskers that flared above its gaping, thick-lipped mouth. Repulsed, I hurried away, nearly tripping over other buckets and cans filled with every variety of frogs, turtles, crabs, and eels, some of which were huge, looking like garden hoses, and others that were small, worm-like, that writhed in slithery mounds. The smell of slimy frenzy was overpowering so I hurried back to rejoin Da Mama. By now she had chosen a fish, which the fishmonger hauled from the drum and put in a plastic bag partially filled with water.

"Here," Da Mama said, handing me the bag. "Time to go home and cook."

Boarding the crowded noonday bus, I was forced to stand with both arms linked around the upright metal poles, balancing precariously between chickens and fish. The chickens were easy passengers, dozing while they hung upside down, but the fish felt as heavy as a sack of wet laundry. As soon as there was room on the bus, I carefully lowered the bag to the floor. I felt a certain satisfaction standing there, as though my burdens designated me a native.

When we got home, the maid took the doomed creatures from my hands, replying to Da Mama's inquiry that Da Bobo was still out. The pullets, still tethered together, were released into the courtyard. They strutted and pecked at the ground, unaware they were living their last moments. I went across the courtyard and tapped on Aunt Lucy's door, finding her at work at her table.

"So, you're leaving tomorrow?" she said, looking up from the pile of papers written in her minute, precise script.

I nodded, my heart suddenly feeling heavy. I glanced at her radio, puzzled by its silence. She saw my look, explained, "They were playing Khachaturian. An opera. Vulgar. Barbarous."

Again the atmosphere felt strained. She sat in her favorite chair-throne while I stood, awash with the familiar sense of the lowly disciple in the presence of the all-knowing. We talked a little about what I had seen and learned on my trip to China. Then I asked her how she felt about Da Bobo's plans to sell the house. She did not hesitate. "It seems the right thing to do. Why hang on to it? With the proceeds we could get two modern places. We are all getting older, after all. This house is too much work. You see how hard it is for your uncle to keep it up."

"But it's Yeh Yeh's house . . . ."

She smiled. Her little eyes, though weak, looked remarkably clear. "That was another time," she said.

It was late in the afternoon by the time Da Bobo finally got back, handing our train tickets to Shangai over to my mother. He didn't explain how far he had gone to meet his contact, but we could tell from the weariness in his face that he had ridden miles. A little while later, Uncle John and Auntie Elsie arrived. They brought gifts of fresh peanuts and a bottle of American whiskey. We sat in the foyer, chatting. Behind us, in the back kitchen, we heard sounds of Da Mama and the maid preparing dinner. I noticed that the pullets were no longer in the courtyard. All that remained were a few white feathers scattered on the ground, and another that had gotten caught in the branches of Yeh Yeh's plum tree.

Dinner began with several cold dishes of pickled cucumbers, thin-sliced stewed beef tendon, and salted duck eggs. For the second round of courses, Da Mama served stir-fried hollow vegetables with mushrooms, eggplant with minced pork, and the pullets I had carried from the market with peanuts and peppers. I passed the remains of the pullets, which proved more tender than any chicken I had ever eaten, to my mother, who savored them, bony bits, cartilage, and all. Finally, Da Bobo presented the pièce de résistance, the fish my aunt had chosen from the roiling barrel that he had cooked in his special fragrant brown sauce. The fish was so large its head and tail flopped over the edge of the platter.

Uncle John raised his teacup and toasted my mother and me, thanking us for coming to China and wishing us a safe journey home. I raised my cup and mumbled a few fractured phrases in Mandarin, trying to tell my relatives that I'd enjoyed my stay and that I was grateful for all I'd learned. I had silently rehearsed the speech throughout the day. At the appointed moment, I heard it coming fast and garbled through my teeth. From the corner of my eye, I saw Aunt Lucy frown and cock her head, like a dog that hears a strange noise, but my other relatives applauded and fussed over me as though I were a precocious two-year-old.

After Uncle John poured the whiskey, the family stories came thick and fast. Some were new, but most were ones I had heard before. The stories were dearly known to everyone, and the evening became a strenuous but cheerful squabble, with everyone vying for the floor in order to tell the story as it truly happened.

At ten o'clock, Uncle John and Auntie Elsie rose to catch the last bus to their borrowed apartment. Uncle John took my hands and said, "Come again," in a tone that sounded familiar and easy, as though we lived next door to one another.

Once again, we accompanied my uncle and aunt to the bus stop and waited until they were safely aboard the bus. Our farewell seemed abrupt, especially for one before what promised to be a long separation, but I sensed everyone preferred it that way.

Back at the house, Aunt Lucy retired to her room, leaving Da Mama and my mother to clear the table. I was about to join them when Da Bobo pulled me aside to the portico to admire the moon, orange-yellow, heavy in the sky and extraordinarily old-looking, glowing as though lit from within. We stood there a while then Da Bobo turned and we followed the path of yellow moonbeam back into the house, pausing in front of Yeh Yeh's portrait and the two scrolls.

"Well, Sung Lien," he said. "Which scroll will you take home?"

I had completely forgotten about choosing. I tried to study the scrolls, but my eyes kept returning to my grandfather's portrait. Looking at his face, I realized he had foreseen everything: the changes overtaking China, Lucy's abdication of her role as his emissary, even Da Bobo's plans to sell the house. I was glad he wasn't there to see it happen.

Da Bobo cleared his throat. "So, what do you think? Which do you choose?"

I looked at the scrolls, admiring the characters flowing in their precise choreography. I knew that taking either one of them would be the first act in dismantling Yeh Yeh's house, and that I neither wanted nor deserved this role. "I can't, Da Bobo," I said.

"But Yeh Yeh left one for you. That's why you came."

I shook my head. "Maybe another time. When . . . if you sell the house."

Da Bobo sucked air into his lungs with a sharp sound. Slowly letting his breath out, he looked up at Yeh Yeh's portrait. "Who knows when that might happen?" he said, in a tone that was half hopeful, half resigned. Then, lightly, "It's all just talk . . ."

He looked at me and saw that I had glimpsed what my grandfather had already seen of the future. His tone became serious. "If we sell the house . . . if that happens, then you must promise you will come back to choose."

I hesitated.

"Because I'm not sending it!" he said, suddenly agitated, observing my reluctance. "You have to come get it. Promise!" I remained still. He jabbed a finger at Yeh Yeh's portrait. "Promise!"

"All right, Da Bobo."

My uncle said nothing more, but seemed satisfied. We stood looking at the scrolls and at Yeh Yeh's face in the yellow moonlight.

That night, my mother and I lay for the last time on the old horsehair bed. As usual, though we lay mere inches apart, we remained in entirely separate zones. Throughout our time in China together I had grown to understand my mother from her stories, her brusque but caring stewardship of me, and her interactions with her family, but still there remained a kind of dead calm between us, an emotional gulf that I had hoped to bridge on this journey.

The stifling heat and the frustrating obstacles of our trip had distracted me from the wish that my mother and I would grow closer, that by literally walking on the ground of her native country I would gain favor in her heart.

Now that I had fulfilled my duty in paying homage to Yeh Yeh, I thought perhaps at least she had nothing left to disapprove of me there. Yet a feeling of restraint and distance persisted. Was it too late? Or did I imagine everything—were my mother and I in fact as close as we could possibly be for two persons who shared a natural reserve? Perhaps it was a matter of language and culture, that we expressed ourselves differently, or that we had different priorities now.

Even as life drew my nearly seventy-year-old mother toward the future, she embarked on another trajectory that was the backward curve of her memory. She had arrived at a point in her life when the pull of the future had become increasingly tenuous. Weakened by her own ailments as well as the declining health of her siblings, her future was eclipsed by the vibrant images of her past. At the same time, my view of life as a thirty-eight-year-old writer and musician was that of a work still in progress.

In a way I was grateful that travel in China had illuminated the nature of this distance between us. Despite her strenuous efforts to enter modernity, or at least her hastily constructed version of it, China's true character still reposed in the past. My mother, predisposed to the past, recognized this characteristic and embraced it. My generation, with little sense of history, attuned to the future, could only flounder in the transitional state of the People's Republic from what had been to what was yet to come.

What, then, bound me to China? Bloodlines? Instinct? Had I, like a salmon genetically programmed to return to its birth waters, been transmitted a sense of origin? Or had I inherited a cultural identity, the days of Yeh Yeh in his prime, the bygone era of the Mandarin, when intellectualism, art, and spiritual investigation remained at the center of life? And then there was what resonated in the family bonds between me and Aunt Lucy, Da Bobo, and Da Mama, beckoning from the seat of the family home. I realized that the history of my family was inextricably tied to China and by being born into this family I inherited its history. It remains a precious legacy of which I am proud. My sadness at what my relatives suffered assures that I will never forget, and that what they have bequeathed to me, while much of it is tragic, remains whole and true. My heritage, like the most exquisitely balanced dish, with equal components of acid and sugar, bitterness and salt, is perfectly Chinese.

26

LIGHTNESS

When I knocked on aunt lucy's door early the next morning to say good-bye, she looked up from the millet ball she was eating and put her finger to her lips. Handel's opera, *Solomon* was playing on the radio.

"Good-bye!" I whispered.

She nodded, smiling absently, her eyes preoccupied with the music. She was not to be disturbed, and as she was still recovering from the effects of the heat wave and our recent excursion to Liulichang Street, I felt perfectly fine saying good-bye to her then and there. From our last parting in St. Paul, I knew Aunt Lucy didn't indulge in dramatic farewells.

Da Bobo and Da Mama came with us to the train station, where there was great confusion, as usual, and we were nearly separated by the masses of people swarming around the platforms. Da Mama began to cry just as we were about to board our train.

"You stay too short! Next time, you come longer, bring Fred!"

I hugged her tightly.

"Get on, the train is leaving," Da Bobo said, handing me the sack of food Da Mama had prepared for us, which felt heavy enough to feed the entire Red Army. His manner was brusque, I knew it was his way of getting through this painful separation. He helped my mother onto the train, hauled our bags aboard, and jumped off just as I climbed on. The conductor hustled the last passengers onto the train, exhorted everyone else to stand back. My mother and I cranked down the window of our compartment and began to wave furiously. The train started to pull away. Standing on the platform my uncle and aunt waved until finally we could see them no more.

Sharing our compartment were an old woman and her middle-aged son, who eyed us suspiciously as we prepared for the twenty-four-hour ride by taking off our shoes and stashing our food under my mother's bunk. The old lady hunched in her corner and barked orders to her son, who complied meekly, rearranging their belongings, unwrapping parcels, wrapping them again.

I decided to ignore our two companions and climbed into the bunk above my mother's to watch the scenery. Occasionally I peeked down to see what she was doing. My bunk was barely three feet above hers, and through the metal slats I was able to read the list she was making for when she got home:

1. Make appointment for new perm.
2. Send away for concert subscriptions.
3. Buy yarn for Jo-Jo's sweater.

And so on. When she finished the list, she took out a scrap of paper from her purse and began to sketch stitch patterns for the new sweater she was planning for my oldest niece, whose birthday was in November. The sweater, like all the hundreds of others she had knitted, would take her a week, at most. She knitted when she watched TV, listened to music, or waited for the kettle to boil, her needles a blur, the knitted yarn flowing from her hands.

The hours passed, the train wheels clicking rhythmically on the tracks. My mother jotted down more Chinese tunes she remembered, sewed on a button. She wasn't idle for a minute.

Late in the afternoon, the old lady and her son left for the dining car. Relieved at their departure, my mother and I opened Da Mama's bag of food and nibbled cold steamed bread, hard-boiled eggs. Our customary silence felt heavy. Now that our long trip together was drawing to a close, I felt compelled to talk about it, to mark it somehow.

"Hey, Mom, remember the flutist on the Yangtze boat?" I ventured.

She thought a moment, hummed a bit of the tune he had played in our cabin.

"What about that tennis match in Xi'an!"

She nodded, resumed chewing her piece of bread.

I suspected she had exhausted her store of commentary about our trip and had nothing more to say. I watched the scenery outside the window. Miles of fields dotted here and there with typical blocky peasant houses flashed by.

"It was nice seeing Auntie Anna, Uncle John, and Aunt Elsie."

At the mention of her siblings and sister-in-law my mother brightened.

"I hope Uncle John is feeling better."

Her face fell. She set her piece of bread down and looked out the window, as if to signal that talk of Uncle John's state of health was too risky.

We listened to the rhythmic click of the rails, which for me had the same effect as minutes ticking away on a clock, indicating our continual, speedy withdrawal from China. I began to feel certain that I wasn't ready to leave, after all. Already I missed Da Bobo and Da Mama, and I was nagged by the thought that I had forgotten or had missed something important to the fulfillment of my trip. I wanted more than anything to turn back. At the same time I felt exhausted, drained by the emotional events of recent days and the monotony of the long train ride.

While I reflected on this, my mother remarked casually that the U.S. Open tennis championships were starting soon in New York. She was far from being stuck in the past, but was already way ahead, thinking of the future. The train ride vaulted her from the past into the future, and she was happy to be getting back. I began to think that what I had concluded about her might not have been true, that she was at home neither more in the past nor the future but anytime, anywhere. Was it that she had accepted what it meant, to have enough, to be content with whatever was at hand? That she had learned about leaping, facing whatever came, as in that moment she had urged her brother Henry to jump from the staircase of her childhood home, saving him from the Red Guards?

When the train pulled into Shanghai early the next morning, we took a taxi to the hotel that Da Bobo had booked for us and checked into a room that was modern and clean. I turned on the television, and, sure enough, *Bonanza* was showing. Ben, Hoss, and Little Joe Cartwright were still speaking their miscued and hyperkinetically dubbed Chinese. It was as though five weeks had not passed at all.

I asked my mother if we were going to contact Shrewin again. She shook her head, giving me a look that said, *Are you crazy?* indicating her understanding of my dislike of running all over the city after our less-than-simpatico relative. We spent the afternoon shopping for souvenirs, strolling along the Bund, and ate an early dinner in the hotel restaurant. Since it was our last night in China, I wanted to say something that would commemorate the time we had spent together, but everything I thought of seemed stilted, artificial. My mother and I sat across from one another like a long-married couple, silent, separated by private thoughts and malaise.

The next day we arrived at the airport, where officials behind the airline counter looked as if they were from Minnesota: big-boned, white, and meat-eating.

"How ma-ny bags?" the man inquired, exaggerating his pronunciation. At first I wondered if he thought I was hard of hearing, until I realized he assumed I was a native Chinese.

"One," I answered, lightly. "To Minneapolis–St. Paul. My mother's is going to Washington National."

Looking at me more closely, the official changed gears smoothly. "No problem. You both change planes in Narita. Have a good flight."

My mother fell asleep soon after takeoff, and slept through the food and beverage service. As the plane hummed along at its high-level altitude, it hit me again that I was flying home, and that in a few hours my mother and I would be going our separate ways. Looking at her dozing next to me, I wondered if she had woken and looked at me during the many nights in China when we had slept next to one another, thinking about who she had made, who I had become. Had she cherished these moments as I had? Had she felt the same lonely sense of separation? I did not know whether other mothers and daughters experienced the same thing, or whether only those set apart by culture and history felt so inchoate and perplexed.

I gazed out the window, seeing nothing but clear pale sky. There were no clouds, no point of reference by which I could locate our place in the world. It was impossible to grasp that we were passing through time zones, outpacing the earth, as it were. Leaping. Exhausted, I closed my eyes.

Different images appeared: mulberry fields, the blood-brown door of Yeh Yeh's house, my grandfather's face framed by his scrolls of calligraphy. I thought again of that windblown night when I stood before the scrolls and received his blessing. My trip had been a memorial, not only to my grandfather, but to my expectations of what he and his house furnished to my life. I had been like a hermit crab, scuttling from one ill-fitting place to another, believing that my true home was with my grandfather, in China. At least that was what his letters had led me to believe. But I realized my history, like China's, was one of change. I could no longer count on borrowed houses, but construct my own in St. Paul with Fred, our dog, the giant maroon and gold dahlias in our backyard.

Next to me my mother shifted a little, murmuring in her sleep. Her hair was mashed against the seat, her jaw sagging. She looked worn out, our five-week trip had taken a lot from her. Now she looked like all of her near-seventy years, and I could see myself developing her Lin family jowls and drooping eyelids. I realized again how much I had to learn from her, because she had rebuilt her house in every season of her life. Only now, at the end of our trip together, I realized what she had endured and accomplished in her life, and who she had become through all of it. They were her footprints I had been unknowingly following in China, not Yeh Yeh's; the lessons she learned were those I needed to embrace.

As we hurtled across the sky, drawing closer to the future, I felt a sense of urgency. I reached out my hand and touched my mother's face. The feel of it—soft, dry, like the skin of an apricot withering in a bowl—made my heart leap in my throat. Here at last we were meeting. It had taken so long and been so difficult, and the future of my ageing mother seemed increasingly fragile, yet I was happy and grateful because I knew finally that we were joined. Before she woke up, before I could weep, I withdrew my hand, because I knew my mother would have preferred not to witness what I had just experienced. She believed, as she lived, that such moments in life were private, even sacred. This particular moment belonged to me.

When the plane touched ground at Narita airport, my mother stirred and began to gather her things. I had anticipated this moment, for I knew what it was I wanted to say. "Mom," I began, but fellow passengers, anxious to get off the plane, crowded our row to rummage in the overhead bins. The moment dissolved in a disorderly shuffle, and the words died in my mouth.

We moved out in two lines, walking up the jetway. In the terminal, monitors flashed with flight information. We saw that my flight to Minneapolis–St. Paul left in less than an hour, as did my mother's to Washington National. My flight departed from the same terminal, and my mother's left from another which could only be reached by taking an underground transport. Blinking lights on the monitor warned that boarding for both flights was already underway. My mother looked around, agitated.

"I'll go with you to your terminal," I said.

"No!" she said, grabbing her blue bag from my hand. "You miss your plane. I go by myself."

"But Mom . . ."

"Bye!" she said, and hugged me, fiercely and briefly. It had taken me so long to understand that this, too, was her way. I saw it was her way of leaping to the next moment, and that I could only stand aside.

"Mom . . . Mom . . . I love you," I stammered.

She nodded, veered away, as though she didn't want to hear. She turned her back, ready for what was to come.

"Bye, Mom!"

But she was already gone.

To this day, when someone lights a match, peels a hard-boiled egg, or sets off fireworks on the Fourth of July, I think of China. To me, sulfurous fumes are the signature smell of this country, its most telling aura. It is the scent of lingering ancient history and bitter suffering, betraying China as surely as reddened hands give away a woman who would pass herself off as a lady, as irrevocably as a slip in accent unmasks the gentleman who would conceal his humble upbringing. Anxious to assume the face of prosperity and power, to overcome its image of a second-class citizen in the world, China detonates nuclear bombs, threatens the borders of her neighbors, issues tough rhetoric at international forums, and ignores the ongoing pleas of her people for social and political reform. China's leaders disregard her innate and intractable sense of time, attempting to hurry a giantess whose slow internal rhythms were established eons ago. I picture petty administrators scurrying to dress her up, piling on baubles and glitter, placing a sword in her hand, then presenting her, with much pomp and ceremony, to the company of the world. Even then, though China makes for an awesome presence, a tiny tendril of scent escapes, a smell of rotten eggs, of primitive smoke and incipient fire that expose her. Even today, though she is more modernized and forthcoming about her internal affairs, she is regarded by Western nations with caution and fear. Her growing wealth and power are viewed as threatening. Mistrust of her transfers to me because I share her face. For this reason, I feel sympathy for her situation. I try to tell people she is not innately bad.

I wish I could say that Yeh Yeh's house stands today, but sixteen years after my trip to Beijing it was torn down, a high-rise built in its place. Da Bobo put up a real fight, circulating petitions, convincing Beijing big shots to designate the house a historical landmark, even managing to get sympathetic television coverage. He instigated an uproar among Chinese citizens who sensed with the advent of cheap high-rises comes diminished human values. In the end, the government claimed eminent domain and sent the bulldozers. I have a picture of Da Bobo standing in front of his house the day before it was knocked down. Though he wears his trademark look of the brave, he looks hazy, blurred, as though he were already moving out of range of the camera, bolting for the future. Now he and Da Mama live in a high-rise apartment of their own, on the outskirts of town in a suburb. To me, though they say they are content, there is something incongruent and sad about their move, as though they were once magnificent and wild and true and now they have been captured and made to live in a box. Aunt Lucy did not live to share this fate. A few years before the house went down, just after completing her translations of Mark Twain, she complained of indigestion, went to the hospital, and died.

China's rush toward modernity remains breathtaking, as demonstrated even in the exchange students she sends to Minnesota. No longer morose and concave, emanating hunger and truncated adolescence, this bright, fast-talking group rushes about with laptops in hand, cell-phone holsters flapping, crunching numbers and spouting software-speak, the newest national dialect.

From the sidelines, my boomer Chinese-American generation looks on, amazed by the ferocity of this new class and its mounting successes. At the same time, we observe how easily Chinese and Asian elements have been folded into contemporary American culture, at least superficially. Stereotypes still exist, but we are struck by overwhelming evidence that what was distinctly ours has become mainstream American. Wonton skins are now routinely substituted for ravioli skins. Our Mandarin sense of dignity and forbearance has eroded into crass materialism and a habituated sense of entitlement like any other upwardly mobile group. Though there are clear benefits to frictionless assimilation, is this what we want? If the foundations of our ancient homeland transform into Western mores with their distracted and fractured views, where are we left to look for our philosophical mooring?

My mother, now in her eighties, solves the dilemma by living in America with her American friends and visiting China on a nearly annual basis. I can never reach her by phone since she is off doing aqua aerobics, playing tennis, performing on her recorder at senior citizens' homes, or attending concerts with her many friends. She travels to China with her two brothers, Richard and David, who currently reside in California, to visit Anna, her only other surviving sibling and her daughters Sho Mei, Sho An, and Sho Sung and their children. *You don't believe China today,* she tells me. *Beijing has roads everywhere, so many cars!* She doesn't see this necessarily as bad, as I do, with my fear of pollution and distaste for poor city planning and sterile architecture, her view being that life goes on.

She goes back to China because Anna and her extended family are getting older, and each visit may be her last. In the not-so-distant future, Auntie Anna, who now lives in Guangdong Province, turns ninety, and my mother has asked me to go with her to celebrate this important milestone. I am somewhat surprised by her invitation because although we went back to China together in 1994, more recently she has gone with her two brothers and I have gotten used to being out of the loop. I haven't yet promised my mother I will go. Part of me resists going to a country whose most recent actions are appalling and heartbreaking—ignoring the current plague of AIDS in outlying poor villages caused by contaminated blood distributed by the knowing government, and the Yangtze River Dam project, which has displaced hundreds of thousands of people from their homes. The Chinese have tried to mute the AIDS disaster while trumpeting the feats of their hydroelectric engineers. How consistent it is with their historical practices that they have as much to hide as show.

Perhaps I am also reluctant to go because I don't want to see Da Bobo and Da Mama living in a high-rise. This would shatter the very last of my treasured memories from the trip my mother and I took in 1987. Damming the Yangtze River is bad enough, but to see my relatives living anywhere else but in Yeh Yeh's house is something I sadly fear. I resist proof that China has become a place where houses such as Yeh Yeh's stand no longer.

Of course any trip I would take to China now wouldn't be about the policies of its government or my self-centered notions. I look ahead in my calendar to see if I can make myself available because of Auntie Anna and my mother. Secretly, I think my mother already knows that I'll go. She always seems to know how things will turn out in the future.